Creating a Perfect World

Ohio Bicentennial Series

Editor: Clarence E. Wunderlin, Jr.

H. Roger Grant, *Ohio on the Move: Transportation in the Buckeye State*

Phillip R. Shriver and Clarence E. Wunderlin, Jr., eds., *The Documentary Heritage of Ohio*

Stephane Elise Booth, *Buckeye Women: The History of Ohio's Daughters*

Catherine M. Rokicky, *Creating a Perfect World: Religious and Secular Utopias in Nineteenth-Century Ohio*

Creating a Perfect World

Religious and Secular Utopias in Nineteenth-Century Ohio

CATHERINE M. ROKICKY

Ohio University Press
Athens

Ohio University Press, Athens, Ohio 45701

Printed in the United States of America

Ohio University Press books are printed on acid-free paper ∞ ™

10 09 08 07 06 05 04 03 02 5 4 3 2 1

The publication of this book was made possible in part
by the generous support of the Ohio Bicentennial Commission.

Frontispiece: "The Cradlers," 1888. *Ohio Historical Society.*

Library of Congress Cataloging-in-Publication Data
Rokicky, Catherine M., 1967-
Creating a perfect world : religious and secular utopias in nineteenth-century Ohio / Catherine M. Rokicky.
p. cm. — (Ohio bicentennial series ; 4)
Includes bibliographical references and index.
ISBN 0-8214-1438-0 (alk. paper) — ISBN 0-8214-1439-9 (pbk. : alk. paper)
1. Utopias—Ohio—History—19th century. I. Title. II. Series.

HX806 .R575 2002
335'.9771'0034—dc21

2001058817

For Samantha Selena and Amanda Marie,
my little pieces of Heaven

Contents

Acknowledgments

I would like to offer my gratitude to several people who played key roles in the completion of this manuscript. Clarence E. Wunderlin, the editor of the Ohio Bicentennial Series, deserves special thanks for giving me the opportunity to contribute to this project. I would also like to thank him for his helpful critiques of early drafts of this work. I extend much appreciation to David Sanders, director of the Ohio University Press, for his encouragement and patience throughout the project. I would also like to thank Sharon Rose, project editor, and Tammy Oberhausen Rastoder, copyeditor, for their efforts in the preparation of the manuscript.

Several research facilities merit thanks. I thoroughly enjoyed conducting research at the Western Reserve Historical Society, and I would like to thank Barbara Billings and the entire staff for their help in making the society a great place to work. I also thank the staff of the Ohio Historical Society and the Cincinnati Historical Society. Shirlee Muse, librarian at Cuyahoga Community College, helped me throughout this project, and I thank her as well as Carol Toth and the library staff at CCC.

I would not have completed this volume without the help of my family, and I extend much appreciation and love to them. Special thanks go to my mother, Marie A. Tedeschi, my sister, Mary Tedeschi Vittardi, and my grandparents, Peter and Esther Tedeschi, for their help and encouragement in the writing of this project. I thank my daughters, Samantha and Amanda, for the love, patience, and laughter that have constantly reminded me of the greatest joys in life. To my husband, Paul, I say thank you for your unflinching encouragement and unselfish character throughout this project. Without your love, humor, and patience, I would have never completed this book. Thank you for this and for so much more that I do not need to put into words.

Introduction

DURING DIFFERENT ERAS OF AMERICAN HISTORY, INDIVIDUALS have responded to changes in the economic, social, and political sphere by searching for alternative ways of living. Because of the severe crisis of the Great Depression in the 1930s, some Americans participated in New Deal communities that experimented with cooperative forms of living. Most recently, the decade of the 1960s, rocked by the Civil Rights movement, the Vietnam War, and the subsequent political polarization, led people to establish communes with less conventional ways of living that members viewed as superior to those accepted by society. Many of these havens were founded in California, a state still known for its experiments with various lifestyles.

The communal movement of the 1960s moved scholars to delve into America's past to understand other periods when people attempted to create a more perfect world on earth. The nineteenth century holds a rich tapestry of people who acted on different philosophies, beliefs, and ideas to create perfect havens. Although hundreds of utopias dotted the American landscape in the nineteenth century, they never altered significantly the course of American politics or economics. Socially, however, they demonstrated the possibilities in American culture for experimentation as well as the limitations that culture imposed on groups that pushed too much for change.

In the early nineteenth century, Americans were dealing with the political, economic, and social transitions brought on by westward expansion and by industrialization. The movement of people westward across the United States along with the increasing separation of home and the workplace led some to search for more control and order in their lives. The Second Great Awakening, with its evangelical fervor, influenced many Americans to take an active role in altering society, and evangelicals such as Charles G. Finney encouraged followers to participate in reform movements, such as temperance and abolition, that targeted societal evils. Indeed, Americans were optimistic that they could perfect society. Just as they could participate in politics to alter government, they could also shape society. The belief in progress led many to challenge traditional concepts and institutions. Americans also felt compelled to respond to the changes around them to gain more control in their lives.[1]

The limited goals embodied in reform efforts seemed inadequate for those who saw the opportunity to bring greater change. Some Americans chose to create self-contained communities where they experimented with remaking society entirely, as they hoped to create a perfect world on earth. The establishment of such a haven would help to bring peace and harmony to advance the Second Coming of Christ on earth, or the millennium. Utopianists believed that spiritual changes would ultimately lead to social and economic transformations.[2]

The idea of the perfectibility of man and the acceptance that the millennium was upon them were concepts shared by both utopianists and reformers. Despite this connection, they never worked together for the goal of perfecting society. Yet this philosophical connection also discloses the ties that did exist between evangelicals, reformers, and utopianists. Utopianists differed from reformers in that utopianists saw the opportunity in the United States to bring quick change without overturning the government. Members of utopias hoped that their communities would serve as models for others to follow, a goal similar to that of John Winthrop and the Puritans in founding the Massachusetts Bay Colony as a "city upon a hill" in the seventeenth century. Utopianists wanted others to realize the true order of God and to help end the chaos around them. While utopias did attract much curiosity and attention, they did little to transform and affect all of American society.[3]

Utopianists introduced their own ideas about religion and the social order, and some distinctions can be made between the religious and secular communities. Religious utopias emphasized the maintenance of unique forms of worship and unorthodox beliefs and practices. They saw themselves as a select number of chosen people who would create a haven secure from the outside sins of the world, or a City of God as St. Augustine phrased it in the fifth century. Often, their religious doctrines combined some elements of mainstream Protestantism with their own particular beliefs. In fact, utopianists often viewed themselves as returning to the origins of Christianity and the true faith. They found justification for their particular practices and philosophies in Bible verse.[4]

While preserving their theology, members of religious utopias also established a society different from the norm. Indeed, both religious and secular utopias challenged the existing social and economic order, including the concepts of marriage and the nuclear family, sexual practices, distribution of property, wage labor, and the social order. Although communities might have emphasized particular purposes, either religious or secular, they often combined these goals within their communities. Also, while they rejected the outside world as evil and corrupt, they still maintained connections to society in order to increase the chances that others would follow the example they set.[5]

Utopian communities attempted to limit and control the interaction with the outside world. Hence, the communities usually appointed a small group of people to deal with the outside world. The vast majority of the group would thus remain uncorrupted. This separation worked well for groups without political aspirations, including members of Zoar and other German-speaking groups in the United States and, to a lesser degree, for the Shaker communities. The Shaker communities prayed for those who had to interact with nonmembers so that they would escape corruption.[6]

In establishing their new economic and social order, utopianists did not reject progress but worked to control it for the benefit of all. In fact, the successful communities survived for so long because of their ability to adapt to the economic realities of the period through development or adoption of new means and methods of production. The strands of individualism in American life did not disappear in these communities as utopianists attempted to apply American individualism in a manner responsible to all. Members believed that their unique way of living would create a higher state for the individual and better human relationships in contrast to the selfish individualism running rampant in the industrializing nation.[7]

The utopian groups that existed in nineteenth-century America were generally small, many attracting fewer than twelve people. Even groups that attempted to unite large numbers and had thousands of members at their peaks, such as the Shakers, found it difficult to maintain so many people.[8] Larger communities meant greater numbers for the group to support and also a greater likelihood that division might break apart the haven.

Utopianists are often perceived as intellectuals struggling to forge a new order. However, the rigorous physical demands placed on members served as a natural limitation on who joined the groups. Furthermore, many utopias established an authoritative order necessary for the survival of the community. Utopianists had to suppress strands of individualism to assure the survival of the group. Most members of utopian communities were ordinary people who chose to participate in something extraordinary. The factors driving individuals to join these experiments ranged from the charisma of a leader to the attainment of freedom, either spiritual or temporal.[9]

Between 1787 and 1919, approximately 270 utopian communities existed in the United States. Demographic studies show that utopias were established in large numbers in certain time frames. One-third of the communities were founded in two periods: fifty-five in the years 1842–48 and thirty-six in the years 1894–1900. Research suggests that there was an ebb and flow to the popularity of such communities. One study indicates that utopias emerged during periods when Americans underwent long-wave crises pertaining to economic development. The utopian communities provided alternatives to capitalism, a system that utopianists criticized during these surges. While the antebellum era usually receives much attention for its wealth of experimentation, the late nineteenth century also saw the creation of many utopias as people struggled with the rapidly changing economic and social order resulting from industrialization. An examination of these post–Civil War communities, however, does not uphold the connection between utopias and economic crises because people claimed to have received God's word in both good and bad economic times.[10]

Most utopian communities emerged not only during particular time frames but also in specific areas affected by evangelicalism and reform. Utopias were founded in rural areas near urban centers from which they drew their members. These communities did not emerge on the frontier but rather in rural regions near commercial centers.[11]

Some areas of the nation experienced the firestorm of religion, reform, and the establishment of utopian movements to a greater degree than did others. The area of New York known as the Burned-Over District earned its name because of the intensity and degree of religious excitement and reform. The district stretched from east of Utica to west of Buffalo and from the Adirondack Mountains in the north to the Finger Lakes in the south. The region followed the route of the Erie Canal, and religious activity and reform surged with the canal's opening in 1825. The westward migration of peoples from New England to New York and then to areas further west like Ohio and Indiana helps to explain the levels of religious zeal and experimentation in these regions.[12]

The state of Ohio and the Western Reserve in particular played pivotal roles in the religious, reform, and utopian communities of the nineteenth century. The Western Reserve or "New Connecticut" consists of the northeastern portion of Ohio from Lake Erie extending south to the forty-first parallel and stretching 120 miles west from neighboring Pennsylvania. This includes the counties of Erie, Huron, Lorain, Medina, Lake, Cuyahoga, Geauga, Ashtabula, Trumbull, and Portage as well as portions of Mahoning, Summit, and Ashland. Because of the westward migration patterns, Ohio lay in the position to receive those affected by the movements in the East, especially those from the Burned-Over District. Ohio far surpassed neighboring western states as a haven for utopian groups, with twenty-one in total. In fact, between 1830 and 1860, Ohio had the largest number of utopian experiments by state. Eleven utopias were created in Indiana, and a smaller number of communities developed in Wisconsin, Illinois, and Michigan.[13] Ohio's utopian experiments were a continuation of the activities in western New York.

Why did so many people in search of creating a perfect world look to Ohio for refuge? As noted, migration patterns naturally led people from the East to the state in pursuit of new opportunities. Ohio offered land at affordable prices, giving people the opportunity to advance economically. Transportation also existed to facilitate migration. Consequently, the population of the state increased rapidly in the early nineteenth century. In 1810, the population was 231,000. This figure had more than doubled, to 581,000, by 1820, and by 1830, 938,000 people lived in the state. Furthermore, Ohio in the pioneer phase of the late eighteenth and early nineteenth centuries attracted people from many diverse backgrounds so that no particular religious group dominated the territory. The mix of cultures in Ohio provided a tolerant atmosphere for those motivated to create communities based on new ideas.[14]

This study examines the nature of Ohio utopias that thrived in the nineteenth century. These include the United Society of Believers in

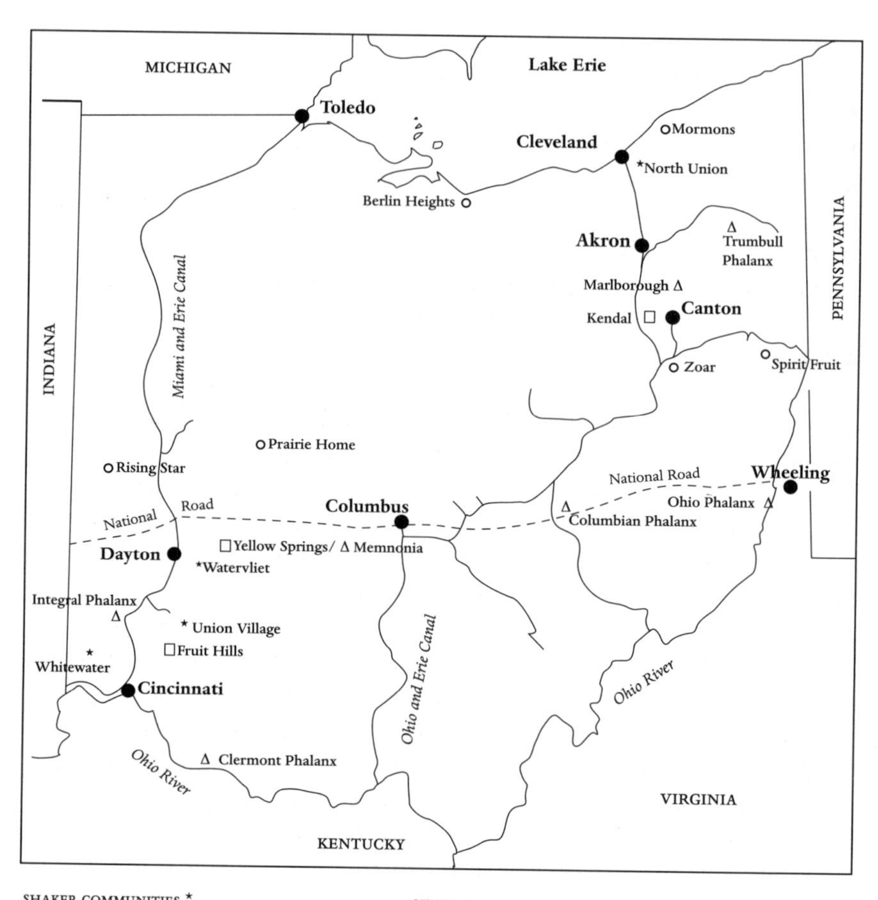

SHAKER COMMUNITIES *

Union Village *(Turtle Creek)*	1805–1912
Watervliet *(Beaver Creek)*	1806–1910
North Union	1822–1898
Whitewater	1823–1907

FOURIERIST PHALANXES Δ

Marlborough Association	1841–1845
Ohio Phalanx	1844–1845
Clermont Phalanx	1844–1846
Trumbull Phalanx	1844–1848
Columbian Phalanx	1845
Integral Phalanx	1845–1846
Utopia *(on former Clermont site)*	1847-1858
Memnonia Institute	1856-1857

OWENITE COMMUNITIES □

Yellow Springs	1825–1826
Kendal	1826–1829
Fruit Hills	1845–1852
Equity *(not shown—exact location in Tuscarawas River Valley unknown)*	1833–1835

OTHER COMMUNITIES ○

Zoar	1817–1898
Mormons	1830–1838
Prairie Home Community	1844
Brotherhood, or Spiritualist Community *(on former Clermont site)*	1846–1847
Rising Star Association	1853–1863
Free Lovers at Davis House *(Berlin Heights)*	1854–1858
Point Hope Community / Industrial Fraternity *(Berlin Heights)*	1860–1861
Berlin Community, or Christian Republic *(Berlin Heights)*	1865–1866
Spirit Fruit	1899–1904

Christ's Second Coming, or Shakers; the Society of Separatists of Zoar; and the Mormons. Other ventures, many short-lived in the state, include Owenite communities based on Robert Owen's model at New Harmony, Indiana, and the Fourier Phalanxes, founded on the philosophy of French utopianist Charles Fourier. Additionally, this book explores the establishment of such communities, their leaders, the involvement of women and gender roles, economic activities, successes and failures, and reasons for abandonment. The examination of these many havens helps to provide a greater understanding of all the utopian endeavors that dotted the American landscape in the nineteenth century.

The communities that developed in Ohio had various origins. Some groups had roots in Europe while others were wholly American phenomena. The Shakers had characteristics of both. Mother Ann Lee, leader of the "Shaking Quakers," shaped by religious developments in France and England, brought a small group of Believers to America in 1774. The group experienced success unknown in Europe, and membership increased. The organization of communities, systematization of doctrine, and increase in numbers took place after Mother Ann's death, when leadership fell to American converts. Thus, Shakers cannot be considered an authentic European import.[15]

On the other hand, the Society of Separatists of Zoar had their roots firmly planted in Europe. The group came to the United States from Wurtemberg, Germany, hoping to find a haven in which to practice their beliefs and escape famine. Led by Joseph Bimeler, they purchased five thousand acres in the Tuscarawas Valley in northeastern Ohio and founded a community in 1817. Communal ownership was established out of necessity rather than out of philosophy, as many of the more than 150 original men and women were poor. Residents also agreed to celibacy so that they could concentrate on repaying the money used to purchase the land instead of trying to support a growing population. The Separatists gained financially when the Ohio and Erie Canal was set to pass through their territory. The state sought out their aid to construct the canal. This enabled the community to pay back its debt and to establish industries. However, the community could not keep pace with improvements in industrialization and had to abandon segments of its economic activity. Furthermore, Bimeler died in 1853 with no member ready to accept the leadership role. The society underwent decades of decline and disbanded in 1898. At its peak, the group numbered five hundred.[16]

Another religious utopia established in Ohio that ultimately attained much success outside the state was the Mormon community, or the Church of Jesus Christ of the Latter Day Saints. This sect (a religious body holding beliefs that differed from mainstream religious doctrine) was one of several that emerged in the Burned-Over District. However, the Mormons differed in the success they would ultimately achieve. The migration of the Mormons to Kirtland in Lake County, Ohio, illustrates the movement of people and ideas from the Burned-Over District to the Western Reserve. Joseph Smith, the prophet and founder of the Mormons, saw visions and received golden tablets in western New York that served as the basis for *The Book of Mormon*. Two Campbellites, Sidney Rigdon and Parley Pratt, invited Smith to move his sect from Palmyra, New York, to Ohio. Rigdon assured Smith that Ohio would provide many converts to the new faith. Smith decided to move his flock to Kirtland in 1831. Two years later, the Mormons began to build an awe-inspiring temple as the center of their movement, a structure that still stands. Nearly twenty-five thousand people joined the Mormons in Ohio, but the controversial sect eventually found itself unwelcome as suspicion and hostility descended upon the group. Some people looked negatively on their communal ownership of land, and word that they engaged in nontraditional sexual practices alienated others. Also, the Mormons experienced hostility because of unsavory financial dealings surrounding the establishment of the Kirtland Anti-banking Company. These problems led Smith and most of his followers to leave Ohio to establish their haven in what is now the state of Utah. However, Smith's leadership of the group ended with his death at the hands of a mob in Carthage, Illinois, in 1844. Those followers remaining in Kirtland fused with the Reorganized Church of Jesus Christ of the Latter Day Saints.[17]

Other utopian communities rooted in the secular, rather than the religious, world took shape in Ohio. Unlike the Shaker villages, Zoar, and the Mormons, these groups lasted in Ohio for only brief periods of time. The ideologies guiding the Owenite communities and the Fourierist phalanxes had European origins.

Robert Owen of Great Britain determined to establish a utopia to reconcile the impact of industrialization on society. He proposed settlements where individuals cooperated together, sharing labor and property without giving any thought to religion. This ideal went against the competitiveness of the capitalist system and challenged the religiously charged atmosphere of the antebellum period. While the most famous of these settlements was New Harmony, Indiana, several such groups were formed in Ohio: Yellow Springs, 1825–26; Kendall, 1826–29; Equity, 1833–35; and Fruit Hills, 1845–52.[18]

Still other secular settlements evolved from the philosophy of Charles Fourier of France. Fourier felt his phalanxes had more to offer members than the outside world did. Members determined to work together for the community, and individuals could decide how much work they would complete. Because of the voluntary nature of work, these communities did not last long. Several developed in Ohio: Marlborough Association, 1841–45; Social Reform Unity, 1842–43; Ohio Phalanx, 1844–45; Clermont Phalanx, 1844–46; Trumbull Phalanx, 1844–48; Columbian Phalanx, 1845; Utopia, 1847–58; and Memnonia Institute, 1856–57.[19]

Several other utopias chose Ohio as the site of their experiments in living. These include the Rising Star Association, 1853–63, and the Spirit Fruit Society, 1899–1909.[20] The period following the Civil War had challenged some to find solutions to the problems plaguing society because of industrialization. Some people found answers in these havens.

Chapter 1

The Shaker Communities

THE UNITED SOCIETY OF BELIEVERS IN Christ's Second Coming, or the Shakers, came to the United States from Manchester, England, as a result of the influence of Ann Lee Stanley. However, the sect had its origins in seventeenth-century France with radicals known as the French Prophets or Camisard Prophets. This group believed the millennium was at hand and rejected all hierarchy. They viewed physical actions as the sign of religious excitation, and so trembling and dancing held importance in their worship. From 1598 until 1685, they could practice their faith under the protection of the Edict of Nantes. After the revocation of the edict, they fought for twenty-five years to maintain their autonomy but ultimately were defeated. In 1705, a small number migrated to England to practice their faith.[1]

The French Prophets attracted some followers in England, primarily from the laboring classes. Two former Quakers, Jane and James Wardley, became leaders of a group centered in Bolton, England, a town near Manchester. The Wardleys had wanted to return to the former emotionalism of the Quakers, an element lost as Quakers had gained more acceptance in England. They also brought key Quaker doctrines to their sect, including pacifism and the equal participation of women as members and preachers. They fused these elements with the millennial teachings and ritualistic dances of the French Prophets. The sect had earned the name "Shaking Quakers" or Shakers because of the intense dancing, shaking, and shouting that characterized its religious rituals.[2]

Under the influence of the Wardleys, Ann Lee joined the Shakers in 1758. Born in 1736 into a large family, Ann Lee lacked education and came from poor circumstances. She had worked in a textile mill and also as a cook. Her entrance into the Shaker faith began nine years of religious tribulations as well as personal suffering that affected her beliefs. In 1762, Ann Lee married a blacksmith named Abraham Stanley, a union that brought her little happiness. In the following years, she endured four difficult deliveries. All of her children died in infancy or by early childhood, and she thought that their deaths served as punishment for the sexual sins she had committed. These personal sufferings led her to believe that individuals could only devote themselves fully to God by giving up sexual relations. This philosophy greatly troubled her as a married woman, and she tried to avoid sexual relations with her husband. She applied these thoughts to all humanity and asserted that sex was the major cause of suffering in the world. In 1766, after losing her last child, she devoted more time and energy to the Shakers, which seemed to offer her comfort from the tragedies.[3]

The more active role in the Shakers brought Ann Lee further personal suffering and led her to become a key figure. The Shakers added several controversial doctrines that led to their persecution in England. Because of her experiences, Ann Lee introduced celibacy to the Shakers, asserting that individuals could fully devote themselves to God only by refraining from sexual relations. The Shakers also denounced secular influences on the churches, and they refused to observe the Sabbath. They proselytized in the streets and were often imprisoned for their actions. In 1770, Ann Lee served some time in a Manchester prison. The imprisonment galvanized her as she received visions from Christ, who assured her that the evil of humanity rested in the sin of sexual intercourse. Upon her release, she preached with more resolve and took a leadership role in the group. As her importance grew, so did the number of times she was imprisoned and the actions taken against her. Mobs threatened to silence her by removing her tongue with a hot iron. While she was in prison, authorities had attempted to starve her. Because of these trials, Shakers began to view Ann Lee as a martyr.[4]

During her incarceration in 1774, Ann Lee received another revelation naming her "Mother in Christ" and directing her to lead the small group of followers to America. The Shakers had not attained much success in England, only persecution. They hoped that they might experience the freedom to worship in America. In the summer of 1774, with eight others, including her husband, Mother Ann left for America. After their arrival in New York, Lee and her husband parted ways as she refused to engage in sexual relations with him. She then devoted herself to Niskeyuna (later Watervliet), the small Shaker community that the group established northwest of Albany, New York.[5]

The sect struggled to survive economically during these early years in America. Other residents thought them loyal to the British government during the American Revolution. Mother Ann helped to add to the Shaker membership by taking advantage of a religious revival that spread through New Lebanon, New York, in 1779. For those who could not accept the message of the New Light Baptists, Mother Ann offered the Shaker doctrine. During the revival, she succeeded in converting the leader of the revival, Joseph Meacham. She carried the Shaker message throughout New England, where mobs often demonstrated their hostility to the group. The Shakers seemed suspect because of their English origins and their refusal to bear arms. This led people to think them treasonous, and Ann Lee faced imprisonment because she was accused of being a spy. The Shakers likewise faced persecution from the population at large who believed that Mother Ann undermined the family with her doctrine of celibacy. Despite these problems, Mother Ann's work established the foundation for Shaker settlements in Connecticut, New Hampshire, Massachusetts, and Maine. She added new members into the group with her simple manner of imparting the message of salvation. She presented herself as a dignified, honest, and pious individual, which led people to accept her claim of divine calling. She died in 1784, before the Shakers experienced their largest growth in America. Shaker members recognized the significance of Lee as a leader. One wrote, "After the testimony of Mother's gospel was opened in this country, one observed that the work of the revival was not the work of God but the work of Ann Lee."[6]

The death of Mother Ann brought a critical juncture for the sect. The loss of their leader could have meant the end for the Shakers. However, other members stood poised to take charge. James Whittaker, one of the original group of eight from England, took over as leader. Until his death in 1787, Whittaker helped to begin communities in Maine and New Hampshire while strengthening the group's commitment to communal living.[7]

In 1787, two leaders from among the American converts rose to positions of power. New Englanders Elder Joseph Meacham and Eldress Lucy Wright played pivotal roles in the expansion and organization of Shakerism in America. Meacham selected Wright, who had assisted Mother Ann in Niskeyuna, to serve with him as lead minister so that the leadership would reflect their commitment to the equality of men and women. Meacham and Wright were the spiritual parents of the Shakers. One Shaker referred to Mother Lucy as the "Light of the body." Some evidence exists to indicate that Wright's claim to leadership did not emanate from Meacham but from Mother Ann. Lee and Wright had maintained a close relationship, and Lee had acknowledged Wright's claim to leadership before her death. Furthermore, in a community where the sexes were segregated, a separate male/female leadership structure was pragmatic.[8]

Both Meacham and Wright gave tighter organization and structure to Shaker theology, making possible the group's expansion. The two established the authoritative structure of the church, requiring members to follow without question the anointed leaders of the ministry. Meacham also established the structure of Shaker communities while outlining key Shaker doctrine. He created the model of the Shaker groups at New Lebanon, New York. The main purpose of Shaker communities was millennial in nature. Shakers chose to establish havens to create a heaven on earth. Meacham divided members into "orders" according to the level of their spiritual development. He also organized the group into male and female leadership. In a series of publications, he explained that God had sent both Jesus and Mother Ann to lead people to salvation. Meacham also outlined that God held a masculine and a feminine side as Father and Mother. This conviction justified the joint leadership of men and women in Shaker communities, as leadership would be a reflection of God.[9]

The concept of Mother Ann as the feminine side of God held great importance for Shakers. Uncertainty remains about whether Ann made this claim during her lifetime. She did refer to herself as Christ's lover and his bride. However, she also called herself God's servant and never declared herself to be omniscient. After her death, a key component of Shaker belief affirmed that the Second Coming of Christ had occurred through Mother Ann. Shaker communities that developed throughout the nation in the late eighteenth and into the nineteenth centuries emphasized this idea. Shakers showed acceptance of this doctrine at the turn of the century. In 1808, the *Testimony of Christ's Second Appearing* by Benjamin Seth Young enunciated that Shakers believed Ann Lee to be a female savior. In the covenant of the church at Watervliet, Ohio, named after the community in New York, believers stated it thus: "our Lord and Savior Jesus Christ did make his second appearance, by his Spirit, first Ann Lee, whom we acknowledge to be the *first Mother* of all souls in the work of regeneration, and the first spiritual head of the Church of Christ then in the body." Richard Pelham of Union Village, Ohio, stated it as follows: "yet Christ Jesus in his *second appearing* simply means *Ann Lee!*"[10]

In 1856, when Shaker communities enjoyed a peak in their membership of over thirty-eight hundred, Harvey Eads wrote an essay over 130 pages long on the nature of Christ and Mother Ann's connection to it. His extensive explanation and the testimony of other members in Shaker communities indicate that Shakers felt compelled to declare their adherence to this doctrine. They recognized the unique orthodoxy that they maintained and tried to defend it through logic and scripture, which they interpreted literally. Eads stated: "The *Anointed Jesus* did appear the second time in Ann Lee." In another passage he wrote, "The same process which made Jesus the Son of God made Ann the daughter of God and will make us sons and daughters of God." Christ's presence in Ann showed "in her miraculous power, in her self-denial," and "in all the fruits which she the *Anointed Ann* produced did the Anointed Jesus re-appear." Just as Mother Ann during her lifetime stated that original sins of sexuality began with Adam and Eve, Eads made reference to this: "'The seed of the *woman* who were to bruise the serpents head' are the Children of *Ann,* the 'free woman' who are to do it in themselves."[11]

While members accepted this view of Mother Ann, many found it difficult to look to women as leaders and as the equals of men. Meacham attempted to make this doctrine and the appointment of Eldress Lucy Wright more acceptable by claiming that his actions followed "revelations" that he had received. Nonetheless, it took followers almost a decade to acquiesce to these roles for women. Eldress Wright had to encourage women to take an active role and exercise their leadership rights.[12]

Meacham and Wright created the order and structure of the Shaker church to reflect the interpretation of Mother Ann as the feminine side of

God and to increase acceptance of female equality within the sect. The ministry at New Lebanon, New York, the model for the Shaker world, served as the ultimate authority for Shaker churches. This ministry consisted of four members, two males and two females. The head person in the ministry held the power to select or replace the other members of the group. This ministry also had the authority to appoint, approve, or replace the elders and eldresses leading communities throughout the nation. The ministries of all Shaker communities mirrored the composition of the head group at New Lebanon, and the elders and eldresses lived in separate quarters. The Shaker governmental structure was authoritarian, not democratic. Most utopian groups established such a hierarchical system to prevent dissenters from threatening the order.[13]

When Meacham died in 1796, eleven Shaker villages had been established in New England. Eldress Lucy Wright ably succeeded him to continue the growth of the order. Wright led the Shakers for twenty-five years, and membership in the East increased from more than thirteen hundred in 1800 to more than twenty-three hundred in 1830. Many small farmers and craftsmen joined the Shaker communities. Several factors contributed to the number of converts. Many learned about the Shaker doctrines through preaching and publications and found truth in them. The revivalistic aspect of the Shakers with their shaking, dancing, singing, and stamping also gained much attention. Furthermore, some people wanted to participate in the economic order established in Shaker villages, which had brought prosperity for the groups in the early 1800s.[14]

In the early 1800s, Eldress Wright acted upon news that religious revivals had overtaken parts of the West. The southwestern corner of Ohio experienced much religious excitement influenced by the Kentucky Revival of 1800–01, and the ferment went on for several years. At the time, Ohio had a population of approximately forty-five thousand, mostly farmers. The Shakers believed that they would find fertile ground for new converts since they shared several things in common with the revivalists, including physical manifestations of conversion and worship, public confession of sins, and perfectionist beliefs. To recruit new members, Wright appointed three men, Isaachar Bates, Benjamin Youngs, and John Meacham, who traveled on foot to Ohio. They left New Lebanon, New York, on January 1, 1805. Confident of the Shaker way of life, these missionaries helped create seven new communities in the West. Four communities took root in Ohio. The first and largest Shaker haven established in Ohio was Union Village, also called Turtle Creek, founded in 1805 north of Cincinnati. Members of Union Village branched off to form Watervliet in 1806 and North Union, located southeast of Cleveland, in 1822. A fourth community, Whitewater, was founded in 1823 as another branch of Union Village.[15]

Meacham, Youngs, and Bates experienced early success in their missionary endeavors in 1805 with the establishment of Union Village. The three men converted two influential figures to start the village: Malcolm Worley, a wealthy citizen, and Richard McNemar, a Presbyterian minister. Both men helped to add to the number of Shaker converts. Within a year about 370 people had united in the Shaker way of life at Union Village. The members of the new community demonstrated a willingness to serve and obey God since they had "separated [themselves] from the course of the world to seek a union and spiritual relocation to each other in the order of God." The ministry of New Lebanon selected David Darrow to serve as the leader of the ministry, a position he held for twenty-five years. The settlement at Union Village served as the center of Shakerism in the West.[16]

The community of Union Village fostered the organization of communities in other parts of Ohio. Watervliet was located on Beaver Creek near Dayton and was also known by the names Beaver Creek, Beulah, and Mad River. McNemar had preached in this area during the revivals of 1802–03. After his acceptance of the Shaker faith, he spread the message to Beaver Creek, and many converted to the group. Upon the formation of the society, John Stewart was named first elder.[17]

Union Village also played an important role in the establishment of the North Union society near Cleveland. The Society of Believers at North Union was established under the leadership of Ralph Russell of Warrensville, Ohio, who encountered the Shaker way of life in 1821 at a visit to Union Village. Russell found the Shaker principles so impressive that he resolved to move his family to the Warren County community. The elders at Union Village convinced Russell to create a new community in northern Ohio so that he might convert others in the area to the Shaker faith. Ralph Russell founded the community on land he owned in Warrensville and land owned by early converts who were relatives and friends. He established an area on the land as the heart of North Union based on a vision in which he saw a ray of light near his log cabin, and the ray of light "rose in a strong erect column and became a beautiful tree." The North Union Shakers called their settlement the "valley of God's pleasure."[18]

In 1822, Richard W. Pelham and James Hodge from Union Village arrived in Warrensville to help with the first meeting of the society, held at the Russell home. Although only twenty-five years old, Pelham persuasively explained the Shaker way of life to those in attendance and answered all of their questions. Consequently, Russell's three brothers, Elisha, Rodney, and Return, converted to the Shaker faith.[19]

While the Russell family thus formed the cornerstone of the North Union settlement, other early members took on important roles for the society. These included Chester Risley, a neighbor of Ralph Russell, and Prudence Sawyer of Mentor, Ohio, who joined the community in 1823. In 1826, James Sullivan Prescott entered the community after laboring as a stonemason to construct the Center House for the Shakers. This close contact with the community led Prescott to join. As a member, Prescott recorded the history of the community. The Shakers added more new members from the surrounding area and from travelers. In 1828, eighty-nine people signed the covenant to form the North Union society. At the height of its development, the North Union society consisted of more than five hundred people and 1,500 acres of land.[20]

Just as a Union Village convert helped to form the North Union community, Miriam Agnew, who joined the Shakers at Union Village in 1823, helped to extend the Shaker reach to her home of Whitewater, north of Cincinnati. At Whitewater, Agnew spoke about the Shaker doctrine and reported to the Shaker leadership that the people of the area received her words with interest. The Shakers sent Richard Pelham of the North Union Society and George Blackleach to start a community. By the fall of 1823, the community at Whitewater had attracted thirty believers. The leadership of Union Village decided to combine the Whitewater group with a settlement that had taken shape earlier at Darby, located seventy miles northeast of Union Village. The Darby community had had difficulties since its beginnings in 1818. The land of the Darby village was also claimed by the military, so the Shaker leadership feared losing the settlement. Hence, they determined to join the Darby and Whitewater groups to forge a strong Shaker community.[21]

The communities established in Ohio followed the structure and doctrines of other Shaker villages. The ministries of each community oversaw the leadership of "families." Each village was divided into families, and the number of families was determined by the size of membership. Families consisted of between thirty and one hundred people, and each family had a female and male component, reflective of the lead ministry at New Lebanon, New York. Two women and two men governed the respective sides of the house, and these leaders had absolute authority.

These elders and eldresses listened to confessions, preached, conducted meetings, engaged in mission work, and made decisions on the admittance of new members. Beyond this, they determined work assignments and served as conduits to the outside world. The church at Union Village chose the first elders and trustees, and those selected usually held their positions for life. The elders and trustees in turn usually selected their successors. While the Shakers believed the shared governance between men and women provided equality for women, in reality it left most Shaker women subject to the ultimate rule of leaders who had been chosen by superiors in the hierarchy. The majority of Shaker women held no political power. Furthermore, even women leaders did not enjoy equal authority with their male counterparts. Rather, they enjoyed power in their sphere, that is, power over the female sides of the communities. The property of the societies remained legally owned by males who served as trustees. Also, the division of labor into traditional male and female tasks left men in charge of the industries producing the most wealth in the communities. Many Shaker women accepted the belief that men were their superiors as representatives of God on earth. Women, reflecting Mother Ann, served as coworkers in their delegated sphere.[22]

The ministries of each community had control over other important factors. Elders and eldresses chose trustees who held control over the property of the community. These trustees also were selected to conduct business with the outside world along with trading deacons. To avoid corruption by nonbelievers, they traveled in groups of three and could not remain outside the communities for more than four weeks. Members regularly prayed for trustees and deacons at church services so that they would resist the temptations of society. Members gave up considerable decision-making powers to the trustees for the good of the community.[23]

The Shakers took much effort to recruit new members since, with their commitment to celibacy, they could not depend on natural increase to sustain a population. The Shakers attracted larger numbers than did other utopian groups, and they founded several communities throughout the nation. At the height of their membership in the 1850s, they had more than thirty-eight hundred members. After this the society experienced a steady decline, numbering 1,849 in 1880 and 855 in 1900. The Shakers recruited many people who found truth in Shaker doctrine, whose "whole end, design and purpose . . . is to receive and diffuse the manifold gifts of God to the mutual comfort and happiness of each other as brethren and sisters in the gospel."[24]

They also recruited people who had grown wary of their Protestant sects. Richard Pelham, an important leader who helped to establish the communities of North Union and Whitewater, converted to Method-ism at a young age but did not feel wholly satisfied with this faith. Several years later, in 1810, he visited his cousin who lived at Union Village and found his religious home with the Shakers. He recollected, "The Shakers had stolen my heart, absorbed my affections. To me there was but one lovely spot on earth, and that was Union Village."[25]

Luther Gould of Connecticut endured the loss of his mother at a young age. After her death, his father remarried and had all his children baptized as Presbyterians. As an adolescent in Massachusetts, associated with acquaintances of questionable character, Gould confronted the issue of the salvation of his soul. A Shaker visiting his father explained to Luther that the Shakers served God. This left an impression on Gould. He learned more about the Shakers in his early twenties and in 1841, at forty-three years old, joined the Shaker community at North Union, where he thought himself fully in the light of true salvation.[26]

Religion was an important factor in Shaker conversions, but people also joined for other reasons. In their recruitment efforts, the Shakers sought out people who engaged in their particular industries, such as broom and barrel making and the cultivation of herbs. James Prescott of Massachusetts had learned about the Shakers during his teenage years, when he attended a Shaker meeting. However, he first became a Baptist. A mason by trade, he moved to Cleveland in 1826 and was employed by the Shakers of North Union to construct their first dwelling house. Members at the time lived in log cabins and needed people who could build new dwellings. Prescott grew interested in the faith, studied its doctrines, and entered the order. He served as an elder, teacher, and trustee for the society during his life with the Shakers.[27]

Those people who wished to become Shakers first entered the "Gathering Order," "a door to the Church; into which all must enter and through which all must pass before being admitted into the true Church of Christ upon Earth." Those in the gathering order would, they hoped, undergo conversion and fully enter the Shaker faith. The Shakers wanted people who would seriously enter the faith, and they discouraged people from making quick decisions that they could not follow. The covenant of the Church at Union Village cautioned new members that joining the sect required caution and deliberation. Some individuals stayed only briefly in the gathering order before completely entering into Shaker life. Others stayed for an extended amount of time and never embraced the Shaker way of life.[28]

Some who entered the gathering order never intended to become Shakers. "Winter Shakers" were people who would enter in the fall and receive food and clothing from the group throughout the winter. When spring arrived, they would leave the order. At the beginning of spring 1879, at the time that Shaker communities throughout the nation had declined in number, the Church Family of Union Village noted that John Parks had left the community. The other members were not surprised at this because "he never was anything of a Shaker." Apparently, the Shakers had experienced difficulty maintaining recruits as the records noted: "In this day very few persons come among Believers who are in the least degree prepared for the saving discipline of Shakerism. Most of those who apply are in want of a second shirt, and almost as destitute of principle."[29]

Shaker recruits differed from converts in other communities in that Shakers accepted a number of young people, and children formed an important component of Shaker society. Although members took vows of celibacy, children entered Shaker communities when their parent(s) or persons with legal right over them joined. Upon the establishment of the North Union society, Elisha Russell entered the group with his wife and five children, and other families joined as well. His brother Return brought his eleven children into the faith. A child could not become a full member of the church until age twenty-one. At that age, if the person left the Shakers he or she would receive a share of the parent's property. Many adolescents and young adults joined the Shakers. Young people in difficult situations at that time had no public social welfare service on which to rely. The Shakers willingly offered such youths a home, family, and structure when they might have felt uncertain about the future.[30]

The Shakers declared in their statement of purpose that they would provide "for the relief of the poor, the widow, and the fatherless." Richard Pelham, the youngest of eight children, had endured much difficulty in his youth before finding a home with the Shakers in his early adulthood. His mother died when he was young, and his father gave him to his uncle, a physician and Methodist preacher, to raise. On his 1810 visit to Union Village, he found his spiritual home and converted to Shakerism. Of his personal journey, he said, "Who can doubt that all was the direction of intelligent design." Pelham served the Shakers as a leading missionary, and he helped to establish the communities of North Union and Whitewater, Ohio, and Groveland, New York.[31]

The Shakers made clear provisions about the status of children who wished to enter the church. Those underage youths seeking to enter the society had to express their desire to become a Shaker. They also needed the consent of their parent(s) or guardian to join. If they met these conditions, children still could not become full church members until they reached age twenty-one. Orphans also could not become full members until age twenty-one. The Shakers thought that children could not enter the faith with full knowledge of the commitment. Also, children could not give their property to the community legally. However, they did fall under the care and government of the church as youths. The covenant of the Shakers also indicated that children could not be employed by the church to earn money.[32]

While the Shakers desired younger members to insure the continuation of the group, youths also posed many problems. Most did not bring any property into the community, and older members did not think this fair. Youths at times acted inappropriately. As many had not undergone a religious conversion or a revival experience, some found the Shaker practices and rituals amusing and laughed at them. The Shakers had difficulty recruiting youths serious about joining the order. Accordingly, they made provisions in their covenant to disinherit "disobedient and rebellious" youth who would "not subject themselves to our lawful authority." Furthermore, fewer than 20 percent of those people who became Shakers remained for the duration of their lives. Some chose to leave when they could support themselves, and others left the order because relatives removed them.[33]

The effort of relatives to remove children caused some chaotic encounters in Shaker communities. In December 1813, James Bedle, a former Shaker who had leveled charges against the group for years, attempted to remove his children forcibly from Union Village. Bedle had bound his children as indentured servants to Peter Pease and wanted them back. After Bedle failed in a violent attempt to take the children, Pease agreed to give them up to end the conflict. Bedle removed his two youngest children from the community against their will. His two oldest children and their mother left the community to avoid any further violence.[34]

An incident in 1819 involved Phoebe Johnson, a young woman allegedly held against her will by the Shakers of Union Village. Phoebe and her siblings had entered the Shakers with the consent of their parents and had lived among the Shakers for thirteen years. During this time, the mother had passed away. Before she died, she requested that the Shakers raise the children. The father, a non-Believer, had agreed to his wife's wishes. The *Western Star,* a publication with an aversion to the Shakers, had encouraged people of the area to liberate the Johnson children, and subsequently a mob formed in August 1819. The mob spoke with Phoebe, who assured them that she wanted to remain a Shaker. The group insisted that she leave the Shakers, and Phoebe had to go to prevent the mob from forcibly carrying her away. A few days later, a larger mob of several hundred returned and beat Shaker men and women with their fists, clubs, and whips. Some of the Johnson children hid to escape removal. The Shakers allowed the children to leave with their father, who urged them to be patient and promised that he would help. The Shakers also aided those Johnson children who wished to remain.[35]

Another matter that the Shakers addressed in their covenants concerned the status of married persons who wished to enter the order. By the time of the establishment of the Ohio communities, the position of the Shakers on marriage had changed. During the late eighteenth century, the Shakers had suffered persecution when one spouse embraced the faith more enthusiastically than the other. The lukewarm partner sometimes raised mobs in response to the marital problems evolving from the conversion to Shakerism. The Shakers followed the practice that if a wife embraced the faith and the husband did not, she had to remain with her spouse. If the husband let her go freely, the Church would admit her. If a husband joined without the conversion of the wife, he could enter the faith. The Shakers encouraged men in such situations to leave the wives and take the children if they chose. In this case, the Shakers followed the law, which gave rights to men over women regarding children and property.[36]

In the nineteenth century, the Shakers in Ohio communities expressed a different doctrine on marriage and membership. If a married person converted to the Shaker doctrine and the spouse did not, the Shakers acknowledged the right of the unbelieving partner to leave the community. According to the covenant, "the parties have an indisputable right to agree to such a separation, and to make a just divide of their interest." The Shakers urged those leaving marital relations to settle questions of children and property in a manner acceptable to both parties. The Shakers, however, admonished those spouses who would prevent their partner from "acting according to his or her own faith and sense of duty to God."[37]

The dissolution of marriages when members joined the Shakers proved controversial, and some Shakers took pains to defend it. James Prescott, in his chronicles of the Society of North Union, explained the effects that entering the society could have on a family. In 1825, William Andrews brought a wife and four children with him when he joined the North Union community. According to Prescott, although Andrews had a wife and children, "he now became as though he had none, according to St. Paul's injunction . . . he now put away the office of a wife and became a brother in the Lord, and the wife . . . became a sister in the Lord." All members of the Andrews family joined the Shakers.[38]

Prescott also discussed Mr. O. Wheeler, who converted to the Shakers from Methodism in 1825. When he joined North Union, his three children came with him while his wife stayed behind. Prescott wrote that "a mutual parting and separation took place . . . growing out of a change of religious sentiments of one of the parties, which resulted in breaking up of the family—a practical illustration of the false charges brought against the Shakers of breaking up families, while they may be perfectly innocent. Families are often broken up from other courses, over which the Shakers had no agency or control, and the parties may afterwards, one or both, go and join the Shakers as the consequence of having changed their religious sentiments."[39]

In this assertion, Prescott attempted to defend Shakers against allegations that they undermined the sanctity of families, and he introduced another issue. In alleging that spouses and families often broke apart before one partner joined the Shakers, he raised the question as to whether an unhappily married person could find a socially acceptable way to exit the marriage and family by joining a celibate religious order. The individual could claim that religion caused him or her to take the unconventional action of leaving a spouse. In other words, the Shakers provided an alternative to a person in an unhappy marriage.

Apparently, the state of Ohio recognized the effects that the Shakers had on family life. In some cases when married persons chose to join the Shakers they left their marriage partner behind in difficult circumstances. In 1807, a law was proposed for the relief and support of women who might have been abandoned by their husbands. The law was passed specifically in response to the establishment of Shaker communities in Ohio because "women have been abandoned by their husbands, robbed of their children and left destitute of the means of support."[40]

To thwart such circumstances the law addressed cases in which a man refused to live in a conjugal relationship with his wife by joining a sect that required renunciation of the marriage covenant. In such cases, the woman could file a petition in the Court of Common Pleas or in the Supreme Court. The man had to appear before the Court to answer questions about his relationship with his wife. If the Court judged that the man had renounced the marriage covenant, then the Court would determine the amount of property that the woman received. Furthermore, if the man and woman had minor children, "the husband so violating the marriage covenant shall be considered as having renounced and divested himself of all the authority he could otherwise have exercised over his children." The Court would then determine the amount of the remainder of his property that would go to the support of his children, and the children would remain under the care of the mother "provided that the Court shall have power if they shall deem it necessary to appoint a guardian or guardians for such child or children—and provided also that if the Court shall deem it necessary they may direct such child or children to be bound to apprenticeship." If the man gave any money to the sect or group that detracted from the support of the wife or children, then the property could be retrieved and given to them. Beyond this, the law fined in an amount not to exceed five hundred dollars any person who intently persuaded a married man to renounce his marriage or to abandon his wife or children, or those who persuaded a person to join a sect that called for the renunciation of a marriage.[41]

With this act, the Shaker doctrine of celibacy that would require the renunciation of a marital contract inadvertently gave more power to women. Normally, a woman did not have access to her husband's property or to guardianship of any children if their marriage ended. In the circumstances outlined in the act, however, women had more equal treatment with the right to equitable distribution of marriage property and perhaps guardianship of the children. For women to receive this treatment before the law, however, the court had to determine that the man had committed a wrong by renouncing the marital contract.

In spite of the efforts of Shakers and the law to prevent difficulties when families broke apart because of one spouse's conversion to the group, problems still arose. In 1810, a group of five hundred men armed with guns and swords approached the community at Union Village. This mob originated because of controversy surrounding the conversion of James Smith Jr. to Shakerism and the subsequent dissolution of his marriage. Smith left his wife, Polly, to join the Shakers, and he took his children with him. Polly then appealed to others, including her father-in-law, Colonel James Smith, to retrieve her children. Colonel Smith, fueled by the reports of former Shaker apostates John Davis, John and Robert Wilson, and John Bedle, made several accusations against the Shakers in the public press. He alleged that the Shakers abused the children under their care by whipping them brutally and that the Shakers denied children an education. Also, Colonel Smith accused Elder David Darrow of controlling all of the material resources of the community and living lavishly off the work of others. Richard McNemar denied these charges but could not prevent the formation of the mob on August 27, 1810.[42]

Led by Colonel Smith and other men dressed in military garb, the mob intended to remove the Smith children and force the Shakers to leave the area so that the members could return to their former way of life. Both the attorney general, J. Collet, and the county sheriff, T. McCray, warned members of the group the day before the planned attack that their intentions were unlawful, to no avail.[43]

The mob arrived at Union Village at one o'clock in the afternoon. They dispatched a committee of twelve to discuss their grievances with several of the founding members of the Shakers. Three Shakers agreed to meet with the twelve in the woods. The committee, led by Matthew G. Wallace, a Presbyterian minister, indicated that the people in the area believed the Shakers had caused great disturbances because of their beliefs and practices and threatened both civil and religious society. Wallace charged that the Shakers held members in bondage and oppression and that nonbelievers would no longer accept this. The Shakers and the twelve men discussed several children living in the community with a parent or parents who had grandparents asking for their release. The Smith children were among those mentioned. The committee demanded that the children of the deceased James Watts be given to their grandfather as their father had wanted. The Shakers answered that the children were under the mother's care, and they had no control over them. If the mother wanted them to leave the Shaker community, they would not prevent their departure. The committee also demanded that the Shakers give up their ritual dancing and their efforts to recruit new members. The Shakers responded that they could not take children away from their parents, and they would not give up their faith.[44]

After several hours of maneuvering by each side, the Shakers allowed a committee of six to search the community and see if anyone was being held against his or her will. The committee found all in residence there to be happy. The committee also spoke with the Shaker school children, who told them the Shakers fed them well and did not abuse them. When the committee conveyed these reports to the mob, it dispersed.[45]

Although the Shakers attempted to anticipate problems regarding membership, they had to endure further accusations that they held people in their communities against their will. In 1812, Nancy Dunn asked the Supreme Court of the State of Ohio to help her free her daughter, Sarah Naylor, from the Shakers at Union Village. According to Dunn, her daughter Sarah was taken without any authority by Richard Whemer and one or two other Shakers. Dunn believed that her daughter was being deprived of her liberty and kept by Whemer and the Shakers unlawfully. In response to the court, Whemer replied that Sarah, known as Magy amongst the Shakers, was not being illegally held by the group. Whemer stated that Magy had joined the Shakers seven years earlier and was at liberty to leave the group at any time. As to the accusations made by Dunn, Whemer reported that Magy went with him and another Shaker to visit Dunn, and Magy returned "to her own habitation from which some have taken occasion by groundless slander." Since that time, Magy, with her husband's consent, had left on a journey to Kentucky, and no reason existed for concern about her well-being.[46]

The explanation offered by Whemer did not satisfy the court, and the case went to trial. Nancy Dunn appeared before the court and offered her account of the events. Dunn related that she frequently visited her daughter and was treated well. Sarah accompanied her mother home several times and said that she wanted to leave the Shakers. Dunn asked if Sarah would leave her children, and Sarah replied that she would leave them with John Naylor. One Sunday, Sarah visited her mother and announced that she would visit her relatives in Pennsylvania with her mother. The next day, Sarah returned with two Shakers. When they left, Sarah went with them and indicated that she could not go on the trip. Dunn alleged that Sarah did not receive food from the society and that Sarah's husband, John Naylor, did not support Sarah. She insisted Sarah wanted to leave the society and made accusations against Whemar and the Shakers.[47]

In response to these accusations, Whemar replied that Sarah was in Kentucky, and a witness testified to seeing her in Cincinnati. John Naylor also testified on behalf of the defense. He indicated that he had married Sarah twelve years earlier and supported her to the best of his ability. He just met Dunn the previous summer, and Dunn indicated that she was Sarah's mother. John had never met the woman before and did not know her identity. He also stated that Sarah had said she wanted to go to Kentucky, and he acquiesced. He expected her back when she wanted to return. Another witness testified that Magy had gone to Kentucky of her own free will. Given this testimony, the judge dismissed the case.[48]

Although the Shaker villages did encounter some difficulties pertaining to their members, some people joined the communities for the security they could provide. Shaker communities tended to have large numbers of the elderly and a greater number of women. The Shakers offered the elderly care, friendship, and compassion, in sickness and in health. The elderly made up a larger percentage of the members because those who joined the group at a young age often left the community and the older members behind. While women also made up a greater number of the group, their percentages did not substantially increase until the post–Civil War era. The longer life span of women contributed to this phenomenon.[49]

Some women in difficult circumstances decided to make a home with the Shakers. In 1838, the society at North Union welcomed the entrance of Mary Ann McCleary, a twenty-four-year-old whose husband and two children had died. Before moving to Cleveland, she had read a Shaker hymnal from one of the Eastern societies. This led her to investigate the Shaker faith, which she embraced at North Union. One member stated of McCleary that "very few have a brighter mind naturally and it has been well improved by as good an upbringing and education as the world does often afford."[50]

When people joined Shaker communities, they had to adhere to the religious doctrine of the Shakers as well as to their communal way of life. They required new members to confess fully their sins so that they would be able to begin to live a virtuous life. New members had to settle all debts and right all wrongs before joining so that nothing could prevent them from being "united in a joint interest, according to the gospel" and living "the most perfect order of God on earth."[51]

To enter into the communal way of life, new members had to agree to work and serve the family to which they joined and to use their property for the benefit of all. By eliminating personal property, members entered into a joint church where they could leave behind the business of the world. Joint ownership of property helped to keep the Shakers separate from the rest of the world. Members entered into a community interest "where no man has right of the things he possesses he calls his own, but they have all things common." No distinction would be made among members based on how much property they brought into the community but "all should have just and equal rights and privileges, according to their needs."[52]

If a member chose to leave the community, which he or she could do freely at any time, that person could take the property he or she had brought into the family. Frequently departing members took tools from the trade they had learned from the community as well as some clothes and cash. However, a member who left could not claim debts or damages against the society. When Thomas Cohoon left the Society at North Union in 1843, he settled monetarily with the group and promised not to bring debts against them. Members signed agreements stating that they understood these provisions. In 1806, William and Robert Wilson signed a covenant when they joined the community at Union Village. They agreed that they entered the group of their own faith. They stated that they gave themselves and their services freely and would not charge the community any debt for labor or service completed by them. In 1846, Henry Rickerd certified that he joined the North Union community for religious reasons. He promised "never to bring any charge or demand" against the community "for any labor or service or any benefit I may or have rendered them beyond what I may receive in communion with the rest, in such as food, clothing, lodging, nursing" while he lived with the Shakers. Other new members at North Union in the 1840s signed similar statements.[53]

Although the Shakers mentioned the principle that individuals leaving could not make claims, troubles sometimes arose. Mary Ann Swayer, also known as Mary Ann Calder, sued the community at North Union for payment for services she rendered while she resided with them during different periods over fifteen years. She estimated her labor to be worth thirty-five dollars, or $110 per year. She based her claims on the fact that she had worked as an individual with a handicap as she only had one hand. She also argued that she signed the covenant when she was not of age. Her lawyer argued that even had she been of age, the contract was null and void because it denied members the right to marry. Swayer offered testimony that the Shakers forced people to sign the covenant and then held them against their will. She also claimed that the Shakers did not uphold good government or good morals. According to her suit, if the society continued in its actions, the institution of marriage was threatened.[54]

The Shakers employed L. Starkweather to rebut these charges. Starkweather demonstrated through testimony that the Shakers were founded for charitable purposes. Moreover, members had the free will to sign the covenant and leave the society of their choosing; none were held in bondage. Starkweather also stated that he had served as attorney for the Shakers for twenty-one years and he had never known them to act immorally but only as true Christian models. This defense met the approval of the jury, which found in favor of the Shakers.[55]

The Shakers succeeded at institutionalizing the concept of community-held property and establishing dynamic villages that changed with the economic realities of the times. Shaker communities usually were founded with an initial donation of land and then grew substantially. In the case of North Union, the settlement started with land given by several members: Ralph, Elijah, and Elisha Russell, Chester Risley, and Riley Honey. Seven log cabins dotted the original landscape, and frame buildings eventually replaced these dwellings. The Shakers constructed the Center House, the first frame building of the settlement, in 1826. In their architecture, as in their daily lives, the Shakers let practicality guide them. In the first twenty years after its establishment, North Union developed substantially, adding several barns and a grist mill. Members also converted their original dwellings into work areas to make brooms, brushes, and other items. By 1874, the community included a woolen factory, church, school, office, tannery, blacksmithy, and several buildings housing the different families.[56]

The addition of the new stone grist mill in 1843 held much importance for the Shakers, and the Mill Family, named for it, managed it. The mill was built on the bank of a creek running through the village and stood four stories high to make it level with the land. The mill was constructed of wood except for the basement, which was made of sandstone. The Shakers used the mill to grind grain for themselves to make flour and coarse feed. People in neighboring towns also depended on the mill for these functions, and it attained a reputation as one of the best mills in the country, bringing much income to the Shakers. By 1886, though, the mill had outlasted its utility and become a financial burden to the community, so the society blew it up as part of the Fourth of July celebration.[57] In 1889, not long after the grist mill, the pride of the community, was blown up, the North Union society disbanded. The grist mill thus represented both the rise and fall of this particular community.

The Shakers kept detailed records of buildings that they added to their communities, seeming to indicate that they equated the success or vitality of their group with such progress. The Shakers of Union Village, Watervliet, and North Union recorded the growth of their communities

1.1 Shakers, North Union: Grist Mill (James Prescott on left). *Western Reserve Historical Society, Cleveland, Ohio*

from cabins to the construction of mills, barns, and new residences for the families. Visitors to the Shaker villages also took note of the mills and the successful industries that propelled their economic life. The North Union Shakers possessed a plentiful supply of timber, which enabled them to expand their buildings when necessary. They also had an excellent sawmill, which allowed them to put the timber to good use. In 1854, they used their resources to construct a woolen factory standing four stories high on its north side and three stories high on the south side. The upper story had a spinning jack and two power looms for weaving cloth. The Shakers used the machines to manufacture most of the wool into stocking yarn. Another story contained an iron lathe, which they used for turning broom handles since broom manufacturing was a major Shaker industry.[58]

In the construction of their buildings and in their industries, the Shak-

1.2 Shakers, Union Village: Main Dwelling of Church Family. *Western Reserve Historical Society, Cleveland, Ohio*

ers demonstrated ingenuity and thoughtfulness. To power three mills, the North Union society needed to harness water power. Doan's Brook, the creek running through the center of their land, provided this water source. The Shakers used the creek by creating dams and large ponds, which they called lakes. This made it possible to power three mills in a mile.[59]

Members of Shaker communities contributed to the economic progress of the group with their inventions. The inventions developed by the Shakers evolved from the practical necessity to simplify their production methods or to simplify their lives. Daniel Baird of North Union invented Babbitt Metal, a soft metal necessary to reduce friction caused by harder metals that made the bearings of machinery heat up, thus requiring the brethren to stop machines until they cooled. Others recognized the utility of this invention, and Ward and Company employed this metal on their lake steamboats. Baird sued the company but lost the case. The company offered Baird a lifetime pass on its lake boats, indicating that it probably had copied his invention.[60]

The members of the Shaker communities in Ohio placed importance on their commitment to key Shaker doctrines, including the duality of God as masculine and feminine. In a testimony of faith, Chester Risley, a leader of North Union, explained, "We therefore claim Jesus Christ the son of God and the founder of the first Church of God on Earth to be our Spiritual Father and the Daughter of God and eternal wisdom who dwelt in the person Ann Lee to be our spiritual and ever blessed Mother." Another North Union member rationalized: "St. Paul preached *Jesus* and the resurrection, but in this day we preach Mother and the resurrection. You talk of a child of God—if God was its Father, who was its Mother? Who ever heard of a child being born of a father? How could there be a father without a mother? Does not the very idea of a father *imply* a *Mother* in the Deity?"[61]

Since the millennium was upon them and had originated "from *God* the *Eternal Mother,*" Shakers did not need to reproduce and accepted the doctrine of celibacy. They believed celibacy was an essential component to attain salvation because members needed to attain full repentance. The Shakers did not condemn marriage in cases where fit subjects could improve the race "if they keep it where it belongs in the Adamic order." However, they viewed sexual relations as a civil rather than a Christian right, and they refrained from them as did Jesus Christ and his Apostles. They thought that sexual relations belonged to a person's animal instincts and needed to be eliminated to achieve "the highest and holiest, and happiest life."[62]

1.3 Shakers, North Union: Girls' Home, Dwelling House (built 1826). *Western Reserve Historical Society, Cleveland, Ohio*

Richard Pelham of the North Union society explained his personal experiences that led him to embrace a celibate life: "At this early age I had some serious and perhaps some uncommon reflections concerning the intercourse of the sexes. I was strongly impressed with a sense of the impurity and deep degradation of everything of the kind." During his adolescence, he indulged in pleasures of the flesh, "the greatest enemy of my soul." After this prayer, he entered into a life of celibacy and did not stray. While other Americans of the era shared the view that the end of sexual relations would bring about a higher spiritual state, few supported eliminating sex altogether. The Shakers expressed their unconventional adherence to celibacy in the Covenant of the Church at Union Village: "We have neither been flattered with the prospect of any carnal delight nor threatened with any corporal punishment as the means of bringing us into the present faith."[63]

By incorporating celibacy and renouncing the sin of carnal desires, the Shakers created an atmosphere for more equal treatment of women, who could no longer be subjected to their husbands' authority in marriage or be viewed as sexual objects. Originating with Ann Lee and her personal difficulties with childbearing, the doctrine of celibacy helped to eliminate the burdens of pregnancy, childbirth, and child rearing for women. Although this opened new avenues for women, the Shakers still seemed to adhere to patriarchal ideas about male leadership. At the height of her leadership and charisma, Ann Lee still deferred to males. When Joseph Meacham joined the order in 1780, he questioned a church with a female leader when St. Paul had denounced it. Through a male intermediary, Lee replied that a man naturally leads a family, but in his absence, a woman takes over. Furthermore, Ann Lee viewed Christ as her leader. She also told women to follow Jesus and instructed married women to obey their husbands.[64]

These philosophies (duality of God and celibacy) provided the backbone for the separation of the sexes in the community, including the dual hierarchies of males and females. Shakers constructed their leadership between female and male heads not out of a concern for equality between the sexes, but because celibacy necessitated the division. Males and females occupied different sides of the house, and many dwellings had separate entrances for the sexes. Physical contact between men and women was strictly prohibited; they were not even permitted to shake hands or touch. In fact, hallways had extra-wide dimensions so that members did not brush against each other. Men and women ate on opposite sides of the dining room, and they also sat separately at religious services. Even in death, males and females remained separated on different sides of the graveyard. The sexes were separated so successfully at North Union that James Prescott, who wrote the chronicles of the community, did not know vital information to provide sketches of its female leaders and members. Three or four times a week, women and men met at union meetings where they would sit facing each other—men in one row and women in another. Sisters had designated male counterparts matched to them according to age and interests with whom they could converse. Such meetings took place to foster a positive relationship between genders and to extinguish any negative feeling that would have formed because of the forced segregation.[65]

The daily routine of Shaker men and women revolved around work and worship. The rank-and-file members consisted of people who wanted assurances of salvation and who wanted to live their newfound revivalism. Those who stayed in the Shaker communities for their entire lives must have liked the purpose and structure of the group. Many devout Shakers thought the order brought them closest to God. The religious beliefs of the Shakers influenced each aspect of their daily lives. The Shakers carried out their tasks as part of their love and respect for God. Shaker villages noted the peacefulness, order, and simplicity. The Shakers structured their days around prayer, worship, work, and nourishment.[66]

Shakers arose between 4 and 5:30 A.M. as did other Americans engaged in agriculture. After prayers, members began their chores. They ate breakfast between 6 and 7 A.M. Before each meal, brethren and sisters gathered in small groups to say grace. Then they entered the dining area with the elders and eldresses leading the way. Men and women ate at separate tables in silence. They prayed again after their meals and then returned to work. The workday ended between 7:30 and 8 P.M., and Shakers devoted the rest of the evening to prayer and worship. Depending on the day of the week and the community organization, members would pray in their rooms, worship at services, or practice their songs and exercises.[67]

Worship services held much importance for Shakers and helped to distinguish them from other utopias. Members looked to religious meetings with anticipation because they used song and dance as a form of release from their routines and simple daily lives. Shaker services began as unorganized meetings and developed into more structured rituals. Archibald Mencham of the Whitewater community explained the importance of the society's meetings: "We have lively and refreshing Meetings often with a manifest of a good measure of life and power. We have been laboring for a number of months past to break our bonds and be free souls in the gospel so that any of the Brethren and Sisters old or young can express their faith and good feelings in Meeting without any embarassments."[68]

The defining ritual of the Shakers was their unique dances. At the Whitewater meetings, members united "in various exercises just as the Spirit seems to dictate such as Marching, Shaking, Bowing and Speaking . . . Singing Songs of prayer and thanks." The Shakers developed formal dance patterns such as the "Square Order Shuffle" introduced by Father Joseph Meacham, who had received inspiration from a vision of angels. Other Shakers also claimed divine inspiration in their introduction of new aspects to Shaker worship. On December 31, 1845, the Shakers of North Union received a gift from God instructing them to build a fountain in their meeting room to "unite to wash and bathe." The Shakers recorded the specific dance God had ordered them to perform, and they included a diagram of the dance in their records.[69]

As in other aspects of Shaker life, pragmatism played a key role and dictated the structure of the meeting houses. Meeting halls had plain decor with blue walls. Members sat on benches without backs, which they could move to perform their dances. During the dances, brethren and sisters did not touch, although they danced at the same time. The Shakers also included a section in the meeting hall for visitors to observe the worship service. The North Union society provided raised benches for visitors so that they could see the service unencumbered. The Shakers usually opened their meetings to the public on Sundays during the spring and summer. In 1838, Archibald Mencham of the Whitewater community reported that they regularly welcomed more than one hundred visitors to their services, and "sometimes some individuals . . . cannot refrain from shedding tears." In the 1840s and 1850s when Shaker communities experienced many periods of spiritualism, they closed their services to outside visitors.[70]

Another component of Shaker worship was inspirational music, which Shaker communities shared with each other. Along with dances, Shaker songs and tunes became the property of the society. The Shaker archives include a large collection of Shaker hymns and music. Members practiced their songs for Sunday service in weekday meetings. The songs deeply affected members, and some included the words of their favorite hymns in their reflections. Philander C. Cramer of North Union apparently found meaning in "A Little Treasure," which spoke "Of Mother's pretty love," and he recorded a verse for reflections with his religious beliefs.[71]

Music served to unify the various Shaker villages. The Shakers also strengthened ties with each other by frequently sending visitors to the other communities, a practice that began in the 1820s. Members from other villages offered inspiration to their Shaker counterparts. Two hundred fifty miles separated the communities of North Union and Union Village, and members frequently made this trip. Many of the Ohio societies welcomed and sent visitors to the New York communities, including New Lebanon. At times, visits lasted for extended periods of time. In 1824, the North Union society welcomed Elder Matthew, who stayed for the entire winter.[72] Practicality may have dictated the length of his stay, since winter travel was more difficult.

While the Shakers gave high importance to religion and worship each day, they also acknowledged the significant task of educating the children. They believed that the best members entered the community in their youth. They also held the philosophy that they needed to discipline and govern the children as parents. The natural parents of children raised by the Shakers at Union Village made a statement about their children's care. The community at Union Village outlined these principles: "We have an indisputable right to teach them the fear of God; to debar them from evil company—to restrain them from vice and wickedness—To guard them from all corrupt and pernicious principles, and to point out to them their duty at all times, and to see that they submissively do it." The Shakers attempted to instill virtue in the children through education in the classroom and in their daily labor. Children "should be taught to make a profitable use of their time, filling up their leisure moments with readings." Males remained under Shaker care until age twenty-one and females until age eighteen. Those who remained faithful to the Shaker religion received a joint interest in the church.[73]

As with the adult community, children were segregated by gender in their living quarters and in their schooling after the 1820s. When the North Union society began, children lived together in a log cabin. When the society grew in number and constructed more buildings, the Shakers enforced segregation of boys and girls. Boys went to school for four months in the winter so that they could help with the harvest in the summer. Girls attended school for the same amount of time in the summer.[74]

Men and women shared the tasks of educating the children, and the most qualified members had this responsibility. In the 1830s, Prudence

Sawyer taught the girls at North Union while James Prescott had charge over the boys. Prescott held this position for forty-four years. The Union Village community first opened a school in 1808 with John Woods in charge of the boys and Malinda Watts in charge of the girls. For many years, boys and girls received separate educations at Union Village, but eventually they received schooling together. The Whitewater society formed a school order in their first five years and appointed James Wells and Susannah Farnum to lead the boys and girls.[75]

Children received moral, social, religious, and literary instruction. Academically, the instruction was comparable to the education received by children in the public schools in the area, and the Shakers received public money according to the number of students they taught. Shaker teachers, appointed by members, instructed students in reading, writing, spelling, grammar, geography, arithmetic, natural history, and vocal music. At North Union, the brick schoolhouse consisted of stationary seats, desks, and platforms for the teachers, as well as blackboards, books, globes, and maps for instruction. In addition to the academic subjects, boys learned farm work or a trade while girls received training in domestic work such as cooking, sewing, spinning, and canning. The Shakers believed in a division of labor between the sexes and accepted some of

1.4 Shakers, Whitewater: School and Scholars. *Western Reserve Historical Society, Cleveland, Ohio*

the social norms. The Shaker communities gave the students a busy schedule, and little time remained at the end of the day for play. However, the youths did enjoy some recreational activities such as sleigh rides and picnics.[76]

Although the Shakers put forth much effort with the youths of their communities, the majority of Shaker children never converted as adults. The Shakers faced many challenges with youths, especially in persuading them that they should embrace a celibate life. The wisdom of suppressing their "carnal desires" became especially difficult to convey to the youths when they reached puberty. The Shakers attempted to use prayer and moral suasion to help lead youths to conversion as adults, but the small number of Shaker youths who did embrace the faith indicates that the Shakers largely failed in communicating their religious mission. Those youths who did convert had enjoyed a close relationship with an older member who had served as a mentor.[77]

In their establishment of separate communities, Shakers did not participate in politics or vote in elections. However, they did pay taxes as required by law, and they did respect days of thanksgiving and fast as stipulated by the government. They refused to bear arms, and this caused conflicts with the government during periods of war. During the War of 1812, members of the Union Village community, including Elder Samuel Rollins, were called into the army. The Shakers responded by articulating their unique status as members of a religious community who had separated "from the common cause of the world . . . to be a particular people consecrated to God." Consequently, they believed they were "lawfully exempted from the contaminating service of a military life." For those members called into service, they would "in no case violate their vows and obligations to God." Eventually, those Shakers called to serve in the War of 1812 were discharged.[78]

During the Civil War, Shakers once again had to address the military issue. Some young members enlisted on their own while others were drafted. The refusal to bear arms caused trouble. George W. Ingalls of North Union was drafted by the U.S. Army, and it took a meeting between a trustee of New Lebanon, Benjamin Gates, and President Abraham Lincoln to attain a reprieve from duty. Later, petitions secured the exemption of Shakers from military service after Lincoln offered exemption to all true Shakers.[79]

Although Shakers were not compelled to bear arms, they did not stay removed from the conflict. When a Sanitary Fair was held in Cincinnati in

1863 to gather supplies for the Union troops, the Union Village community donated fruit, catsup, brooms, and other materials. Shakers also held opinions about the burning issues of the time. The record keeper for the Church Family at North Union lamented that there could be no "life, Liberty, and the pursuit of happiness while four million of souls are condemned to hopeless involuntary servitude under the same constitution and Laws." The record keeper continued, "I do not expect any great victories by the federal forces until they are willing to acknowledge the African to be a man, and prove their sincerity by making him a free man and defending his rights."[80] These observations were made just before the Battle of Antietam, which paved the way for Lincoln's issuance of the preliminary Emancipation Proclamation, which freed the slaves in the states in rebellion.

In the economic aspects of daily life, segregation was enforced. Because of their commitment to celibacy, the Shakers did not want males and females to interact unless necessary. Work was a vital component of everyday life in the Shaker villages, and Mother Ann had encouraged discipline in everyday life as she urged her followers to put their "hands to work and their hearts to God." Economically, men controlled the activities that brought the most wealth to the community, indicating that the Shakers held some traditional views about gender relations.[81]

The elders and deacons determined the work assignments for the families and members, and they used a building in the community as their office to make the decisions. They assigned members to tasks in pragmatic fashion so that they had enough laborers when a certain task, such as the harvesting of crops, needed completion. Every day, "caretakers" or "overseers" took the members to their assignments. Although the Shakers had few idle moments, they labored at a natural pace and varied their tasks to meet the needs of the family to which they belonged.[82]

Because the Shakers produced so many goods that they sold to the outside world, they designated certain people as "trading elders" who conducted business for the communities, including selling and purchasing products for the community. The Shakers conducted all business transactions in cash, and they did not compile annual reports for the members. Trustees held all property in their names for the communities, and the individual families of each community kept records of their own affairs.[83]

Since Shaker societies had to meet the needs of all members, they produced a variety of agricultural and manufactured goods. Men carried out the bulk of agricultural activities—planning and planting fruit orchards and growing berries. At North Union, the cultivation of apples held much importance. Elijah Russell devoted himself to the fruit orchards, including apples, peaches, pears, plums, cherries, and grapes, and he took great care to develop fruit of the finest quality. If a tree did not produce the best fruit, Russell would use grafting techniques to alter it so that it produced fruit of the finest quality for several years. He also made adjustments in his planting because of the poor quality of the soil. He planted his trees on topsoil and built up the soil around them rather than planting the trees on clay. The innovations of Shakers such as Russell help to explain the longevity of Shaker communities. The Shakers grew far more apples than they needed to consume, and they sold their surplus to people in the Cleveland area. The North Union Shakers also cultivated between two thousand and four thousand pounds of sugar annually from the sugar bush on their land.[84]

The communities at Union Village and Whitewater also developed diversified agriculture, which males headed. Union Village men grew sweet corn, potatoes, barley, oat, rye, peppers, mangoes, cabbage apples, tomatoes, and cucumbers. The brethren also produced sugar from maple trees, manufacturing up to five thousand pounds in some years. Like the North Union society, they sold their surplus in the surrounding area and had little trouble finding a market for their products. They also had customers from more distant locations in Cleveland and Baltimore. The brethren at Union Village took charge of raising bees and livestock such as hogs. At Whitewater, crops grown included corn, broom corn, apples, and peaches. The men there also raised hogs.[85]

The production of dairy products held great importance for the North Union society because hard clay beneath the topsoil made cultivation difficult. Samuel Russell headed the efforts to find the best breeds of cattle. He searched both the United States and England to procure superior breeds. The Union Village community likewise imported cattle from England. In 1876, North Union claimed the largest dairy herd in the state with over forty cows. The Shakers had a good market for the milk in Cleveland, making twenty-three hundred dollars from the business in 1873. These dairy products accounted for a good portion of their income.[86]

At North Union, men also took charge of raising silkworms, although the Cleveland climate did not provide the perfect conditions for this economic activity. In 1843, the society had an estimated eleven thousand silkworms. While the men raised the silkworms, the women were responsible for reeling and spinning the silk.[87] This division of labor again illustrates how Shaker men and women worked together for common goals and the fact that women engaged in traditional activities.

Appropriately, since the society emphasized order and cleanliness, the manufacturing of brooms grew into one of the key Shaker industries. The North Union society made a large number of broom handles that were used by members of the Union Village community as well. Even during the period when the Shaker groups began to decline, they depended upon the manufacturing of brooms and broom handles for survival. In December 1876, Brother Charles Clapp of Union Village sold forty-five dozen brooms to a purchaser in Cincinnati. In 1881, the Center Family of North Union noted that their greatest income—$1,239.85—came from brooms. To maintain this industry, the North Union Shakers depended on purchasing their corn brush in Illinois.[88] The Shakers, who embraced market society to sell their surpluses and the goods of several key industries, thus did not entirely reject American society.

Since the Shakers believed in the division of labor between the sexes, women took responsibility for laboring in tasks traditionally relegated to their gender, and their roles mirrored women's sphere in the outside world in the early nineteenth century. Shaker women worked mostly indoors, and they had the task of caring for the men. Shaker women did the cooking and serving of food, as well as the washing, ironing, and mending of clothes, which they completed every other week. At North Union, the community had water piped into the Mill Family residence, and the other families came to this house to do the laundry with this convenience. This gave the sisters from the different families a chance to socialize with each other. Each sister was responsible for washing and mending the clothes of her assigned male counterpart. Sisters entered the male side of the house each day to clean up after the men and to make their beds. Shaker sisters had the task of informing their male counterparts if they did not exhibit orderliness, a key Shaker virtue. This relationship was the closest Shaker equivalent to the marriage partner. Although assigned these traditional tasks, not all Shaker women had to fulfill the role of mother to the young members of the society. Usually women cared for and schooled the girls, and male members did the same for the boys.[89]

In fulfilling their roles as nurses to the sick and dying, Shaker women made significant advances in the use of medicinal herbs, one of the society's most successful endeavors. Because Shakers believed in developing a self-sufficient community, they wanted to provide treatment for the ill from within. However, they did call on doctors in cases where they could

1.5 Shakers, North Union: Women Bleaching Wool, 1874. *Ohio Historical Society*

not provide adequate treatment for the ill. For medicinal as well as culinary purposes, Shakers pioneered the collection, drying, and packaging of herbs, and men held an important role in the basic work of the industry. Women processed the herbs. They had developed medicinal plants by 1825, long before the American society at large had adopted the practice. This industry held importance for the colonies at Union Village, Ohio, which had the largest herb industry in the state, and Mount Lebanon, New York. From their herbs, Shakers produced extracts, oils, distilled flavoring, and fragrant waters. The outside world noticed their advances, and customers from the United States and abroad, including Paris and London, purchased their herbs. The Shaker communities worked together in this important enterprise. For example, women in the Mill Family at North Union traveled to Rockport and Northfield to collect lobelia for their own society and wintergreen berries to send to Union Village.[90]

Shaker women also manufactured products that they could sell outside of the community. Sisters in the Mill Family of North Union used flax to make towels, and they sold approximately ten dozen per year. The sisters used yarn spun in the woolen mill to knit stockings. However, they seemed to save this task for leisure time. They also made bonnets, mittens, and socks. The sisters of Union Village made mittens and gloves initially by hand. In 1861, the society added a knitting machine for the production of these goods, selling them for six dollars per pair.[91]

Although women did not engage in planting, they did help to pick berries, including blackberries and strawberries. They also canned and preserved fruits, work that brought income into the communities. The Records of the Church Family at Union Village notes, "The sisters are industriously canning cherries." Women made apple butter to sell and also marketed surplus catsup, horseradish, and dried pumpkin.[92]

While women made such contributions to the economic well-being of the community, it remains unclear whether or not they had control over all of the wealth they generated. Most of the products women made did not produce much income for the communities. Financial records indicate that the accounts for the female and male sides of the families were kept separate. Women did use their income to pay for the necessary expenses to manufacture their products. However, males serving as deacons assumed responsibility for the general finances of the families, thus further limiting the economic roles of women in Shaker society. Men seemed to hold the ultimate power regarding economic affairs even though they made up the minority of the population.[93]

Despite these indications that Shakers accepted the outside world's concepts regarding gender, they enjoyed a reputation as a group committed to sexual equality. In actuality, they did not consciously emphasize gender equality until the late nineteenth century. Other utopian movements influenced the Shakers in this regard. When utopian experiments failed, some of their former members joined Shaker communities and contributed their ideas about reform, including women's rights. Frederick Evans, an Owenite, joined the Shakers in 1830. He became a prominent Shaker leader, widely respected both within and outside of the order. Evans advanced radical ideas, including women's rights, although not all members of the group agreed. Because of his reputation, however, nonbelievers associated Evans's views with those of the whole community. Evans reported that Shaker women enjoyed equality within their own separate sphere. At age eighty, he acknowledged that women had the same faculties as men and even more.[94]

In the late nineteenth century, the leadership role of the sisters in the economic life of the communities increased. Not until 1880 did a sister hold the position of trustee in a Shaker village. Trustees conducted business with the outside world and recorded the financial dealings of the community. In 1880, the trustee board at North Union was changed from four males to two brethren and two sisters. This change came at a time when the industries of Shaker women took on more importance in the communities. After the Civil War, the sisters began to make fancywork, including fans and dusters, which grew into key Shaker markets. The rise of women trustees also occurred as the proportion of women to men in the order increased. With this demographic change, the sisters' industries grew in importance. Hence, their larger role in the financial life of the communities could be explained by the increase in the value of goods the sisters produced, which coincided with the decline of male industries. The rise of women coincided with the decline of the Shaker order, suggesting that women's roles increased for reasons other than a commitment to greater equality. Not all brethren supported these new positions for women, demonstrating that the order was not entirely committed to equality of the sexes.[95]

Although men held the more prominent position in economic affairs, women felt themselves superior in the spiritual life of the community. This idea reflected views held by the outside world, views in which women were perceived as purveyors of religion and virtue in the home. Consequently women had taken important participatory roles in the Second Great Awakening and in religious movements of the later nineteenth century.[96] Despite this feeling of spiritual superiority, women still felt restrained in their religious roles, as evidenced by the manner in which they expressed themselves.

One of the guiding philosophies of the Shakers originated in a verse from Revelations that appears at the beginning of their records: "What thou seest, write in a book." This laid the groundwork for the creation of an exhaustive Shaker archive. However, men contributed more readily to this archive than did women. As mentioned earlier, James Prescott lamented in his history of North Union that he did not have the data to give the bio-graphical accounts of the sisters, so he mentioned them collectively.[97] The segregation of the sexes partially accounts for Prescott's lack of information about the sisters. However, Shaker women did not fill the void by recording their own experiences and histories in the villages.

Women also felt more reluctant to express themselves in public. In

1871, at a convention for Shakers and Spiritualists in Cleveland, Ohio, Elder Frederick Evans of Mount Lebanon, New York, gave a powerful address in which he called for female Shakers to give testimony to their faith. None spoke. James Prescott of North Union recorded the event and admonished the women in attendance: "All silent!!! I was sorry! If I had been a *good* speaker and had a peculiar feminine voice, I would have got up and spoken for them and made that hall ring in the name of Mother! . . . I would have told them what it was that *first* inaugurated woman's rights, established equality in the sexes, and revealed a Mother in the Deity." The setting of a full Lyceum Hall with people standing in the aisles had perhaps intimidated the women and silenced them.[98]

While women remained more silent than men in recording their experiences and reflections, they found a voice in spirit possession and as sources of inspired writings. The Shakers had emerged in the 1700s at a time when other religious groups viewed spirit possession as part of repentance necessary to achieve full conversion. The Shakers, however, did not correlate spirit possession to conversion. They saw spirit possession as the way in which God communicated to them. The Shakers believed that God selected the people for inspiration, and the message delivered by such individuals might even contradict Scripture or previous Shaker practices. If the Shakers acknowledged that a person had true gifts of revelation from God, they would follow that person's words.[99] In spirit possession, women could attribute words to deceased Shakers as well as distinguished leaders, including Jesus Christ and Mother Ann. As long as the society believed her to be a recipient of God's inspiration, a woman did not have to worry that her words and ideas would be questioned. In such a forum, women held considerable power, and Shaker men accepted their actions as fulfilling their roles as members of the spiritual community.

Spirit possession offered women a way to voice their opinions without taking ownership of them. Women who held little power could create a receptive gathering for their ideas in spirit possession. However, the women who served as instruments appear so frequently in the Shaker record that it seems they truly accepted themselves as instruments of God, as did the community. They believed they were interlocutors for the Divine.

Many of the records regarding spirit possession were made in the 1830s and 1840s, a period of revival among the Shakers. Women played an important role in this spiritual awakening, called "Mother Ann's work."

Prior to the awakening, some Shaker women had already begun to free themselves in their efforts at self-expression. In 1835, the Shakers at North Union listened often to the teachings of Eldress Lucy and Sister Vincy at society meetings. In the late 1820s, Sister Vincy had undergone deep spiritual turmoil and suffered bodily affliction. Eldress Rachel encouraged her to work for God, which she did. Both Sister Vincy and Eldress Lucy set examples for the females in the village to express themselves spiritually: "the grown sisters have been enabled to break their hands and many of them speak occasionally pretty freely, we are in hopes they will never get under such bondage again as they have felt."[100]

The religious excitement in Shaker villages commenced after a trying period for the group. The entire nation had suffered economically as a result of the Panic of 1837, and the Shakers did not escape this crisis. Many people turned to religion because they thought the end of the world was near. Furthermore, society membership had declined, leaving the Shakers without a large pool of people from which to select leaders. A demographic shift in the age of the members also affected the communities. The percentage of children under fifteen and youths aged fifteen to twenty-nine grew, and approximately 40 percent of the members had not known Mother Ann personally. Spiritually, the Shaker communities suffered from dullness and apathy.[101]

Shaker leaders saw the need for a revival that would affect the communities in different and sometimes contradictory ways. Some members looked to "Mother's Work" to reestablish spiritual values and to encourage members to give up their wrongdoings. The youths among the Believers latched on to the energy of the revival and its charismatic aspects rather than focusing on Shaker tradition. Clearly, Shaker leaders wanted the youths to be affected by the revival, as they believed that experiencing full conversion would help them commit to the society.[102]

Women contributed to and initiated periods of spirit possession in the Shaker communities. Perhaps the women felt more open to expressing themselves through the interlocutor of spirits. The religious excitement began in Watervliet, New York, in August 1837, and women greatly influenced the revival. In fact, women initiated the awakening. Girls ranging in age from ten to fourteen began entering trancelike states and experiencing visions. Some scholars believe that the girls started the revival in response to the rigid routines and disciplined work schedules that they followed. Word of the Watervliet revival reached other communities quickly, and other villages began to report visions. The Shaker record contains much material regarding the period of spirit possession. The accounts of the visions in New York match closely with the visions reported in Ohio.[103]

In 1837, Elder Freegift Wells led the Union Village society into "Mother's Work." Elder Wells read a lecture that Lucy Wright had given years earlier as a source of inspiration. Wells urged the brethren and sisters to confess their sins and strengthen their humility while working harder at their spiritual lives. After several weeks of increased feeling, Wells communicated the events that began the revival in New York. Members learned in detail the visions that the girls in New York saw. This led to people receiving visions in Union Village.[104]

In July 1838, members of Union Village visited the community of North Union carrying the message that Mother Ann was with them. After this, several signs indicated that gifts of the Gospel had arrived, and the sisters displayed them. The gifts began with a Shaker woman who spoke three different languages in succession. Then several younger sisters had powerful bodily movements and went into vision together. One member reported: "They were taken by violent aspirations of supernatural power and carried away in vision into the Spiritual World, saw and conversed with Angels, and departed spirits, some of whom they once knew in the body." They exhibited gifts of tongues, prophecy, inspired messages, and repentance. In August 1838, several sisters and one young brother expressed involuntary physical manifestations at one Sabbath meeting.[105]

Those involved in spirit possession, including instruments and observers, underwent an intense experience. John P. Root of North Union described these events: "The Purity, brightness and Glory of these Holy inhabitants of the Heavens especially Christ and Mother Ann was such that the Inspired ones when they came . . . would fall as lead at their feet, then they would be strengthened with Divine power and rise up." Root continued, "On beholding these painful scenes the ones in vision would be thrown in the most extreme suffering and lie as dead before us."[106]

Youths continued to play a large role in "Mother's Work" after their actions to initiate it. In 1840 at Union Village, a fifteen-year-old female who played the violin displayed a solemn gift and delivered a message from Mother Ann. Mother Ann told the elders to gather in a circle around the spring in the meeting house. Then "Mother's children that were justified might come forward (2 or 3 at a time) and kneel down in the Spring, and the elders were to wash them."[107] Such ceremonies helped members to strengthen their faith.

Women held much significance in "Mother's Work," and, in the records of the North Union society, Lucretia Sutton, Charlotte Hart, and Mercy Sawyer appear often as instruments of spirit possession in the 1840s. In one case, Sutton served as the intermediary for Moses, who stated: "I want you to be willing to suffer, for Mother does love souls that are willing to suffer." Moses also expressed his displeasure with the unconverted: "I hate the half-way Shaker; I hate all false Believers." Sutton here disclosed some of her own anxieties concerning the members in the village. In the 1840s, other utopian experiments dotted the nation, and some people searched for the perfect haven. Perhaps it troubled Sutton that some of these half-hearted Shakers found their way into the village and threatened the sanctity of the community.[108]

The words against false believers underscored a problem in Shaker communities. Several visitors instructed the Shakers not to fall away from tradition. Sutton gave voice to the words of Abraham the Patriarch: "So fight, fight on . . . and overcome all evil and Mother will crown you with endless love." George Washington also communicated through Sutton to acknowledge Mother's love: "I am one of those guardian spirits that was sent by Mother to protect her faithful children."[109]

During periods of spirit possession, the North Union society welcomed many other distinguished visitors through sisters who served as instruments. St. Paul instructed the Shakers to live a life of simplicity. The prophet Isaiah stated through Charlotte Hart that Mother wanted "to bless every honest, simple soul." Additionally, the prophets Elijah, Daniel, and Job, the angel Gabriel, the angel Raphael, and Saints Peter, Luke, and John visited the North Union society. In these divine messages, the believers were told to be honest and virtuous. They were instructed to repent their sins and to have confidence because they were loved. Father Jesus and Mother Ann delivered their words jointly to the brethren and sisters: "We your Heavenly Parents unite. . . . We do want you to forsake all worldly pleasures and bear your crosses against your pride and lust." Through Sutton, Elizabeth, former queen of England, called on the believers to live lives of simplicity: "I have possessed much of the treasures of earth. But they never done my poor needy soul any good." Through simplicity, she had become Mother's child. Apparently, Sutton thought she and other Shakers could achieve true greatness through the humility they displayed and the simple life they lived. Many Shakers had fallen away from the core practices of the order, including cleanliness and simplicity in possessions and dress. These messages confirm that the Shakers wanted this spiritual awakening to forestall the incorrect behavior of the members.[110]

The believers at Whitewater also received the words of many distinguished guests, including George Washington, Thomas Jefferson, and Powhatan, through spirit possession. Many of the same themes appeared in their messages, indicating that similar problems plagued the Shaker villages. Jefferson instructed the youth of the community to obey their faith so they would receive rewards in Mother's kingdom. George Washington told Elder Archibald that Mother Ann had blessed him with the joys of heaven, and Elder Archibald would receive the same. Furthermore, Mother Ann had work for the elder to complete. Powhatan answered some questions that Archibald had regarding other Indian chiefs: "They are gathered into Mother's gospel, and they are living souls, and they send their everlasting love and blessing to you."[111]

Men also served as instruments in spirit possession but not as frequently as women. Curtis Cramer of North Union received several messages during a time of personal spiritual crisis. Mother Ann told him how to reconcile his troubles: "When you are obedient to the voice of the spirit then shall the spirit of your Mother gather very close to you." Subsequently, Mother Ann spoke to Curtis, encouraging him to devote himself wholeheartedly to the Shaker gospel. God also instructed Curtis to repent because he had failed to "devote your soul and body your time and all your talents" to God. God told Curtis to make a public confession before the Shakers. If they forgave Curtis, then he could renew his covenant with God. Another brother, William Johnson, received the words of an angel: "O thou child of thy Mother, art thou willing to bear tribulation? Art thou willing to suffer for the cause of thy Heavenly Father?"[112] Cramer's experiences illustrate the Shakers' efforts to strengthen those wavering in their faith.

The revival period slowed in the mid-1840s. Some Shakers who wanted to feel themselves part of the revival had presented themselves as false instruments, leaving leaders to distinguish the real inspirations from those created. Members desired to act as instruments because of the excitement and also because of the notoriety they received for any manifestations they displayed. Also, "Mother's Work" declined as some messages divided the members. In 1841, a message instructed the Shakers to accept the diet advocated by Sylvester Graham, who urged people not to consume meat, alcohol, tea, or coffee. The dietary question plagued the Shakers, as some members accepted the ideas of Graham concerning vegetarianism while others continued to eat meat. Elder Freegift Wells of Union Village returned to Watervliet, New York, in 1843 after seeing the division over the dietary question in Ohio. Wells urged the leaders in New York not to enforce a vegetarian diet in his family. Many other Shakers agreed with him, although they did not voice their opinion. The end of "Mother's Work" led many to leave the society.[113]

In the 1840s, the Shakers looked to Millerism and Spiritualism to increase their ranks, but neither helped to halt the declining numbers of the society. The Millerite movement began in the Burned-Over District of New York. William Miller developed a religious following and claimed that the millennium was at hand. Miller wholeheartedly believed that he had calculated the exact time when Christ would come down to earth for the second time to begin a reign of peace. Several thousand people followed Miller. Cleveland served as home to the Millerite movement of the West, and Cincinnati also attracted a large number of the faithful. Miller had predicted that the Day of Judgment would come in April 1843. Many of his followers clothed themselves in ascension robes and waited at high elevations to make an easier ascent into heaven. When the appointed day arrived without Christ's appearance, Miller recalculated and proclaimed that Christ would come in October 1843. Again, nothing happened, causing Miller to lose his credibility and his followers. The collapse of the Millerite movement meant approximately two hundred new Shaker converts at Union Village. Most of these people were then sent to the Whitewater community.[114]

Many Shakers incorrectly believed that the rise of Spiritualism would add to their numbers. In 1848, Kate and Margaret Fox of New York claimed they heard strange knocking sounds at night that constituted a code from the spirit world. While many people did not believe their story, the Shakers accepted it. Consequently, more Shakers experienced spirit possession. The Shakers even worked with the Spiritualists to gather strength. In 1852, the Shakers held a meeting with the Spiritualists at Cleveland. In spite of such efforts, the membership of Shaker communities did not drastically increase.[115]

After the peak in their ranks in the mid-nineteenth century, the Shakers endured a drop in membership. The decreasing numbers concerned them, and they found hope in any indication that they would gain new recruits. One member of the North Union society expressed optimism that an alleged German prophet who had predicted the assassination of President James A. Garfield in 1881 "predicts that very shortly we shall have more Shakers than we shall know what to do with." Despite such hopefulness, no Shaker revival occurred.[116]

Several factors help to explain the declining numbers of Shakers. Many individuals who entered as youths left the order. Since the group could not depend on natural increase, they relied on conversion, and the sect failed to attract many adults in the late nineteenth century. Those who did enter Shaker communities at this time joined largely for economic rather than religious reasons. Some Shaker leaders tried to encourage more converts based on economic motivations. Because of the changes brought on by industrialization, many began to question the class structure, and the Shakers offered an alternative to capitalism in their socialistic order. Some leaders, such as Elder Frederick W. Evans of New Lebanon, New York, portrayed the Shakers as "progressive" people who offered spiritualism in the increasing secular world. Evans and other Shakers published a periodical named *The Shaker* between 1871 and 1899 to gain converts with this message. However, many Shakers felt this emphasis detracted from the real religious purpose of the order. Elder Harvey Eads of South Union, Kentucky, led the opposition to Evans. Consequently, a schism emerged in the Shakers between Eads and the conservatives and Evans and the progressives. This divide further weakened the Shakers, who needed a united front to combat the declining ranks.[117]

The society at North Union supported the progressive leadership of Evans. One member wrote: "It is now generally conceded at North Union that Elder Frederick W. Evans of Mt. Lebanon, New York, is a better man than what a certain class of non-progressive minds among believers have represented him to be; or even what some of *his own* writings have represented him to be; and as Believers progress (which surely they must) and as the world progresses, he will be more appreciated."[118]

In 1871, Evans spoke at a convention of Shakers and Spiritualists in Cleveland at Lyceum Hall, where members of the North Union society embraced his message. James Prescott reported that the speech Evans delivered on the Sabbath evening to a standing-room-only crowd made the convention a "triumphant success." Inspired by angels, Evans moved the audience in the "Christ Spirit," causing people to tremble, jerk, and twist on the floor. Evans explained the relationship of the Shakers to the other Spiritualist groups. He called Shakers primary, "the root," and Spiritualists secondary, "the branches." Evans stated: "When ye see the branches flourish, ye may know the *root* is holy." According to Prescott, the convention caused the Christ Spirit to flow throughout the city. The convention was received as the best ever held in Cleveland and resulted in a demand for Shaker books and tracts.[119]

Despite this success, the Shaker population did not permanently increase. The Shakers found it increasingly difficult to attract new members when they had to deal with internal division. Furthermore, they found it hard to recruit new members because of the changes brought on by industrialization and urbanization. Consequently, Shaker communities began to close. The North Union society disbanded in 1889; Whitewater closed in 1907; Watervliet ended in 1910; and Union Village in 1912.[120]

The case of the Center Family at North Union helps to illustrate the undoing of Shaker villages. The number of members in the Center Family at North Union declined to forty-eight people by 1876. From 1876 to 1885, the Center Family decreased to twenty-three people, and most of these were elderly members who could not perform many tasks. Consequently, the production of the Center Family declined. The family brought in a significantly smaller amount of money from its major industries of broom making and dairy products. Between 1876 and 1885, the profit margin in this family decreased, too. The North Union family attempted to deal with these changes by renting out farmland since it had lost workers. The community had to sell the stone quarry in 1879 since it could not make a profit from it.[121] The aging of the membership, along with the inability to attract new members, led to its economic slide and ultimately to the demise of the community.

Before the Union Village society disbanded in 1912, the remaining members made efforts to provide for themselves. They had the choice of going to live at another Shaker community or returning to the Methodist Home for the Aged in Cincinnati. The home agreed to care for every member of Union Village, regardless of any illness, for the duration of their lives. These arrangements with the home included the provision that all real estate held in trust by the Shakers of Union Village was transferred to the home. The home also agreed to respect the Shaker faith and to take suggestions from the Shaker residents.[122]

After the last Ohio settlement closed in 1912, only a few Shaker villages remained. The last Midwestern village, South Union, disbanded in 1922. Only two Shaker communities survived until 1961. The small Sabbathday Lake, Maine, community is the sole remaining Shaker haven.[123]

Chapter 2

The Society of Separatists of Zoar

THE SOCIETY OF SEPARATISTS AT ZOAR, Ohio, was a religious commune with origins in Europe. Unlike the Shakers, whose American-born leaders Joseph Meacham and Lucy Wright guided the sect into the nineteenth century, Zoar's German religious foundations served as the basis for the community throughout its long and successful history. The Separatists left Wurtemberg to escape persecution just as Ann Lee had done in 1774; however, the migration of Separatists was much larger than the group of eight that Ann Lee brought to New York.

The history of the Separatists dates back to the sixteenth-century Reformation in Germany. Many religious sects arose in Germany opposed to the Catholic Church, and the Kingdom of Wurtemberg served as home to many such Protestant groups. Although Prussia accepted the Lutheran faith as the state religion, several sects persisted in their particular beliefs and did not embrace Lutheranism. One such group, the Pietists, required members to embrace a morally pure life that began with

2.1 Zoar: Old Church Print. *Ohio Historical Society*

a conscious conversion through God's grace. Pietists called for Bible study and prayer meetings and regarded dancing and cards as sinful. They embraced the teachings of several people, including Frederick Christoph Oetinger. Oetinger had developed some ideas from the mystic philosopher Jacob Boehm. The mysticism embraced by the Separatists included the belief that Christ would come to earth a second time, and they believed this would occur in 1836. Oetinger gained followers from his writings and teachings, which led to the emergence of the Separatists.[1]

The Separatists deviated from followers of Lutheranism in that they refused to accept the rituals of baptism, communion, and confirmation. They did not embrace the ceremony attached to marriage and instead required that witnesses be present to acknowledge such an agreement. Because Lutheran clergy ran the public schools, they did not send their children. Since they believed that all men were equal before God, they did not acknowledge anyone as their civil authority. Consequently, they would not serve in the military or take oaths. As did the Quakers, they demonstrated their beliefs in the equality of all men by refusing to use titles of distinction and by refusing to take off their hats for leaders. Some Separatists accepted more radical doctrines, including celibacy and vegetarianism. Their deviation from accepted social norms led to their persecution, which included imprisonment and floggings. They thus searched for a place where they could practice their faith without fear of reprisals.[2]

Economic and political changes affected the Separatists. The people of Wurtemberg lived in a state of poverty throughout the eighteenth century. This condition arose between 1688 and 1707, when the region underwent invasions from France. The poor administration of the Duke of Wurtemberg, Charles Eugene, prevented any recovery from these problems, leaving the vast majority of the population impoverished. The people's economic strife increased with the French Revolution and the Napoleonic Wars. The people of Wurtemberg could do little as their farms and property were destroyed, and men were forced into military service. The Lutheran Church did little to aid the population during the troublesome period, and some people turned to mystics who spoke of Christ's return to earth. Some Pietist groups made the decision to separate from the Lutheran church in the late eighteenth and early nineteenth centuries, when the Church embraced new ritual elements, including a new hymn book that some viewed as too worldly, and a new liturgy.[3]

The first Separatist group to leave Germany did so under the guidance of George Rapp, a weaver from Wurtemberg. Approximately six hundred Rappists, most of them peasants and mechanics, arrived in Philadelphia in 1804 before moving to Beaver County, Pennsylvania. They bought five thousand acres of land located twenty miles northwest of Pittsburgh and called their settlement Economy. Members agreed to establish a Harmony Society where they would hold all property in common and work together for each other. They stayed at Economy for ten years and then moved to New Harmony, Indiana. After a decade at New Harmony, they sold their land to socialist Robert Owen, who experimented with creating his own perfect haven. The Rappists then returned to Economy, Pennsylvania, in 1824, where they experienced economic success and enjoyed membership escalating to an estimated one thousand people.[4]

The Separatists who established Zoar did so under the direction of mystic Barbara Gruberman. She had moved to Wurtemberg from Switzerland, where she was not accepted. As Mother Ann Lee had done, Gruberman spent hours in trancelike states in which she saw the underworld where sinners went as punishment. The Separatists viewed these states as communications from the Holy Spirit, and they accepted her revelation that God had called them "children of the Most High." They considered Gruberman to be their mother. She instructed her followers to go to America so that they could worship as they chose. Because of illness, she could not lead them, and she died before the group left on its journey.[5]

Religious persecution played a significant role in leading the Separatists to America. Because the Separatists violated civil and religious practices, the authorities dealt harshly with them. Since they refused to send their children to Lutheran schools, they had to pay fines. Furthermore, the authorities took many children from their families and removed them to orphanages, where the parents had to pay for their living expenses. If the Separatists could not meet the heavy fines imposed on them, their homes and property were taken. The men who were imprisoned had to perform hard labor in extreme weather and other difficult conditions. The authorities showed no leniency to women and children in handing out punishments. The Separatist leaders especially suffered the wrath of the authorities, and they took great pains to evade persecution by moving frequently. Both Gruberman and Joseph Bimeler, who would later serve as the leader and spiritual guide of Zoar, found it necessary to relocate often to avoid capture.[6]

In the midst of their persecution and in the wake of Gruberman's revelation that they were God's children, the Separatists outlined their principal beliefs. They believed in God in the Trinity—Father, Son, and Holy Ghost. They looked to the Bible as the source of all truth that directed their lives. The Separatists banned all ceremonies, which they declared had caused their schism with the Church. They also embraced addressing everyone equally, showing reverence and honor only to God. They accepted sexual relations only as a way to continue the race, but they felt abstinence to be a better state. Furthermore, they declared that they could not serve in the military to murder their fellow man. All of these tenets and others provided followers with the way to salvation.[7]

The declaration of their beliefs did little to alter their condition; however, circumstances did change and afford them the opportunity to leave Germany. At first, the Separatists moved near the southern border of Wurtemberg with the help of a friend at the court of King Frederick.

They had to sell all of their property to purchase this land. In early 1816, they were forced to abandon their new homes with little warning. The Separatists petitioned the royal minister of the interior to allow them to move to Brandenburg, and he refused the request. They then asked if they might leave for America, and the government accepted this petition.[8]

During the winter of 1816–17, the Separatists made arrangements to emigrate to America. They made one last attempt, however, to remain in Wurtemberg, as leadership had changed with the death of King Frederick. His son William ascended the throne, and the Separatists asked him for permission to establish themselves in Wurtemberg. William refused, and the Separatists proceeded to plan for their journey. Several traveled to Antwerp to procure passage on a ship. Most of the three hundred members possessed little financial means and were artisans and farmers. Some had attained education and possessed professional abilities. Those who could not afford the passage to America received the help of those Separatists with more wealth. Members sold as much property as they could to obtain the amount needed to travel. The Quakers of England also offered material support to the group.[9]

The voyage to America began in April 1817 as the group left Antwerp. The ocean travel lasted more than three months and proved arduous for the Separatists. They traveled in the steerage compartment in the lower decks of the ship where cattle were usually carried. Many developed serious illnesses including dysentery. The leader of the group, Joseph Bimeler, a man with a lame leg and an eye that protruded, greatly helped the Separatists to endure the journey by helping the sick and offering his religious knowledge to them. From humble origins in Munich, Bimeler, a weaver, had the qualities of a good leader, including a natural speaking ability. He possessed great knowledge of Scripture, which he used to fulfill his role as teacher, as well as business acumen that would serve him in America. Supposedly, before Gruberman's death, she had a vision that a new leader from Munich would emerge.[10] Bimeler's leadership proved invaluable to the Separatists.

On August 14, 1817, the group arrived in Philadelphia, Pennsylvania. The Quakers of the city provided the Separatists with temporary housing until they could find a permanent place to stay. They also offered the immigrants money sent by the English Quakers to help them settle in America. Furthermore, the Quakers established a committee of fifteen to aid the Separatists in whatever they needed. The necessary aid given to the Separatists led John James of Philadelphia to comment, "Kind Providence has been with you from your first setting out from your own land of suffering and Distress."[11]

The main issue facing the Separatists concerned where they would make their permanent home. The Quakers had instructed one of their number, Thomas Rotch, to help in this decision. The Separatists first looked in Pennsylvania for land but found none satisfactory. Rotch was from Canton, Ohio, and helped them find land in Tuscarawas County. George Rapp had considered buying this land for his community. Bimeler purchased a total of fifty-five hundred acres of land from Godfrey Haga, a Philadelphia merchant, for sixteen thousand five hundred dollars, or three dollars per acre. The transaction went through in Bimeler's name, but each member was to have an interest in the society equal to his investment. Bimeler had to borrow fifteen hundred dollars from the Quakers to insure the sale, and he had to accept notes amounting to fifteen thousand dollars.[12]

After the purchase of land, Bimeler quickly made arrangements to move the group of Separatists. He went along with a small group of hardy men and their families to begin settlement in the fall of 1817. At first, many stayed in Philadelphia, including the sick and elderly, who received care from the Quakers. Both men and women found work in this interregnum. With the assistance of the Quakers, women took positions as domestic servants, labored in a trade, or bound themselves out in service.[13]

Not everyone looked favorably upon Bimeler for quickly exiting Philadelphia. Thomas Cope, a member of the committee of Quakers who helped the Separatists, reported to Rotch that Bimeler seemed to exercise undue influence over the group in the decision to move to Ohio. Cope stated Bimeler refused to hire out some of the Separatists who had made such requests. After Bimeler purchased the land with the loan from the Quakers, he would not wait for a better time of year to move. Bimeler also asked for the money raised by the Quakers in London, but the Quaker committee did not relinquish all of the money to him. Instead, the Quakers divided the sum and distributed the money to each member of the group separately.[14]

Traveling by wagon, Bimeler led the advance group of settlers and arrived at the land in November 1817. The land was situated along the east banks of the Tuscarawas River in Tuscarawas County, which was located in the northeastern part of central Ohio. The land was hilly and not particularly suited for agriculture. Many different trees dotted the landscape, including oaks, maples, and chestnuts. The group named the settlement

Zoar after the ancient town on the banks of the Dead Sea. In Genesis, Zoar served as a haven for Lot as he fled Sodom. The meaning fit for these Separatists who fled the oppression they had endured in Germany.[15]

The settlers began the village by building a log hut, followed by homes located around a town center. They had some difficulties in February 1818 as the snow accumulated up to four feet and they lacked adequate food. However, neighbors offered them help by giving them flour and potatoes.[16]

Once spring arrived, the settlers of Zoar awaited the help of members who had remained in Philadelphia. This contingent eagerly prepared for their sojourn to Zoar. Hanna Fisher noted that "they are determined to see for themselves" the settlement of Zoar. Their employers did not want them to leave because they were sober and valuable people. Some of the Separatists could not depart immediately because they did not have the money to travel. Others had to complete the remainder of terms of service for which they had bound themselves. However, Fisher saw that they viewed the move to Zoar as a spiritual matter rather than an economic choice: "They look on Zoar to be the land of Promise, Baumlar, their leader has so infatuated them that they look on him as another Moses." Apparently, Fisher doubted the veracity of such opinions held about Bimeler. In spite of this skepticism, the devout Separatists accepted the belief that the community could not fail because they were inhabitants of a millennial kingdom. They thought that the millennium had begun as God had chosen them to build a community that would be His kingdom on earth.[17]

The questions the Quakers had regarding Bimeler's intentions and character were not limited to remarks in correspondence. Apparently, some members of Zoar, concerned more with property than faith, feared that they could lose the land in the event of Bimeler's death since Bimeler held the community land in trust for the others. Thomas P. Cope indicated that the Quakers would be willing to help the Zoarites improve the land by constructing a gristmill and a sawmill. However, the aid in the amount of six hundred dollars depended on Bimeler signing a declaration indicating that the land and property belonged to the entire community. As Cope said, "We are unwilling to give anything to promote the private views of a few Individuals to the prejudice of the rest." Thomas Rotch then informed the Zoarites of the necessity of such an agreement and sent a declaration for Bimeler to sign. Bimeler sent a letter to the Quaker Committee denying reports that he acted like a despot. He disclosed the functioning of the community in detail and emphasized that the German Separatists and Friends held much in common. He also enjoined the Quakers to help them, saying, "We are in the place where God will grant us happiness and dry our tears. Now offer us your hand and we will in future times praise you as the fountain head of our happiness." Although Bimeler had objections to the declaration, he apparently signed it. In the spring of 1819, the Zoarites established a community of goods.[18]

When the Separatists had initially planned their immigration to the United States, they viewed religious freedom as their primary goal. They did not intend to establish an experimental community where members held all things in common, but ultimately, this type of community evolved. During the first year of the colony, the Zoarites did not produce enough food to carry them through the winter of 1818 to 1819. Each family had the task of cultivating as much land as possible. It was expected that each family would purchase its own portion of the land. A family was expected to sell off the land it could not cultivate. However, since some of the ill and older members were unable to engage in agriculture, the Zoarites began to work for each other. They felt obligated to assist those who had made the journey for religious purposes. In response to the problem, some Zoarites led by Johannes Breymaier suggested the creation of a community of goods where all members held their property in common. Bimeler had his doubts about this proposal because he thought that the members could not forge the close association necessary for its success. However, he supported the idea enthusiastically after the community approved it.[19]

In April 1819, the community of Zoar outlined the principle by which it would live in a constitution. Fifty-three men and 104 women signed this document explaining that their community of property had originated from their desire "to unite themselves, according to the Christian apostolic sense." Each member of the community renounced "every right of ownership" to his property and gave the power to manage the property to the directors of the society. The members of the society elected three directors who managed and took possession of the community property and conducted all business transactions. Members promised to support and obey the decisions of the directors. The directors also had the task of resolving any conflicts in the community as long as they were not involved in the dispute. If a member decided to leave the community, he or she could not claim any compensation for the property or labors unless a majority vote of the society sanctioned it. The society had the discretion to increase or reduce membership. The community would hold elections each year according to the laws of Ohio. Each director served for three years, and the members would vote on one director each year.[20]

The members of Zoar and the Shakers both decided to hold property in the community interest for stated religious reasons. However, the Zoarites felt more pressed to establish a community of goods because they had to care for the elderly and infirm who could not care for themselves. The members of Zoar also had more control over the administration of their property than did members of the Shaker communities. The annual elections of Zoar gave them this power. In Shaker villages, the control was autocratic, since the trustees who managed affairs were appointed by the elders.

Although Bimeler had played a significant role in the community's establishment, he did not serve as one of the society's first directors. Johannes Breymaier, Joseph Georg Ackermann, and August Huber held these positions. Bimeler still held much power and acted as the general manager of the society, and his name appears on the business and legal papers of the community. When the community revised the articles in 1824, members elected Bimeler to the position of arbitrator. According to the Articles of Agreement of 1824, the community would elect one to three arbitrators who would serve as executives, but Bimeler was the only person to hold this position. In the 1833 constitution, the title of arbitrator was changed to cashier and agent general, and the Zoarites elected Bimeler to both of these posts. He served in both capacities until his death in 1853.[21] The election of Bimeler to these leadership positions indicates the community's confidence in his skill and abilities as well as his importance to Zoar. Bimeler had not initiated the community of property, but he did much to propagate it with his administrative abilities.

The successive articles of agreement that Zoar approved in 1824 and 1833 indicate their success in sustaining their community of property as well as their evolving acumen in business affairs. Furthermore, they demonstrate that Zoarites had experienced some problems in their early years as a community of interest and wanted to prevent further difficulties. In the 1824 document, the members continued to give reverence first to their Christian duty. They wanted to "establish and confirm the spirit of love as the bond of peace and union" which would provide "a safe foundation of social order." Out of their Christian love, they wanted "to unite our several personal interests, into one common interest." So their religious ideals would lead to the development of a temporal order.[22]

The 1824 articles also indicate that they hoped the community-held property would preclude any lawsuits or arbitrations. The society "abolished and abrogated" backsliding or excommunicated members' demands for goods and services. These articles elaborated on the status of children as well as new members in the society. The directors had control of children, but they could not bind any children out of the society as apprentices without the vote of a majority of the members. Youths could become full members of the society when they reached adulthood. New members could enter Zoar with the approval of the directors, the board of arbitration, and a two-thirds majority of the society. The approval of new members also depended on their relinquishing all property to the community interest.[23]

In May 1833, the Zoarites amended their articles in response to developments in state law. The state of Ohio legislature had passed in 1832 an act to incorporate the Society of Separatists of Zoar as a "body politic." This allowed the community to function as a corporation that could pass laws as well as hold property in common. They could also engage in business transactions. Interestingly, although women belonged to the community of interest and had full voting power, the Ohio legislature listed only male members in this act.[24]

In response to the law of the Ohio legislature, the community of Zoar decided to revise its entire constitution. The Articles of 1833 served as the basis of the community's government until it disbanded in 1898. The constitution divided the members into two classes, designated as the novitiates and the full associates. Members in the first class, or novitiates, served a probationary period of one year before they could become full associates, or members of the second class. They did not have to relinquish their property. The children of members had to follow this procedure if they wanted to enter into full membership upon reaching legal age—eighteen for females and twenty-one for males. Children of members and those applicants in the first class were themselves admitted as novitiates. A novitiate could enter the second class if the trustees approved and if members brought no objections to the applicant. At the time of admission, the novitiate committed to the provisions of the constitution and gave all property to the community. A person in debt would not receive admission to the society.[25]

The constitution also provided for the democratic government of the community. Three directors or trustees governed Zoar. Each year, an election was held to select one of the three. Both men and women voted in these elections, in which the majority won. The directors controlled the property and managed the community's affairs. In return, they had to act in the best interests of the society and had to provide members with homes, food, and clothing. Furthermore, the directors decided the work that each member performed according to his or her abilities. Additionally, society members elected a cashier or treasurer who took charge of all the financial affairs of the community. Voters also selected a five-member committee, different people from the trustees, that served as a court of appeals to decide cases that the trustees could not resolve. This included cases involving discord among Zoarites. If the trustees could not settle the matter, then one of the party could appeal to the committee. In addition to the directors, members elected an agent general who served as the chief conductor of business transactions with the outside world. This post was considered the most important and highest in Zoar, and only Bimeler held it. This indicates the esteem the society had for him. After his death in 1853, no one replaced him. Instead, the cashier or one of the directors performed his duties.[26]

In return for the democratic government and the community of goods, members had to make some commitments to Zoar. As noted, they pledged their property. They also promised to "bind ourselves most faithfully and industriously to execute all the orders and regulations of said trustees . . . without opposition and murmuring, and we likewise agree to apply our strength, good will, industry, and skill for life to the general benefit of said Society." If a member did not live up to these expectations and acted "contrary to duty and good order," then the society had the right to excommunicate him or her. Also, a member could elect to leave the society. In either case, the member would not have any claim to the property of the society. However, he or she could appeal to the standing committee to receive indemnities.[27]

The constitution also made provisions regarding the children of the society. Members with children agreed to give the trustees the power to direct the youths until they reached legal age. Trustees had legal control over the children as if they held indentures for them. The society agreed to establish a school for the children headed by "such male or female overseers . . . whose qualifications shall be found best suited for said purpose." The standing committee would select the overseers, who committed themselves to giving their best efforts to the children "as well in moral as in physical consideration, the best possible education, thereby having in view not only the attainment of scientific branches of knowledge, but also gradually training them to performing the diverse branches of manual labor." Parents placed their children under the care of the school overseers at age three, and their children would receive education appropriate to their age and faculties. The standing committee supervised the school and decided when youths should be placed under the control of the trustees to perform labor. Once the youths reached legal age, they decided whether or not they wanted to join the society as full members, and they had to go through the admission process.[28]

The society tried to include all matters of importance in the constitution, and its articles of governance had greatly evolved from the initial declarations of 1819. It realized that over time it might need to alter the constitution, and so it made provisions to do so. The society could alter the document at any time if the amendments adhered to "the principles of unity and the preservation of the Society" and if two-thirds of the members supported the changes.[29]

Most of the issues addressed in the constitution concerned worldly matters, although the Separatists had founded the community based on religious principles. Apparently, the German Separatists, like the seventeenth-century Puritans who founded the Massachusetts Bay Colony, found no inconsistency in developing an economically prosperous community in God's name. As indicated in the constitution, the Separatists had established a community of goods so that they could attain security over their land. They did not embark on this economic relationship for the purpose of experimentation. Rather, they wanted to maintain the integrity of their property in a religious community based on their beliefs.[30]

The principles that the Separatists had embraced in Germany they carried with them to Zoar. These included a rejection of all ceremony, equality of all people, a refusal to bear arms, and the acceptance of sexual relations only for reproduction. Joseph Bimeler served as the chief spiritual leader of the community and directed the society members through his preaching about the path that God wanted them to take. The Zoarites believed that they had found the way to attain eternal life.[31]

When Bimeler spoke to the community, he did so without any written sermons. Rather, he spoke through the inspiration of the Holy Ghost. Bimeler believed that he differed from the clergy because he accepted the spiritual work of the Holy Ghost and did not need to learn about God as if acquiring a trade. He believed that these spiritual manifestations were necessary because the spiritual needs of people changed over time. Only the inspiration of the Holy Ghost could meet the needs of the people.[32]

Although Bimeler did not first commit his thoughts to paper, a record still exists of the words that he spoke to the community as their guide. The record began when a young man, Johannes Neef, wrote down Bimeler's preachings from memory so that his deaf father might understand his words. Neef maintained this record from 1822 until 1832, the year he died. Later, another young man continued the record. The community took great pains to preserve this record. When Bimeler died in 1853, the Zoarites found that no one could adequately take his place. They wanted to preserve his preachings so that others might read his words at their services. The community purchased a handpress and hired a printer to do the job. Bimeler's preachings fill three large volumes in German, and few copies have survived. In addition to Bimeler's words, the society also printed a volume containing the poems or hymns written by Terstegen, a mystic of the Reformed Church who lived from 1687 to 1769, which they used in their religious services.[33]

Through his words, Bimeler sought to bring true Christianity to Zoar. He urged his followers to repent and enter into the community of God. The Separatists subscribed to a school of thought known as chiliasm, which held that Christ would come to earth to live for a thousand years before the end of the world. The Zoarites came to interpret the reign of Christ as an inner rather than an outer transformation. Consequently, members had to repent to achieve a state of grace.[34]

Bimeler also addressed worldly concerns in his preachings. While he did not forbid the use of tobacco in the community, he urged against it. He also counseled the members to eat and to drink alcohol in moderation. Bimeler advocated orderly, clean, and industrious lifestyles. He even thought members should work on Sundays if necessary because he believed one day held as much sanctity as any other. Likewise, he did not follow Christian holidays. In his instructions to the community, Bimeler left room for personal choice. He did not want to establish himself as a despot of the community but rather encouraged members to form their own opinions on matters. He did not believe this individualism would conflict with the community of property. He believed that the Separatists could best achieve a godly society in which people did not have concerns about being rich or poor. Without this worry, members would not exhibit selfishness and could love their neighbors fully.[35]

When the village was first organized, sexual relations in marriage were permissible, and several families welcomed children in 1819. The increase in the population, however, affected the labor of the community. Women outnumbered men two to one in Zoar, and their labor contribution to the village held much importance. They worked in the fields and took responsibility for raising and spinning flax and tending to the sheep. They also performed the traditional tasks of cooking and sewing. If they had to care for their own children, the society lost a valuable labor source, and Zoar had to pay off the debt from the purchase of its lands.[36]

In response to these circumstances, the Zoar community instituted celibacy around 1822. The Separatists had already accepted the belief that sexual relations were a necessary evil to propagate the race, so the adoption of celibacy was not a great stretch. Members could not marry, and those spouses already in the village had to live apart. Some married Separatists had already decided to live separately and remain chaste for their faith before they left Germany. Some spouses completely separated before the departure from Germany because one of them held stronger religious beliefs. In such cases, the weaker of the faith stayed in Germany. Bimeler did not condemn marriage during the celibate period, which lasted until 1830. However, he stated that God only tolerated the institution. Bimeler believed that people should pay more attention to the attainment of eternal happiness than to any worldly joy that they might find in marriage.[37]

Despite his preachings, Bimeler attempted to obtain some worldly bliss of his own. He became attracted to a young woman who worked for him in his household. They married, and Bimeler withdrew the antimarriage law in 1830. Those who wished to marry had to receive the approval of the trustees as a formality. Anyone wishing to marry a nonmember had to leave the community. His preachings after 1830 showed him to be in favor of marriage. The society accepted marriage once more after the members had completed the full payment of their debt and the need for female labor was no longer as great. Furthermore, the community began to welcome more Separatists from Germany who could not afford to leave with the initial migration of 1817. These new applicants who had spouses would not have to renounce marriage to enter Zoar.[38]

With the acceptance of marriage, Zoar could depend on natural increase to sustain the society, unlike the Shakers, who were entirely celibate. Furthermore, Zoar received many requests from outsiders to join the society, and the process followed to enter the society differed from that for becoming a Shaker. The Zoar community was more selective.[39]

Individuals who applied to enter the community had to submit letters to the cashier of Zoar, who decided whether a person had the necessary qualifications and possessed a skill or trade needed by the community. Unmarried persons and those with a German heritage were looked upon more favorably. The trustees then evaluated the applicants who met these standards and either accepted or rejected them. Those admitted to the community underwent a one-year probationary period. Following this, they would become full members, as long as no one held reservations about them. Individuals could not enter the society if they were in debt. Children born to society members also followed this process. They did not become full members by virtue of their parents' faith. During the probationary period, individuals did not have to give up their property and received food, clothing, and housing from the community.[40]

The society accepted the greatest number of new members between 1819 and 1834. From 1830 to 1834, Zoar admitted approximately 170 men, women, and youths, most of whom were the family and friends of those who had left Wurtemberg. These persons probably wanted to leave Wurtemberg because of political and economic factors, and their connection to members at Zoar would make the transition to the new country easier. Furthermore, they shared in the religious beliefs of the community. However, Zoar admitted few foreigners from other nations. It accepted very few new members throughout its existence. An outsider would more likely receive admission if he or she married a member.[41]

Most of the people who asked to join Zoar felt that they had led uneventful lives prior to their inquiry for admission. Some of the applicants indicated that they hoped to find meaning in their lives by joining Zoar. Although interested persons declared that they had the necessary religious background to join, few actually understood or knew anything about the Separatists' philosophy. Zoar did accept some individuals who had joined other communal societies, including the Shakers. Some applicants looked to Zoar as a caretaking community for the elderly and infirm.[42]

Many applicants expressed a desire to join Zoar because of the society's communal aspects. In 1872, A. J. Randall of Dayton was disappointed that the society would not accept him, stating "I desire to be with a class of people that are harmonious and work for each others interest." Randall wanted to enter a society "where the greatest object in Life is Peace, love, and harmony." The communal features of Zoar attracted large numbers during times of economic crisis such as the Panic of 1873. The Separatists received an especially large number of requests to join between 1875 and 1880, probably because of the high unemployment of the times. They rejected those who did not have a firm grasp of their religious mission.[43]

Those individuals who were admitted had to conform to the way of life already established. They had to give up their property to the community. Applicants usually had property worth a few hundred dollars, although a few had thousands of dollars in property. They had to declare their financial worth upon entrance. Their economic status did not determine whether or not they could live in Zoar. Rather, the Separatists placed more emphasis on applicants' spiritual beliefs and personal virtue. In return for giving up their property, members would receive food each day and clothing. They would have to commit themselves to attaining only the rewards of serving God rather than earthly acknowledgments. Members had to perform only the labor that they could handle.[44]

While many people applied to enter Zoar, others made the decision to leave the community. Although seceding members could not bring claims against the society, they could present to the standing committee claims to receive indemnities. In 1837, T. Friederich Heim admonished the Zoarites for failure to live up to their promises to admit him into the community. Heim claimed that political reasons kept him in a probationary state for more than three years, during which time the society profited from his labor. He endured injuries as a result of the work he had performed. Heim demanded restitution and threatened to take his case to court outside the community. Zoar ultimately paid him twenty-five dollars to compensate him for his superior services to the community. Women who left Zoar usually could take more property with them, such as clothes and household goods.[45]

While members' religious beliefs and common goals were important, the society lasted for so many years because of its economic success. Many of Zoar's initial settlers had learned trades that helped in the establishment of the village. Zoarites attempted to establish a self-sustaining community, a goal achieved by 1835. They developed several small industries, including blacksmithing, carpentry, and wagon making. Not only did these industries benefit Zoar, they also helped neighboring farmers who paid for these services. In Zoar's first years, members constructed a gristmill and a sawmill. Built in 1821, the gristmill provided services for thirty farmers in the region during its first year. The flour processed at the mill, along with the maple sugar from the trees of the village brought money to the society that it then used to purchase goods it could not produce on its own.[46]

Zoar benefited greatly from the construction of the Ohio and Erie Canal from 1825 to 1833. The State of Ohio wanted to construct a route that would link Lake Erie with the Ohio River. Since the canal needed a water source to fill its channels, the canal had to follow on a parallel course with rivers. The planned route passed for seven miles through Zoar as the Tuscarawas River cut diagonally through the community. James Robertson of the canal committee noted "the excellent natural advantages" of the route through Zoar. Because this project was massive for the time, canal commissioners divided the project into small units of work and hired small contractors to complete certain sections. The Separatists agreed to construct the canal running through their property, and they earned twenty-one thousand dollars for this labor. Both men and women helped complete this project. The male members dug the channel, and the women carried the dirt away in tubs on top of their heads. The society earned additional money by selling food and supplies to other contractors working on the canal. This business allowed Zoar to pay off all of its debt.[47]

The Ohio and Erie Canal provided an even greater benefit for Zoar. When the society completed its section of the canal in 1828, it quickly enjoyed easy access to Cleveland to the north on Lake Erie and eventually had a route to Portsmouth in the south on the Ohio River. This provided new and large markets for their goods in Ohio and throughout the United States. The Separatists also owned and operated at least four canal boats. Initially, nonmembers ran these boats, but members eventually took charge of navigating them. With the additional monies brought in by the canal, Zoar purchased more lands and by 1854 owned 7,500 acres. The society also built a flour mill in 1837 on the canal's banks because they could easily load the grain and flour.[48]

The canal also meant that the community would receive more people from the outside world. In later years, the accessibility of Zoar would help to establish it as a resort town. In 1834, the canal had the negative effect of introducing disease to the community. An ill passenger on a canal boat was forced to disembark from the vessel in Zoar. The Separatists cared for him, but he died a few days later. After the Zoarites buried him, his spouse arrived wanting to collect the belongings on his person. A stranger opened the grave, and subsequently the cholera spread throughout the community. From August to September 1834, fifty-six members, one-third of Zoar's population, died, including Johannes Breymaier, who had introduced the concept of the community of goods.[49]

The canal helped to transport the surplus goods the members grew and produced. The society divided its economic activities into agriculture, animal husbandry, and manufacturing. The members grew wheat, oats, and rye as their main crops. They also produced fruits. The surplus apples, cider, and pears that they produced were sold in outside markets, providing the community with cash income. Zoar earned a reputation for its fine pears and apples developed by one member, Simon Beuter. The members grew vegetables and made wine from grapes, but most of these the community consumed. Each family had a vegetable garden that supplemented the basic vegetables provided by the society. The community was also known for its gorgeous flower garden, and it appointed a special person to care for it. Outside visitors always commented on the lovely garden. The flowers and trees raised in Zoar held much value in outside markets.[50]

Zoarites also raised several varieties of animals for different purposes. From their cattle, they obtained meat and hides for consumption in the village. They sold the surplus in markets from New York to Iowa. The Zoarites maintained a herd of dairy cattle for the production of milk, butter, and cheese. They raised sheep for meat and wool. Other animals used by the community included horses, hogs, and poultry. The Separatists raised silkworms too in the early years of the society.[51]

One economic endeavor that proved challenging to Zoar was the construction and management of two blast furnaces built on the canal. The society decided to pursue this project because of the availability of ore on its land and because they could transport the goods produced on the canal. Zoar also had access to coal, located beneath the ore deposits, that could fuel the furnaces. In 1834, the Zoar furnace was constructed. At first, outside men managed the furnace until members learned the trade. The society built a second furnace, the Fairfield Furnace, which produced pig iron and castings. The community sold these products in Ohio, New York, Illinois, and Pennsylvania. The society kept detailed records of their works, including a diagram of the furnaces. After the discovery of ore on Lake Superior during the years 1850 to 1860, the furnaces in northern Ohio produced a higher grade of ore that Zoar could not match.[52]

Zoar demonstrated the willingness to gain economically from commerce with the outside area in their establishment of a general store and a hotel. Later, Zoar tried to attract visitors for economic gain. An additional hotel was built to serve the workers and travelers on the canal. This hotel had a view of the canal and river and stayed open until 1845. In the senior years of Zoar, the Separatists attempted to bring in more income by attracting tourists to the hotel, and they gained a good reputation for their gardens and serenity. In the twilight years of the society, the hotel was renovated to double its size, a project that indicated its popularity with visitors.[53]

One of the industries that the Separatists established at Zoar was a brewery. The members grew barley and hops for the purpose of making

2.2 Zoar Hotel, 1889. *Ohio Historical Society, Louis Baus Collection*

beer, which members consumed. They drank beer when they had to complete difficult tasks. During the summer, members consumed it to quench their thirst. Men working in the fields received a pint a day for lunch. Women also consumed beer while washing clothes on hot days. That beer not consumed was sold to visitors, including guests at the Hotel and farmers in the area as well as outside markets. The amount consumed by the community usually superseded what Zoar sold. In addition to beer, the community manufactured wine and cider. Some community leaders expressed concern that the Separatists consumed too much beer, wine, and cider; however, cases of drunkenness were rare.[54]

In the late nineteenth century, Zoar, with a population of about three hundred and a village consisting of seventy-five buildings, had established several small industries and was engaged in a variety of economic activities. Members ran a canal mill, woolen mill, factory, foundry, and tin shop. Zoarites welcomed guests to their hotel and garden. Other economic endeavors included a cabinet shop, lumberyard, shoe shop, saddle shop, tailor shop, and tannery. Zoar produced several goods for outside purchase. Members made skillfully crafted woolens, including blankets, stockings, and coverlets. Craftsmen built Zoar stoves, which had a large market because of their efficiency. In the later years of the society, the Separatists closed the stove foundry because their product proved larger, heavier, and more cumbersome in comparison with others available on the market.[55]

The society used money obtained from surplus goods to purchase items it could not make, to pay taxes, and to hire outside labor for work members could not do. For example, Bimeler secured Bibles for the community in both English and German. He also purchased books for the education of the children, including spelling books in English and German. After the cholera epidemic of 1834, the Separatists hired outside laborers to cultivate the fields. In the later years of Zoar, the society grew more dependent on outside labor. In 1850, the society received a letter asking that it consider hiring a recent immigrant from Austria who was an "experienced foundry man."[56]

Bimeler's leadership as agent-general and chief businessman of Zoar helped the community prosper. The year before his death in 1852, the property of the community was worth one million dollars. One reason Zoar prospered under Bimeler's leadership concerned his promotion of invention and industry. He made certain that his community had access to various patent inventions so that they could use them in their labor.

The records of Zoar contain numerous agreements for Bimeler to use, make, and vend to others various inventions. These included a machine for stretching horse collars, a machine for pricking leather, a patent churn, and a patent cooking stove.[57]

The decade before the Civil War marked the peak of Zoar's financial success. Because the Separatists did not publish their estimated wealth, it is difficult to ascertain the value of their property. It is clear, however, that the society did start to decline in wealth after the Civil War. At the time the community dissolved, the property value of the land was listed as approximately three hundred forty thousand dollars, and personal property was worth sixteen thousand dollars.[58]

The men, women, and children of Zoar were instructed to lead clean, simple, orderly lives. Members arose early to begin their daily work. In the first years of the community, a bugle sounded to rouse people to work. It also signaled the end of the workday. Some members had regular work assignments to complete, while others had to ask the trustees for their duties. Women and men worked at their tasks until age sixty. At this time, they engaged in less strenuous labor. Women and men dressed plainly. Women usually wore dark dresses covered by aprons and bonnets. The women usually made their own dresses and also the stockings for the men. Men usually dressed in overalls similar to those other farmers of the era wore. Unlike those in the outside world, the men wore a distinctive beard that covered the sides of the face and the chin and left the other

2.3 Zoar: "The Cradlers," 1888. *Ohio Historical Society, Louis Baus Collection*

skin clean-shaven. Because the Separatists viewed all as equal, the trustees attempted to ensure that all members dressed equally.[59]

Most of the labor that men performed consisted of farming, operating the blast furnaces, and working in the mills. Although at times the society had to depend on outside labor, many did not like the practice. Often, outside workers brought with them unsavory habits such as swearing and using tobacco. The Separatists usually offered these people board and housing as part of their payment.[60]

Women performed some of the same tasks as men. They worked in the fields with the men, and they sheared sheep. Women and girls were almost entirely responsible for the cultivation, harvesting, and spinning of flax. Women also engaged in more traditional tasks such as maintaining the gardens for their homes, preparing meals, and making candles and soap. Additionally, the women of Zoar ran the silk and linen industries. A woman also managed the dairy until 1870.[61]

Because men and women worked side by side, the community leaders attempted to eliminate any possible transgressions that might result from the close contact. In 1848, male member Christian Bauer was asked to give up certain objectionable habits. Specifically he was instructed not to expose his body in the presence of women while working. Also, he was told to take care in his dress and eating habits. Apparently, Bauer had attracted too much attention from the female members of the community who were perhaps embarrassed by Bauer's dress. Community leaders may have feared also that Bauer's appearance might lead females to unclear thoughts or temptations. [62]

The labor that women did, combined with their right to vote in the society's elections, gave the average woman of Zoar more equality with her male counterparts than the average woman in a Shaker community had. The average Shaker woman had to follow the rules of the elders and eldresses and did not have a voice in government. However, the village of Zoar did not have female leaders as did the Shaker communities. Consequently, the women of Zoar did not directly create rules or regulations, although they could vote on matters. Furthermore, since Zoar recognized marriage, the women of Zoar still undertook traditional roles as wives. Their parental role differed from that in mainstream society because children after three years of age were reared in a community nursery.[63]

The Separatists established a community nursery where children lived from age three to fourteen, freeing women for work. At age fourteen, the children usually went back to live with their parents. Girls and boys lived in separate houses, and designated women supervised the children for most of the day except for the time in school. Parents rarely got to see their children. The women who ran the nursery often treated the children harshly. The diet fed to them was poor and the living area inadequate. In the winter, the boys often slept in unheated areas. One of the trustees, Jacob Ackermann, refused to send his daughter to the nursery in 1840. Consequently, parents who protested did not have to comply with this rule.[64]

The education of the children proved important to the Separatists, who had wanted to escape the dictates of education in Germany. Bimeler, especially, recognized the value of freedom in American education; however, he did not want the children of the Separatists educated outside of the community because of concern that the youths' commitment to the faith would decline. Zoar constructed a school that was part of the Tuscarawas County school system. The children of Zoar had classmates who did not belong to the society. Because the township paid the teachers' salaries, school directors appointed them, and the teachers were not always members. Children received an education in reading, writing, geography, and arithmetic and were taught in English and German. They attended school until age fifteen.[65]

Children were expected to complete assigned tasks for the community in addition to their schooling. Boys, for example, helped to maintain the flower garden and to assist the men in the fields. Girls helped with harvesting, herding sheep, and working with the dairy industry. Although little time remained for recreation, children, as well as adults, tried to make their work a diversion. Music held great importance in Zoar. Children sang

2.4 Zoar Band, circa 1870 (from left: Louis Zimmerman, Gustave Schumacher, Jacob Sylvan, Ben Beiter, Carl Zimmerman, David Beiter, Martin Rauschenberger, Simon Beiter, Frank Sylvan, Joseph Breymaier, John Bimeler, William Kuecherer, and Jacob Burkhardt). *Ohio Historical Society*

2.5 Zoar: Peter Bimeler at Organ. *Ohio Historical Society, Louis Baus Collection*

while working, and members sang hymns as part of their Sunday services. Zoar boasted a brass band, led by Louis Zimmerman, and a men's chorus. This affinity for music came from the top, as Bimeler played the piano. In 1873, the society installed a pipe organ built by Bimeler's son Peter. The Separatists possessed this musical talent, although none of the members had received any formal training. Besides music, youths enjoyed sailing in the summer and ice skating and coasting in the winter.[66]

While Zoar did not offer its members much recreation, it did offer them a life largely free of worries, since boarding and material goods were provided. Houses sometimes served two or three families. Many of these homes, along with the rest of the village, had distinctive red tile roofs that members made. On certain days, members obtained the supplies that they needed, including food. The society did not keep record of how much each member or family used. Such accounts were unnecessary because all property was held in common.[67]

Although the Separatists had agreed to the community of property and labored under such articles, some discontented members took their claims before outside courts. In August 1839, Friederich Sieber sued the society in the Tuscarawas County Court. The society had expelled Sieber, but he alleged that the constitution entitled him to a share. Sieber also stated that he and his family suffered in Zoar as they did not receive adequate food. Furthermore, he said that Bimeler had made advances to his wife. The lawsuit went so far as to blame Zoar for his wife's miscarriage because of their poor treatment. The society responded that Sieber had made false claims. They also charged that Sieber had not contributed much labor to Zoar and had grumbled about the light work he did do. The society insisted that Bimeler never seduced women. Additionally, they denied that the society was responsible for Mrs. Sieber's miscarriage. This lawsuit was withdrawn shortly after Sieber filed it.[68]

Another case brought against the society did not have such a quick resolution and eventually received a hearing before the United States Supreme Court. The issue again involved grievances brought against Zoar by a member who was expelled. The case involved John Goesele and his wife, Anna Maria, who had managed the canal tavern. In January 1845, the standing committee charged that the Goeseles had allowed inappropriate behavior at the tavern, including drunkenness, and had misused the funds. The society closed the tavern but allowed the Goeseles to live in the village. The Goeseles, however, would not leave the tavern and continued to run it. Consequently, the society expelled them.[69]

In response, the Goeseles, along with other unhappy members, filed suit in county court against the society in March 1845. The plaintiffs attacked Bimeler's character and motives, saying that he had incorporated the society for the purpose of autocratic rule. They alleged that members received the minimum goods they needed for survival and compared their condition to that of slaves. In contrast, Bimeler lived a life of luxury and maintained his position by keeping the rest of the society uninformed of their civil and political rights as American citizens. The complaint asked the court to look into all past business of the society and take inventory of all the society's property. The plaintiffs then wanted to be given their portion of the property. In November 1847, the court dismissed the case and charged the plaintiffs with the cost.[70]

Before taking their case to a higher court, the Goeseles sought to strengthen it by going to Zoar in search of more dissatisfied members. In May 1849, they went to Zoar and posted notices of their manifesto, asking others to help them. They pleaded for the return of their rightful property. They also repeated their charges of tyranny against Bimeler, accusing him of impugning their religious beliefs in the equality of all. They called upon the members to act and compared their situation to that of the patriots in the American Revolution. However, they felt no animosity toward the other Separatists. They wanted the Separatists to agree to a partition of the property and land rather than leaving it to Bimeler's designs. In the manifesto, the Goeseles and the other plaintiffs continually invoked God in their actions. After posting the manifesto throughout the village, the group took over the meeting house and awaited a response.[71]

The trustees held a meeting in the schoolhouse to discuss the situation. They openly considered the Goeseles' proposal and put the matter to a secret vote. Unanimously, they put down the manifesto and also issued denials concerning the charges made against Bimeler. Furthermore, they strengthened their allegiance to the society by passing resolutions to maintain their constitution.[72]

In April 1851, the matter came to the United States Circuit Court. The lawsuit of the plaintiffs went back to the original settlers of Zoar, which included relatives of Goesele, before the approval of the constitution of 1833 and the incorporation of Zoar. The lawsuit questioned the nature of the society and the legality of the rules under which it functioned regarding property. The plaintiffs claimed that they had a right to Zoar's property based on the claims of their ancestor John Goesele, who was part of the original migration in 1817.[73]

The court ruled in favor of the society. The decision stated that Bimeler had purchased the lands and held them in trust for the society as the members agreed to in the constitution of 1819. The declaration of trust that Bimeler subscribed to did not necessitate a grant, and the 1819 articles adhered to common law. The court viewed the 1819 constitution as a contract that designated all property belonged to the society's members. Members had entered freely into the contract and were bound by it. Consequently, only members of the society could make claims on the property and not the descendants of the members. With this decision, the court upheld the legality of the society, and the plaintiffs lost their suit.[74]

Goesele and his group did not rest with this decision but appealed to the United States Supreme Court. In December 1852, the Court, headed by Chief Justice Roger B. Taney, heard the case. The society's attorneys, Henry M. Stanberry and Thomas Ewing, presented essentially the same arguments they had made to the lower court. They explained original members had formed a community of property that would be passed on to its members. Furthermore, they said that the society constituted a universal partnership, and survivorship was part of the partnership. Thus, the heirs of deceased members did not have a right to the property. Stanberry and Ewing also answered the plaintiffs' claims that the society's constitution contradicted the institutions of the United States. They stated that the society was democratic, not autocratic.[75]

The Supreme Court upheld the ruling of the circuit court, with Justice John McLean explaining the Court's standing. McLean stated that because members agreed to hold all property in common and had no individual property, they could not will any to their heirs. Those members who now benefited from the society's holdings did so under contract. The Court noted: "It is strange that the complainants should ask a partition through their ancestor, when by the terms of his contract, he could have no divisible interest. They who now enjoy the property, enjoy it under his express contract." The Court also looked upon the society as a benevolent charity since the original members helped the aged and the ill. The decision praised Zoar: "By great industry, economy, and good management and energy, the settlement at Zoar has prospered more than any part of the surrounding country." Individual ownership defeated the purpose of Zoar, and partitioning of the properties would cause the dissolution of the society: "If the interests of its members could be transferred, or pass by descent, the maintenance of the community would be impossible." If members left the society, they lost claims to the property, just as new members enjoyed the benefits of the society's property.[76]

The Supreme Court decision also addressed the attacks the lawsuit had made on Bimeler. The Court said that Bimeler's decision to hold the land in trust "was above reproach. It was wise and most judicious, to secure the best interests of the association." The Court had gathered information from respectable persons of Zoar and found Bimeler's character "sustained for integrity and morality." The decision noted that "Bimeler is a man of great energy and of high capacity for business" as seen in the success of Zoar. The Court articulated that Bimeler had a "difficult part to act. As the head and leader of the society, his conduct is narrowly watched, and often misconstrued."[77]

The Supreme Court decision did not stop the Goeseles. They filed another lawsuit in the county court of common pleas, which they also lost. Eventually, the case went to the Ohio Supreme Court, which in 1862 ruled against them. Although the Goeseles involved the society in much litigation, it did not have to confront a lawsuit again until after it dissolved in 1898.[78]

Although many people had questioned Bimeler's leadership and motives over the years, most people reached the same conclusion as the Supreme Court. Bimeler was an honest, hardworking, industrious person. His abilities extended into the medical field, and he served as the society's physician. Yet the society's claims that all members were equal were not entirely accurate. Bimeler did live in a better residence than the other members. Visitors called his home "the palace." Constructed in 1835 and located near the garden, Bimeler's house was a two-and-a-half-story red brick colonial with a basement. Unlike other members, Bimeler also had a carriage. However, his injured leg perhaps justified the luxury to members. Such differences had opened Bimeler up to charges from dissatisfied members. Still, his leadership and administrative skills had much to do with Zoar's success.[79]

2.6 Zoar: Joseph Bimeler Residence. *Western Reserve Historical Society, Cleveland, Ohio*

During the summer of 1853, Bimeler became ill. He died on August 27 at seventy-five years of age. As promised, he had held the society's property in trust, and it now reverted back to the community. True to his character and the religion he followed, Bimeler was laid to rest in a simple, unmarked grave. His death left a void in the community leadership.[80]

After Bimeler's death, the society had difficulty finding a suitable replacement for its spiritual and administrative leadership. The society selected Jacob Sylvan to lead them spiritually. While Sylvan could express himself in writing, he lacked speaking abilities. Christian Wiebel undertook the task of reading Sylvan's sermons. After Sylvan died in 1862, Wiebel read the discourses of Bimeler at Sunday services. In terms of administrative tasks, the society did not select an agent general to replace Bimeler. Instead, the post remained vacant, perhaps to honor him. The cashier and the trustees assumed the responsibilities of the agent general.[81]

The passing of Bimeler signaled that the society had to confront changes without its most trusted leader to guide it. In 1861, the nation confronted the Civil War. Although the Separatists believed it was wrong to bear arms, Zoar could not stay removed from the conflict. The society had not remained separate from politics. In the first decades of Zoar, members had divided their loyalties between the Democratic and Whig parties. After the formation of the Republican Party in the 1850s, Zoarites supported it wholeheartedly because of their opposition to slavery. As pacifists, members denounced the war, but some of the younger members chose to participate. Fourteen young men of Zoar enlisted and served, although the United States government exempted men from the draft who paid two hundred dollars. The society paid this price for the young men who followed the pacifism of the Separatists. Those who enlisted still received supplies from the society. Zoar manufacturing did not make any financial gains from the war. It had received many orders for yarn and cloth during the conflict, but its mills could not handle the large orders.[82]

After the Civil War, the United States industrialized at a rapid pace, and Zoar found that it could not keep up with the changing economy. The Separatists found it cheaper and more practical to purchase many small goods from the outside rather than maintain their small industries. For example, they closed their shoe shop as well as their woolen factory and stove foundry.[83]

The nature of the society changed as outside forces began to influence

Zoar. In 1884, a railroad station was established at Zoar, furthering the communications and transportation available. The Separatists decided to meet the new realities by incorporating into a village. This meant that new governmental positions had to be established including mayor, councilmen, secretary-treasurer, and marshal. The society still maintained its own system of government but now it had to function under both frameworks. The municipal organization never caused any conflicts, however, because members agreed on who should hold the offices.[84]

The addition of the railroad meant that more outsiders came to Zoar. Each week, hundreds of visitors arrived from Akron, Canton, and Cleveland. The railroad advertised Zoar as a tourist place with its lovely garden and quaint character. The society welcomed these people, no longer fearing the influence of outsiders. Zoar needed the extra funds that these people brought to the community. To accommodate the visitors, Zoar expanded the hotel, which was completed in 1892. This enabled people to stay at Zoar for weeks at a time rather than for days. Some people stayed for the entire summer. A group of Cleveland artists made Zoar their summer home and used the village as the subject of their works. The presence of outsiders definitely changed the tenor of the village. Alexander Gunn, a former Cleveland businessman who proved a divisive force in the community, noted the following: "The hotel is crowded today with cheap merry-makers, who come in buggies with their girls and have dinner, roam about the village, and drive home in the evening."[85]

Gunn had first visited Zoar in 1879 and then decided to move there, causing a schism in the community. Gunn immediately caused problems because he was not a member and was not German. Beyond this, he was an agnostic, which some Separatists felt threatened the religious beliefs of the community. Gunn cultivated friendships with the society's leaders and musicians and had them over to his house frequently to eat and drink. Although members disapproved of Gunn's presence, the leaders continued their friendship with him, causing many to lose their faith in the leaders.[86]

The Zoar of the post–Civil War period had taken on a different character than in the society's first decades. The first generation of Separatists who had fled Germany to escape persecution had strong ties created by their circumstances and experiences. They established a town from nothing and believed that God had helped them achieve their success. The population lost its last connection to the past with the death of trustee Jacob Ackermann in 1889. Simon Beuter attempted to assume the leader-

2.7 Zoar: Alexander Gunn Residence (Gunn is seated). *Western Reserve Historical Society, Cleveland, Ohio*

ship role in the community and instill the religious beliefs of the original settlers in the members, but without the religious commitment that held the society together from its inception, the community failed. Seeing that the end was near, Beuter resigned as trustee in 1890.[87]

The declining spiritual climate alone did not bring about the dissolution of the society. Economics played a pivotal role, as did lack of sufficient leadership. Under Bimeler, the society kept pace with the agricultural and industrial techniques used elsewhere in the nation so that Zoar products could compete with manufactures from nearby cities such as Cleveland.

After the Civil War, Zoar did not keep up with the new realities of the industrial nation, nor did the community attempt to modernize. Also, Bimeler had used the community's revenues wisely. He put monies back into Zoar industries. After his death, the society invested its funds in railroads and banks, which led to thousands of dollars in losses. Workers at Zoar grew lazy and began putting more effort into socializing than into working. The older members of the community found it more difficult to perform the arduous tasks. The need for outside laborers showed a weakness in Zoar's economy.[88]

Since a measure of discontent had always existed at Zoar, the emergence of difficulties led some members to vocalize their unhappiness. Ironically, the great-grandson of Bimeler, Levi Bimeler, led the effort to disband. Bimeler, who was educated outside the society, considered dissolution the best remedy for the inequalities that plagued it. He outlined his arguments in a newspaper called the *Nugitna* ("anti-Gunn" in reverse), which he began in 1895. The newspaper disclosed some of the divisive forces at work in Zoar, extolled individual rights, and in its initial publication quoted from the Declaration of Independence. Bimeler reiterated the reasons for which the society had formed and asked members if they had lived up to these ideals. He proposed that the society disband and that members receive the share of Zoar's property to which they were entitled. On December 3, 1895, the society met to consider this proposal. Simon Beuter strongly urged the members not to disband, while Bimeler argued for the society's dissolution.[89]

Bimeler published more issues of the *Nugitna* to continue to agitate for the cause. He explained that circumstances that warranted a community of property in the past had changed. Members lacked a spirit of love and simplicity. Bimeler stopped his attacks on the society only after being threatened with expulsion. In 1896, he published the last issue of the *Nugitna*.[90]

Ultimately, Bimeler's wish was granted. The society continued to decline economically. To cover its debts, it had to sell off its investments. At each society meeting, more people came to support dissolution. On March 10, 1898, the members voted to disband.[91]

The society explained its several reasons for disbanding. First, the society noted its economic difficulties. For forty years, the income of the society could not meet its expenses. Second, the religious faith of the community had declined. Third, many members did not follow the society's constitution pertaining to industrial and economic matters, which hurt the society economically. Fourth, members did not fulfill their roles to help the society and instead acted in their own interests. Fifth, many members had grown opposed to the theory of a community of property and come to advocate individual ownership.[92]

In the resolutions to dissolve, provisions were made for the distribution of property. The land owned by Zoar amounted to seventy-three hundred acres, worth more than three hundred forty thousand dollars. The society had to divide this among 222 members. Three commissioners would preside over the division of the property. Full members received a share of the society's property, and those in the probationary class got a half share. Some of the property remained secure from the distribution, including the cemetery, meeting house, and town hall. Members would keep their clothes, personal belongings, and household furniture except pianos and organs. The manner in which the division was carried out resulted in each family keeping its village home, its land, and two hundred dollars. Some Separatists wanted to sell the properties that made money, including the hotel and store, and divide the proceeds. This did not happen, and those who received these properties as part of their share ended up better off financially than did other members.[93]

On October 13, 1898, the Recorder's Office of Tuscarawas County received the deed that divided the society's property. Once all of the property had been dispersed, the Society of Separatists of Zoar officially came to an end on December 7, 1900. Previous members who wanted a share of the property filed lawsuits, but the courts dismissed the cases on the basis that the society had fulfilled its contract to them. Those individuals who had pressed for distribution of the property felt vindicated by these events; those with more religious devotion to the society experienced sadness that their haven no longer existed.[94]

Although the Society of Separatists of Zoar ultimately closed, the founders had succeeded in establishing a religious community and escaping persecution in their homeland. Zoar serves as an example of a utopian movement originating outside the United States that found life in the young nation.

Chapter 3

Joseph Smith and the Mormons in Kirtland, Ohio, 1830–1838

THE TREK THAT LED THE MORMONS TO Ohio mirrored the path that utopianists and reformers took from the Burned-Over District in New York to the Western Reserve in Ohio. The Mormons had their origins in western New York with their founder, Joseph Smith. The Mormons differed from the Shakers and the Society of Separatists of Zoar because their beginnings were in the United States, not Europe. Like those groups, however, the Mormon communities had their origins in religious beliefs. Smith had brought his followers to Kirtland, Ohio, claiming that he had a revelation from God to move the group to Zion in Independence, Missouri. According to Smith, the first place that the Mormons should stop was Kirtland.[1]

Joseph Smith established the Mormon faith, the most successful of the millennial groups, and served as the head of the church throughout his life. From a poor family, Joseph Smith Jr. was born in Vermont in 1805 to Joseph Smith Sr. and Lucy Mack Smith. His family moved frequently, and his father labored in various occupations, including farming. Smith's mother came from a family that had experienced revelations and visions, and she sought earnestly to find a church that offered her spiritual peace. Her husband, on the other hand, seemed indifferent to religion. In 1816, the family moved to Palmyra, New York, because of economic troubles they had suffered in Vermont.[2]

Palmyra offered more opportunity as a location on the Erie Canal that connected the Great Lakes to New York City. The opening of the 363-mile canal signaled dramatic change for the region in the economic and social spheres. The canal helped to encourage manufacturing along the route since goods could be shipped easily. The shifting economy affected social conditions, and people turned to religion to help them adjust to the new realities. The area along the canal experienced intense periods of religious revivalism, and Smith would contribute to religious change there.[3]

Palmyra in the 1810s seemed to offer more opportunity for the Smiths. The area had opened to settlement in the 1790s. By 1810, Palmyra had twenty-six hundred residents. The Smiths worked several jobs until they could purchase property to farm. Their improved financial status helped to support the family of nine children. Lucy Smith's religious discontent still prevailed, and she continued her quest for religious truths, as did many others in the Burned-Over District. Joseph Smith Jr. grew up in an area overcome by religious fervor. Revivals frequently occurred, led by Baptist, Presbyterian, and Methodist ministers. Nothing in his youth seemed to indicate that Smith would become the most successful religious leader of the region. In fact, Smith appeared to his contemporaries as an amiable youth who often told exaggerated stories and spent his free time in search of buried treasure in the form of Indian artifacts or Spanish gold. Such tales had prompted similar searches in New England among desperate farmers. Furthermore, the area of western New York where Smith lived was purported to be the site of a settlement of Indians known as the mound builders. Many people went in search of their artifacts. Smith had a great fascination with these people. In March 1826, Smith faced charges of disorderly conduct and being an impostor in Bainbridge, New York. Smith admitted that he led searches to unearth buried treasure and that he dabbled in magical arts. This testimony led the court to find Smith guilty of disturbing the peace.[4]

The accounts of Smith's youth vary; even the reminiscences that he wrote differ. In 1834, he had written a brief history of his life in response to criticism of his religion. He followed this with an autobiography written after he had attained a following as a prophet. The autobiography

3.1 Joseph Smith, Founder of the Mormons. *Ohio Historical Society*

offered a different version of his formative years, as Smith claimed his visions from God stirred up much ill feeling from prominent members of the community. Because of the contradictory accounts, it is difficult to offer a thorough analysis of Smith's origins as a prophet. However, it remains clear that Smith possessed the personal attributes to attract followers for his various endeavors.[5]

In the 1830s, Smith became influenced by "ultraism," a form of millennial revivalism that reached its peak in the Burned-Over District in the 1830s. During this period, Smith began to reveal episodes of the past that held importance for the establishment of Mormonism. Smith interpreted the past events of his life and stated that God was communicating through him. Beginning in 1820, Smith had received several visions that served as steps in the rise of Christ's church. Smith viewed the 1820 vision, in which angels told him not to join any existing religion, as his personal conversion. Smith claimed that both God and Jesus had appeared to him. A few years later, in 1823, Smith stated that a visitor from God, an angel named Moroni, had appeared to inform Smith that he had special work to do. This work would bring strong opposition, and the established churches would reject him.[6]

Moroni explained that there existed a book of golden plates that included the history of those who had previously inhabited the continent. Furthermore, the golden tablets contained the meaning of the Gospel as Christ had given it to the ancient inhabitants. With the plates, Smith would find two stones fastened to a breastplate that were like ancient "seers," and these would help in the translation of the golden tablets. Moroni also quoted Scripture to inform Smith that the world would end soon, and Smith had the task to make way for Christ's return. The angel then appeared three more times to confirm the message.[7]

Smith said that he found the tablets buried in Manchester about three miles from his family's farm. Three others also said that they saw the angel and the golden tablets, giving validity to Smith's claims. His family and friends viewed him as a prophet, and his visions brought tears to his family. Such acceptance made Smith less reluctant about communicating his visions. Between 1827 and 1830, Smith used the seer stones Urim and Thummim to decipher the golden plates that became the Book of Mormon.[8]

The Book of Mormon explained the history of a group of Hebrews who came to America in 600 B.C. Similar to the Bible, the Book of Mormon was written by prophets and divided into books. In America, the Hebrews divided into two groups, the Lamanites and the Nephites. The Lamanites did not follow their faith and turned into the savage American Indians. The other group, the Nephites, thrived as Jesus taught them, but in 400 A.D. they were destroyed. The Prophet Mormon left behind the words of Jesus on the golden plates, which his son Moroni buried. Moroni became an angel and returned to earth fourteen hundred years later to disclose to Smith the location of the plates.[9]

Smith obtained a copyright for the Book of Mormon so that he could publish it, although he never gained financially from it. It did not receive a warm reception in Palmyra when it appeared in 1830 because it seemed to challenge Christianity. Many people in the surrounding area promised not to purchase the book, and the boycott resulted in low sales. However, Smith's publication received notice in other parts of the nation, including Ohio, Massachusetts, and Vermont. The newspaper critiques of Smith characterized him as a religious fraud attempting to make money just as he had previously tried to make money searching for buried treasure.[10]

The negative critiques did not stop Smith from continuing with his mission. He preached that people had to prepare for Christ's Second Coming by seeking salvation in the latter days. From this idea, the name the Church of Jesus Christ of Latter-day Saints emerged. According to this new system of beliefs, Smith as a prophet had to lead his followers, the modern Israelites, to Zion to await Christ's Second Coming. They would construct Zion as a New Jerusalem in America. Smith would take his followers on this journey and offer them spiritual leadership and guidance. Under Smith, the Mormons attempted to build a cooperative community based on his Law of Consecration and Stewardship.[11]

In April 1830, not long after the appearance of the Book of Mormon, Smith began to form his church at Fayette, New York. Smith met with more than fifty people, including his brother Hyrum, Oliver Cowdery, Peter Whitmer, and Samuel Smith, at the Whitmer residence to establish the church. They reported the presence of the Holy Spirit, and Smith prayed that others would receive the Spirit. Smith also gave instructions as to how the church should grow and develop. He wanted his sect of Christianity to forge a bridge between the old and the new world. His followers thought that God had chosen them specifically, and anyone who did not accept the Mormon faith would end up in hell. Smith's followers increased rapidly, and in 1831 the Mormons numbered more than one thousand people.

Because their faith conflicted with mainstream religions, the Mormons made many enemies. Consequently, Smith found himself arrested several times for disturbing the peace. Because of this opposition, he decided to seek a new home for his church, and he instructed missionaries to look for it.[12]

In October 1830, Smith sent four of his followers, including Peter Whitmer and Parley Pratt, to preach in the West and to investigate the establishment of their Zion. Smith had received a revelation that the Mormons should establish Zion near the western border of Missouri. Smith's plan to travel to Missouri and establish a New Jerusalem discloses yet another philosophical side of the Mormons. At the time that Smith founded the group, many people in the United States and Great Britain were interested in the millennium. People differed about when and how the Second Coming of Christ would take place. Those who thought that Jesus would come back to earth before the thousand years of peace were called premillennialists. They thought those who committed sins would face horrible destruction, so people had to work on earth to correct their behavior. Postmillennialists believed that Christ would come after the thousand years of peace. They thought that people would help to create the millennium by conversion and reform. The Mormons accepted views of both the premillennialists and postmillennialists. In line with premillennialism, they thought that great destruction would come to the wicked. They also believed that they needed to build the New Jerusalem, a belief that places them with postmillennialists.[13]

En route to Missouri, the Mormons made a preliminary stop at Kirtland, Ohio, as Pratt wanted to visit a friend, Sidney Rigdon, a notable preacher and minister. Pratt had initially lived on a farm about thirty miles from Cleveland and fell under Rigdon's influence because he preached ancient components of the gospel, including faith, repentance, baptism, and belief in the Holy Ghost. Pratt found Rigdon lacking only in the commission from God to serve as an apostle. Pratt found this authority after he left Ohio and traveled east on the Erie Canal. By inspiration, he left the canal route and went into the country, where he met and talked

3.2 Sidney Rigdon, Mormon Elder. *Ohio Historical Society*

to Hyrum Smith. Pratt found in the Book of Mormon the commission or authority from God that he had not found in Ohio. He believed he had the mission to make ready the path for Christ's Second Coming. Now he wanted to share the message with Rigdon.[14]

Kirtland had endured many religious changes, and, in 1830, circumstances proved favorable to the Mormon missionaries. Since the start of the nineteenth century, the Baptist Church had wielded great influence in Mentor Township near Kirtland. The Baptist Church suffered a loss in membership when one of its number, Alexander Campbell, formed his own sect. Campbell preached that people should return to the teachings of the Old Testament. Originally a Baptist minister, Sidney Rigdon converted to Campbell's new group, known as the Disciples of Christ or Campbellites. Previous to this, Rigdon participated in the utopian movement at Economy, Pennsylvania, led by George Rapp. The Rappites had come to America from Wurtemberg, Germany, the home of the Separatists that had established Zoar. They, like the Zoarites, had come to America to practice a faith that differed from the Lutheran Church, and both groups established societies in which all property was held in common. Rigdon adopted these ideas and called for community property, which created a rift between Rigdon and Campbell. Rigdon stressed to his followers millennialism, the return to the ancient order.[15]

When Rigdon left the Campbellites for Mormonism, he influenced many to convert. The decision of Pratt to stop in Kirtland proved beneficial to the Mormons as they baptized more than 120 new members in the Chagrin River after only a week in Ohio. The Mormons began to enlist some of the new converts to take leadership roles. Rigdon rose to a prominent role in the expansion of the Mormon Church as he served as the group's liaison with the outside world. Rigdon traveled to New York to meet the Prophet, who delighted in the fact that a thirty-seven-year-old established minister had come to meet him, Smith, who was only twenty-five years old.[16]

The success in Kirtland motivated Smith to alter his plans. In Ohio, Mormons enjoyed more followers than anywhere else. Perhaps Ohio eclipsed New York with its membership because Ohioans did not know about Smith's questionable past. Smith made the decision to move to Kirtland after receiving a vision that instructed him to go to Ohio before continuing in his work of translation.[17]

The entrance of Mormonism into Ohio influenced Rigdon and his followers. Just as he had led some of his congregation to the Campbellite movement, he led one hundred into the Mormon faith. Rigdon had accepted the Book of Mormon as true because he did not think that Smith, at the age of twenty-five, could have written a book containing so much biblical knowledge. The conversion to Mormonism did not constitute a dramatic shift for Rigdon and his Campbellite followers in Kirtland and Hiram. Mormons held some of the same tenets as the Campbellites, including faith along with the repentance of baptism as necessary for the remission of sins. The difference between Campbellite and Mormon faith lay in Mormonism's emphasis on the ancient order and in Mormons' belief in revelations. The Campbellites looked to the Bible for religious truths. One individual, Stephen Hart, a wealthy citizen of Mentor who gave testimony about the Mormons, stated that he had listened to Rigdon preach weeks before Rigdon's conversion to Mormonism. Hart repeated statements by members of Rigdon's church who said that Rigdon had declared that the Bible "in a short time . . . would be of no more account than an old almanac." Furthermore, Rigdon allegedly said that "there was to be a new Bible, a *new* revelation which would entirely do away with this."[18]

At the time that the missionaries arrived, Rigdon lived with some of his followers in a communal settlement known as "The Family." Rigdon had founded this communal group of Campbellites in Kirtland in 1827, and he used some of the ideas from his experiences in the Rappite settlement of Economy. The Rappite communities, like Zoar, established a society where all property was held in common and members shared the same religious faith.[19]

Buoyed by the progress of Mormonism in Ohio, Smith and his wife, Emma, moved to Kirtland in February 1831. Among the newly converted, the arrival of the Prophet elicited much enthusiasm. He also drew reactions from a nonbeliever who lived in Chardon. B. Fowles wrote, "Smith was a fine looking man viewing him from full face—but not as good looking from a people view—He was a hard worker." Smith and his wife stayed at the home of a new convert, Frederick G. Williams. Emma was pregnant at the time. In April, she delivered twins, a boy and a girl, who both died within three hours of their birth.[20]

At the time of Smith's arrival, the Mormon converts numbered about 150. Smith learned that these individuals displayed unbounded religious zeal. During prayer meetings, people went into fits and trances. Some who accepted Mormonism rolled on the floor and outside onto the cold winter ground. Others spoke in tongues. Smith feared that such stories would discredit his sect and, in his first revelations at Kirtland, proclaimed that such actions were false.[21]

Because of the initial success at Kirtland and his failure to gain acceptance in New York, Smith decided to build his temporary refuge in Ohio. He claimed that Kirtland was the eastern boundary of Zion that extended to the Pacific Ocean. Mormonism evolved considerably at Kirtland under Smith's leadership. Influenced by Rigdon's "Family," Smith declared that he had received a revelation to establish a communitarian society. According to one account in the papers of Mormon critic A. C. Williams, "Smith had started a 'fanatical society' . . . in which all property was to be held in common," and Rigdon promoted it. According to Stephen Hart, who knew the Mormon leaders, the group established a "Communistic Society on [Isaac] Morley's farm." He had attended Rigdon's preaching and "heard him urge the church to put their property into the common fund." The community of property did not work out well because some members took it to mean that they could have access to other brethrens' property wherever they chose.[22]

To counteract these problems, Smith issued the Law of Consecration and Stewardship in February 1831. Smith hoped to achieve a society where members enjoyed economic equality and could maintain self-sufficiency. According to the plan, members would give their property to the community, where it would be held in storehouses. Bishops would then divide the property among the members according to their needs. Members would receive property such as a farm tools to support themselves. Any additional profits made from the "inheritance" reverted back to the community. The presence of some individualism in this economic plan demonstrated that Smith wanted to reconcile communal aspects practiced by Rigdon and his followers with the individualism of the group from New York. The plan did not work out as intended; Smith found that members were more motivated to make a profit if they could keep some of it. Subsequently, he reverted to private property for members, and he told them to help the poor out of their own good will.[23]

While the arrival of Smith empowered the new converts, it displeased many in Kirtland. The new converts had undergone dramatic changes as they demonstrated their new faith. Several reported experiencing revelations and participating in other spiritual events. Members of the community did not like the aggressive posturing of the Mormons. Wesley Smith disliked the Mormons so much that he declared that the God of Smith and Rigdon was the devil. Perkins also said that the Mormon meetings where girls had visions reminded him of an "orgy story." The sheriff warned Smith to leave because he believed he would be a drain on Kirtland. Others tried to scare Smith with the threat of violence.[24]

The local newspapers did not look favorably upon the entrance of the new religion. In the preface of his book, Smith addresses those who would question him: "I would inform you that I translated by the gift and power of God." Detractors did not accept his account. After the Book of Mormon arrived in Kirtland, the *Painesville Telegraph* ran several stories criticizing the Prophet for stealing followers. The newspaper said that one of the Mormon missionaries, Oliver Cowdery, "pretends to have seen angels and assisted in translating the plates." Since many alleged that the Book of Mormon was fraudulent, they explained its true origins. A letter from Palmyra, New York, that ten people signed said that Smith first got the idea for the Book of Mormon from a juggling fortune teller. The *Cleveland Herald* said that Smith and Oliver Cowdery "have taken the old Bible to keep up a train of circumstances, and by allocating names and languages have produced the string of jargon called the 'Book of Mormon' with the intention of making money by the sale of their Books."[25]

Some religious leaders likewise questioned the Book of Mormon. A well-respected minister, Thomas Campbell, wanted to debate Sidney Rigdon in February 1831. Rigdon had a respectable background as a preacher and possessed vast knowledge of the Bible. Rigdon and Campbell were friends, but Campbell had strong feelings against the Book of Mormon and wanted to disprove it. Rigdon and Campbell were also connected because Campbell's son, Alexander, had founded the Disciples of Christ and had converted Rigdon. This debate never took place in public, but individuals must have weighed the merits of both Rigdon's and Campbell's arguments as they decided whether to remain a Campbellite or accept the Mormon faith.[26]

Alexander Campbell had founded not only the Disciples of Christ but also, in 1827, the Mahoning Association. This group united seventeen Baptist churches under Alexander's leadership and began with five hundred members. The Campbellites and their Baptist associates went their separate ways in the 1830s. After Rigdon entered the sect, he converted about five hundred to the Disciples in 1828. Campbell enjoyed a good national reputation as a minister. When he offered his scathing comments on the Book of Mormon, they carried weight.[27]

The younger Campbell's critique first appeared in his own newspaper, and the *Painesville Telegraph* reprinted it. Campbell called Smith an ignorant knave and accused him of fabricating and writing the Book of Mormon himself. To prove this, Alexander Campbell cited the many grammatical errors and also the elements of Smith's social and cultural background contained in the book. Furthermore, Campbell stated, the author of the book lacked knowledge of Christian and Jewish history.[28]

While many attempted to disprove the Book of Mormon, others embraced it wholeheartedly. Parley Pratt read the book intently and found himself unable to eat or sleep until he had completed it. Pratt believed that while reading the book the spirit of the Lord touched him. Samuel Smith had given the book to people around Palmyra, New York, without arguing about the book's authenticity. He expected that the spirit would move people to accept it. Among those who did was the wife of Methodist preacher John P. Greene. After she and her husband converted, she brought the book to her brothers, Phineas, Joseph, and Brigham Young. Brigham Young would rise to a position of prominence in the Church.[29]

Smith hoped that he would achieve more converts by displaying powers that only God could grant him. However, he did not always succeed at his attempts. Nonbelievers gave accounts of Smith's efforts to perform such miracles. Lucia Goldsmith recorded the following regarding Smith's attempt to walk on water, which she called "his first baptism" in Kirtland: "There was a shallow place in the river there, where he was to *perform the miracle.* A moonlight eve was chosen, a crowd had collected. Smith started boldly out for a few feet when his *faith—or something, failed,* and down he sank. Some wicked one had removed the support of that piece of the plank he had placed just under the surface of the water." In 1885, Joel Miller gave testimony that matched Goldsmith's account. Miller stated that Smith had worn a white robe and spoke of faith while he walked slowly below the water's surface. After he went down, the nonbelievers laughed. The Prophet never again made this effort.[30]

In another attempt to demonstrate his powers, Smith, according to a number of personal testimonies of eyewitnesses, attempted to raise a child from the dead. A. C. Williams, a critic of the Mormons, recorded these accounts. According to Reuben P. Harmon, a wealthy citizen of Kirtland, Smith claimed in the summer of 1832 that he would "heal the sick and lame and revive the dead." The announcement led to the assembly of a large crowd, which Harmon estimated at over a thousand, in the back of Isaac Morley's house. Rigdon told the crowd that Smith would not preach that day. Harmon went into the house and found a dead child. He wrote,

"I felt its face and hands which were warm and pliable. I thought opium had been administered. It did not breathe. It was about two years old, daughter of Mr. John Gould." James Thompson, who had married Gould's daughter Harriet, recollected similar events in 1885: "I have often heard my wife and her parents tell about Joseph, the Prophet, attempting to restore to consciousness their child which they claimed had been drugged. The child was buried." The parents of the child blamed Smith and the elders for telling them not to seek medical treatment.[31] From the testimonies of the Mormon critics, it is difficult to know whether the child was drugged for pain relief or to make her appear dead. The incident caused more ill feeling toward the Mormons.

When Smith had trouble performing miracles in Kirtland, he explained that Kirtland was not consecrated ground. The promised land was in Independence, Missouri, a new frontier town located near Indian lands about 250 miles from St. Louis. Smith hoped that his group would serve as missionaries to the many Indian peoples as well as whites. Smith traveled with Rigdon and other elders to Missouri, and he settled the group on land located between Independence and Indian lands. The Mormons dedicated a site for a temple, and they built the first cabin in an area that would later develop into Kansas City. Despite Smith's optimism, the efforts of the Mormons to gain converts proved difficult. Several elders expressed disgust with Smith's decision to leave Ohio for this remote location. Rigdon, especially, pushed Smith to return to Kirtland, which he did. Subsequently, the Mormons had two orders: one in Ohio and one in Missouri led by Cowdery. The two groups, however, found it difficult to communicate and make joint decisions. The Kirtland Mormons remained the more influential group because of Smith's presence.[32]

From Kirtland, Smith attempted to expand his Ohio numbers. In September 1831, Smith stated that God had instructed him to go to Hiram, a community of the Western Reserve, so that he could continue the work of translation. Rigdon had moved to Hiram and established a small Mormon church in 1830 after his conversion and the decision of his Mentor church not to provide a residence for him. Many people in Hiram belonged to the Campbellite faith. When Smith and other Mormons arrived, the work of conversion had begun. Smith attracted many people. Even nonbelievers viewed him as "a very entertaining man" who "would interest an audience in a remarkable degree." Many in town were intrigued by Mormonism after hearing that Mrs. John Johnson had experienced the healing power of the faith. After a visit to Kirtland the previous summer, she regained the use of her palsied arm. Smith and his family stayed at the Johnson household in Hiram.[33]

Although Smith's initial entrance into Hiram seemed successful, things quickly deteriorated. He began to lose converts. The sons of John Johnson detached themselves from the Mormon church, as did Symonds Rider, a well-respected minister who previously was a Campbellite. These and others found aspects of Mormonism suspect, including the nature of some of Smith's revelations. Because of this turn of events and problems in Missouri, Smith planned to end his Hiram stay.[34]

Those people who had grown disillusioned with Smith planned to expedite his departure. On March 25, 1832, in the early morning, a mob attacked Smith at the Johnson residence. They dragged him from the house, stripped, beat, and tarred and feathered him. The mob also absconded with Rigdon, who was staying in a cabin on the property. They dragged him over the hard, cold ground, cutting and bruising his head and face, before they tarred and feathered him. Rigdon fell into delirium for a few days after the attack. Smith, however, healed quickly from the ugly affair. His wife, Emma, and her friends nursed him through the night, and the following day he preached. Some of those who had assaulted him came to the assembly and expressed surprise that Smith was there. But the Smith family suffered more than temporary injuries from the matter. The couple had adopted a set of twins whose parents had died. One of the children went out into the cold the night of the attack to see what was happening. This exposure combined with a case of measles resulted in the child's death.[35]

After this, the Smiths left Hiram. Emma went to Kirtland, and Joseph Smith went with Rigdon to Independence, Missouri, to help with problems there. In Missouri, Smith established a government for the branches of Mormonism in Ohio and Missouri. Smith was elected as president and would work with a nine-member board that he appointed. The board would supervise the shared property of the Missouri and Ohio groups. With these issues settled, Smith returned to Kirtland in May 1832.[36]

After the problems in Hiram, the Smiths enjoyed some success in northeastern Ohio in 1832. Their conversions in Kirtland continued to increase, and Smith seemed more comfortable with his role as leader. Personally, Smith and his wife had cause for joy when Emma gave birth to a son, Joseph Smith III. This child would later take on an important role in the development of the Mormon Church.[37]

Another future leader of the Mormon Church came to Kirtland. In 1832, Brigham Young arrived in Ohio with his father and a friend, Heber Kimball. Young had learned about Joseph Smith and influenced his father to sell their Vermont farm to learn from the Prophet himself. In Vermont, Young had labored as a painter and had experimented with different religions. When Smith first met Young, he was impressed with him. At this meeting, Young displayed his "gift of tongues."[38]

The Mormon leadership in Kirtland came to center on three people: Smith, Rigdon, and Young. Smith gathered converts with his preaching, and Rigdon gave the intellectual underpinning to the group. A critic described their relationship as follows: "uncouth Smith had the stronger nature of the two, and it became Smith's creed. What Smith lacked in education, Rigdon supplied, and the devilry in each . . . drew upon." Brigham Young masterfully handled the business of the group and their relations with the outside world.[39]

A nonbeliever who lived in Chardon when the Mormons were in Kirtland recounted the following about the Mormon leadership: "Brigham Young was a young man when the Mormons were at Kirtland but remarkably intelligent. He was quite handsome—more whiskers—while Smith was always more cleanly shaven. He was then considered one of the ablest in the sect, in fact I heard it stated that he was the best preacher. Rigdon was one of the highest of the priests. He was a scholarly man."[40]

On May 6, 1833, Smith declared that God had instructed him to build a Mormon church in Kirtland as a gathering place for the converts. Smith sought financial help from across the nation before he could buy land and materials for the temple. He also expected Mormons in Kirtland to give money and labor to the building. After raising some money, construction began, and most of the materials, including the stone, used to build the temple came from the area, though the Mormons did use glass from England in the structure.[41]

Every day, Smith would tell people what to do on the construction site since God revealed to him the required actions. Mormons made up the bulk of the labor force, although some craftsmen were paid for the project. Smith instructed and helped the stonecutters while Rigdon worked as a mason. Brigham Young contributed work as a plasterer. Women helped on the project by completing traditional tasks including cooking for the workers and making their clothes. They also gave their china and glasses, which the builders ground down and added to the plaster to make the walls of the temple shine.[42]

Lucia Goldsmith, a nonbeliever, recollected her experiences visiting the temple in the autumn of 1835 before the dedication. Goldsmith went to hear Smith preach. At the time, only the center pews were completed, and wood shavings covered the floor. She sat on a workmen's bench located outside the center pews. About six other people attended the preachings. Goldsmith states, "I think Smith had a chair and another near it. The Prophet, a tall spare man, rose when we came in and commenced a short discourse." Smith also said that he would heal "by the laying on of hands." A man approached Smith from the congregation and knelt before him. After an inaudible prayer, Smith laid his hands on the man's head and shoulders. After the man arose, "Smith extended his arms and dismissed us *with his blessing.*" Though Goldsmith makes no comment about the legitimacy of the particular healing, her tone suggests that she considered Smith a fraud.[43]

After several years of labor, the Mormons dedicated the temple on March 27, 1836. The temple was an impressive structure, standing two stories tall with an attic. Inside, the doors, pulpits, pews, and stairs were constructed of native woods that were molded, carved, and made by hand. Much skill went into the construction and design of the temple.[44]

Several thousand members of the Mormon faith, along with four hundred of their elders, priests, and teachers, attended the festivities to dedicate the temple. Although Smith had previously denounced followers for claiming revelations and displaying dramatic scenes of religious zeal, he wanted the outpouring at the temple dedication. He practiced rituals with leaders of the church days before the dedication. Many preliminary celebrations took place, and some male members stayed in the temple for two days and two nights praying, anointing, and prophesying. The revelers felt that angels rejoiced with them that day. On the final day of celebration, Smith and Oliver Cowdery led a large audience from their pulpits. Veils were lowered, and the two men prayed hidden from the view of the congregation. When the veils were taken back, Smith and Cowdery said they had seen God in all his glory. They also claimed to have seen Moses and then Elijah.[45]

The Mormons hoped that the temple would serve as their center for missionary work. To meet the needs of the many who came to the temple, a hotel was constructed across from it. Because of the people needing transportation, the stagecoach line between Richmond and Hudson went through Kirtland.[46]

The dedication of the temple indicated that the Mormons intended to stay in Kirtland. They took further actions to confirm this. Smith had visions of constructing a city of twelve temples. The city would consist of square blocks of the same size. Farms would be located outside the city center. Although this plan never took shape in Kirtland, Brigham Young used it to establish the future home of Mormonism in Salt Lake City, Utah.[47]

In 1837, the Mormons made plans for the establishment of Kirtland City. They planned to purchase more than two thousand acres of land to develop the city, which would have a town center surrounded by farmlands. They planned on accomplishing this by purchasing a little land at a time. The Mormons began to accumulate debt as a result of this plan.[48]

In the midst of the construction of the temple, Smith learned that other Saints in their Missouri Zion were experiencing difficulties. The Mormons had added many converts in Independence, and their numbers had grown to more than twelve hundred. Many non-Mormons in the area felt threatened by their presence. To them, the Mormons displayed an attitude of superiority that they were God's chosen people and had a right to all the land. Others disliked the Mormons because they believed the Saints would create antislavery sentiment since the sect welcomed free blacks to join them in Missouri. Furthermore, the Mormons sought to live peacefully with the Indians, an unpopular idea in a region near the border between white settlement and Indian lands. All of these factors led to violence against the Mormons, including the beating of the men, the torching of houses, tarring and feathering, and the destruction of their press, the *Evening and Morning Star.* With all of these difficulties, the Missouri followers asked the Prophet for assistance.[49]

Smith realized that if he went to Missouri, he would further enrage the nonbelievers. Thus, in the spring of 1834, Smith organized a group of two hundred men, which he named "Zion's Camp," to defend the Missouri Mormons. In May 1834, they left Kirtland for Missouri. Upon their arrival, they found that they could not defend themselves and the Missouri Mormons because the forces united against them were much larger. The Kirtland Mormons aggravated the situation because they seemed to pose a military threat to the locals. Smith and his followers endured further setbacks when a cholera epidemic struck many in the group. Smith escaped this situation by saying that God had told him to return to Kirtland to raise money to buy out their enemies in Missouri.[50]

The problems in Missouri demonstrated to Smith the great animosity nonbelievers had against the Mormons. He realized that the community property especially enraged people in Missouri. Hence, Smith decided to end joint ownership of property in Kirtland in April 1834. At this time, Smith hoped that the end of common property would lessen the ill feeling from nonbelievers while also ending arguments among the members. Smith declared that he had a revelation to divide the property.[51]

As the Mormon population increased in Kirtland, residents grew anxious about the arrival of so many people, several of whom were poor. By 1835, approximately five hundred Mormons lived in Kirtland and an additional one thousand Mormons resided in the surrounding area. So many Mormons came to Kirtland that every available facility to house the people was in use. Many of the incoming Mormons came from fifty to one hundred miles away. Some even came from New England. The large numbers of Mormons threatened nonbelievers who wanted to discredit Smith and stop the influx of his followers. In 1834, a committee of ten men, including O. A. Crary and James H. Paine, printed a challenge to the validity of the Book of Mormon in the *Painesville Telegraph*. The committee had asked D. P. Hurlbut to study the Book of Mormon and Smith's declarations of being the Prophet. Hurlbut concluded that the Book of Mormon was a work of fiction and imagination. Moreover, he stated that Smith did not occupy such a high place as a prophet.[52]

Another critic of the Book of Mormon, Eber D. Howe, editor of the *Painesville Telegraph,* worked with Hurlbut to discount the volume. Howe had shown an aversion to secret societies governed in an authoritarian fashion that seemed conspiratorial in nature. He had led the anti-Masonic movement in Geauga County. He demanded a thorough investigation of Mormonism.[53]

In their research, Howe and Hurlbut discovered that some people from Conneaut, Ohio, thought the Book of Mormon sounded like the words written by Solomon Spalding, who at one time had lived in Conneaut. The residents recalled that Spalding's book included some of the same events and stories as Smith's volume. Hurlbut questioned Spalding's widow, who offered him some of her husband's writings about a migration of Romans to America that was different from the Book of Mormon. Hurlbut and Howe searched for answers about Spalding's lost manuscript. They concluded that Sidney Rigdon had acquired Spalding's book in Pittsburgh, where Spalding had pursued a publisher for it. Rigdon added religious elements to the story, which then became the Book of Mormon. It made perfect sense to Hurlbut and Howe, who always thought Smith did not possess the knowledge and ability to write the Book of Mormon and found the Mormon faith. They did accept that Rigdon could have done it. They hypothesized that Rigdon ensured that the manuscript reached Smith, and then Rigdon pretended that he converted in 1830 when the missionaries reached Kirtland. These findings appeared in a book called *Mormonism Unveiled*.[54]

Others found the theory about Rigdon's authorship of the Book of Mormon plausible. In the papers of A. C. Williams, an avowed critic of the Mormons, the following account of the church in Kirtland is given: "In 1831 the first Mormons moved to Kirtland, Ohio, where the real author and founder of Mormonism, Sidney Rigdon, had been actively planning to locate a permanent Mormon colony. Here the new sect prospered in a wild wave of fanaticism under the management and preaching of the eloquent Rigdon."[55]

Williams also possessed the statements of many people about the Mormons, including James Harris Fairchild, who served as president of Oberlin College at the time he wrote a letter to Mr. Deming in 1887. Fairchild wanted to disprove the legitimacy of the Mormons and offered this advice to Deming: "If you can obtain evidence that Rigdon was at Smith's house in 1827 or '28, you will disprove the account of Rigdon's conversion to Mormonism, at Mentor, as given in Howe's book, and also the statement in Pratt's pamphlet . . . that he first introduced Smith and Rigdon to each other after the Mormons began preaching in Ohio. . . . You will prove that the conversion of Rigdon at Mentor was a device for deception, planned in advance." Perhaps to give more validity to these claims, critics called Rigdon "the brains of the church."[56]

Reports and actions that signaled the Mormons wanted to make Kirtland their permanent home did not endear them to the public, especially because of some controversial aspects of the group. Allegedly the Mormons began to engage in some practices different from the social norm, including polygamy. Part of the problem may have stemmed from the Mormon belief in revelations. Smith's revelations provided the basis for the principles of Mormonism. In Kirtland, this led to trouble as other Believers claimed that they too had revelations involving polygamy. According to some accounts, male members claimed revelations that gave them permission to take on more than one wife if the first wife was very ill or close to death. In response, Smith called a Council of Elders and decided that the only true revelations came from himself, Rigdon, and Cowdery. After this declaration, the revelations of other members ceased.[57]

As the issue of polygamy surfaced, questions emerged about Smith's alleged extramarital affair with Fanny Alger. Cowdery accused Smith of this relationship in 1837. Seventeen-year-old Alger had lived with the Smith family for a time. When Emma Smith found out about the affair, she drove Alger from the house. Alger moved to Indiana. She never responded to questions about the nature of her relationship with Smith. Some believed she was Smith's first plural wife, and it seemed as though Smith had implemented polygamy without the knowledge of others. The Mormon Church accepted polygamy in the 1840s following a series of Smith's revelations, and later Mormon writers viewed Alger as Smith's first plural wife.[58]

In 1835, the Mormons at Kirtland had issued their first statement against polygamy. When this proclamation passed, Smith was in Michigan. However, nonmembers thought that they accepted the practice, and they interpreted the Mormon statement regarding polygamy as proof that some Mormons had subscribed to it. Nonmembers believed that they did practice polygamy because many who had converted to the faith left their spouses. They also cited the Mormon faith for breaking up so many families. The converts remained legally married since divorces were difficult to obtain. If converts wanted to marry a Mormon, they could not because of their first indissoluble marriage. At the time, several different groups, including the Shakers, had deviated from socially acceptable practices regarding marriage. During the 1840s when Smith received the revelations on plural marriage, utopianists, including John Humphrey Noyes of the Oneida Community in New York, were also implementing new concepts of the marital relationship.[59]

The questions surrounding the Mormon marriage practices increased because Smith illegally solemnized marriages on the basis that God had given him this power. The courts in Geauga County did not grant the Mormons the power to solemnize marriages because they were not regularly ordained ministers. In addition to Smith, other Mormon leaders, including his father, brother, and Rigdon, presided over civil marriages. Consequently, they had to answer to a grand jury for assuming this power without a license. Rigdon had to pay a one-thousand-dollar fine. According to one account, Smith's father evaded his charges by leaving the proceedings through a window. Apparently, the charges against the Prophet were dropped.[60]

Joseph Smith had his revelations on polygamy in the 1840s in Nauvoo, Illinois. He justified polygamy by arguing that Old Testament leaders such as Abraham and Isaac had multiple wives. Smith viewed polygamy as a type of celestial marriage that would outlast life on earth, in contrast to secular marriage. The Mormons did incorporate polygamy once they moved to the Utah territory but gave up the practice so that they could apply for statehood. It remains unclear whether or not the Mormons secretly practiced polygamy in Kirtland.[61]

With all the questions surrounding the Mormons, the group was increasingly subjected to violence at the hands of nonmembers. In 1835, Grandison Newell, a leading anti-Mormon spokesman known as the "Mormon persecutor," led a group of people who stoned the Mormon Orson Pratt. Because the authorities did little to protect the Mormons, they had little recourse. In 1836 they did send a letter to a judge, Ariel Hanson, whom they believed they had helped to elect. The Mormons asked for his resignation since he had allowed mobs to attack innocent men, women, and children without any retribution for those responsible.[62]

The Mormons attempted to strengthen their position by entering political life. In 1836, Mormon leaders ran for three different offices, including clerk, overseer of the poor, and constable. The Mormons running for these offices tied in the vote with non-Mormon candidates. Lots were cast to break the tie, and the non-Mormon won for each office. The Mormons did succeed in electing members Frederick Williams and Oliver Cowdery as justices of the peace in 1836 and 1837, respectively.[63]

On the burning issue of slavery, Joseph Smith spoke out against abolition. Smith believed that any support of the reform would alienate potential converts in the South. The Prophet went further to find a defense of slavery in the Old Testament. Oddly, he articulated his argument in connection with his self-proclaimed revelations regarding ancient Egyptian papyri that Michael Chandler had brought to Kirtland.[64]

In 1835, Chandler traveled to Kirtland with four Egyptian mummies and several papyri. At the time, Americans were quite interested in this ancient civilization, and Smith was no exception. Smith had been studying languages, and he attempted to translate the papyri. No one knew for certain whether they could be translated. Smith gave up his efforts and instead claimed a revelation from God that one papyrus was the Book of Abraham and another the works of Joseph of Egypt. Smith never attempted to translate the works of Joseph of Egypt, but he did offer his version of the Book of Abraham, which later masters of Egyptian hieroglyphics would label as ludicrous and inaccurate. In this Book of Abraham, Smith addressed the issue of black slavery. His translation agreed with the arguments used by southern ministers to justify slavery, that blacks constituted a cursed race destined to be slaves. After the translation of the Book of Abraham, Smith published articles stating that the North had no business interfering with the institution. He went further to criticize abolitionists. Two factors account for this position. First, his statements matched the prevailing opinion of most Northerners. Second, the persecution by their neighbors that Mormons endured in Missouri because of their welcoming reception of blacks likely influenced his opinion.[65]

Other reform efforts affecting the nation, including temperance, which enjoyed the largest following in the nation, touched the Mormons. Smith disclosed a revelation in 1833 that Mormons should not use tobacco, alcohol, or hot drinks. He suggested this to his followers rather than demanding it. Also, he stated that wine should be consumed only at communion, and members should eat meat only in the winter. The Prophet himself did not always follow his own advice. In 1836, Rigdon, to Smith's disapproval, introduced total abstinence for the group. Smith accepted this because it was well received by other members.[66]

The financial difficulties that confronted the nation in the 1830s affected the Mormons. After the Second United States Bank at Philadelphia lost its charter, local banks chartered by the states opened their doors. These banks increased the money supply by printing bills without the specie to back it. Consequently, Americans engaged in speculation. The land values quickly increased in Kirtland at rates as high as 800 percent. Farmlands once valued at ten or fifteen dollars an acre skyrocketed to 150 dollars an acre.[67]

In the fall of 1836, Smith and the Mormon leaders, including Rigdon, brought the Church into a land speculation scheme that resulted in the Church's removal from Kirtland. The group had amassed large debts with the building of the temple and their plan to buy up land parcels to establish a Kirtland city. When they needed money, they decided to start a bank. According to nonbeliever Warren F. Parrish, Smith declared "that the audible voice of God instructed him to establish a banking institution." However, they could not get the state legislature to charter their bank. The legislature had also refused to issue charters to other banks. An attorney recommended that the Mormons create an unchartered bank.[68]

In response, the Mormons decided to amend their constitution to form the Kirtland Safety Society Anti-Banking company in 1837. Mormons bought shares and invested money in land on credit. Additionally, the Society issued bank notes signed by Smith and Rigdon to the general public. However, the notes held little value for local merchants. After the Society opened, the value of the notes plummeted. The Mormons had not purposely cheated their creditors but had wanted to find a way to use the wealth they possessed in property. Similar situations occurred throughout the nation as the Panic of 1837 began. The Mormons hoped that the notes issued would be backed by their property at Kirtland. When local merchants refused to accept them on faith, however, they lost the bulk of their value. The Mormons attempted to use the notes for goods and traveled to New York and Canada for this purpose. Smith declared that the currency lacked value because the Society could not pay its creditors.[69]

Consequently, many filed lawsuits against the officers of the Society, including Smith and Brigham Young. The defendants had to pay twenty-four thousand dollars in damages and ten thousand dollars to settle claims out of court. Although the bank did not constitute an official part of the Mormon Church, the officers of the bank were leaders of the church. Consequently, the Mormons had to sell the printing offices and temple at auction to meet the debts. It remains unclear what exactly happened to the temple. The Mormons owed a forty-five-hundred-dollar mortgage on the structure, which was valued at forty thousand dollars. No official records show that it was sold at auction. In 1880, the Lake County Court declared that the Reorganized Church of Jesus Christ of the Latter Day Saints owned the building. Because Smith and Rigdon did not possess the proper license to run a bank, they were arrested and had to pay a thousand-dollar fine. Many Mormons left the faith as a result of these events.[70]

More problems lay ahead for the group. In 1838, Smith faced charges of soliciting two men to commit murder. According to the allegations, Smith asked two of his followers, named Denton and Davis, to kill Grandison Newell, the leading agitator against the Mormons. Supposedly, Smith stated that "if he [Newell] commenced suits for unlawful banking against any of the Mormons, [then we] ought to put him where the crows could not find him." Denton also reported that Smith appealed to the Bible to justify the killing, stating that God wanted it. One defense witness, Warren Parrish, believed Smith was set up in the matter because Denton had disliked the way Smith treated him while working in the Mormons' printing office. Rigdon testified that he had heard a conversation in which Denton planned to kill Smith. With little evidence, the case was dismissed without prosecution.[71]

As a result of the banking scandal and the other problems the Mormons confronted, the community began to deteriorate. Many Mormons left the faith. Smith forced others, who he claimed had departed from his message, to leave. In 1837, thirty-one people were expelled, including leaders such as Warren Parrish, Parley Pratt, and David Whitmer. While some of these asked forgiveness and reentered the Church, others retaliated. Three of those purged, Luke Johnson, Lyman Johnson, and John Boynton, attempted to remove Smith from power by force, attacking the temple armed with knives and pistols. Although their effort failed, they frightened those inside and faced no formal charges. The prosperity of the Mormons in Kirtland drew to a close as Smith lost support.[72]

The anti-Mormon forces took action against the church in 1837 and 1838. In the winter of 1837, a mob chased Brigham Young out of town. A few weeks later, in January 1838, both Smith and Rigdon fled Kirtland with the Mormons divided. Smith had learned that Grandison Newell had obtained a warrant for Smith's arrest for banking fraud. Because of their lost leadership, the Mormons who remained in Kirtland decided to leave as a group known as the Kirtland Camp. The Prophet had apparently seen a vision compelling the Mormon community to leave. In March 1838, more than five hundred Mormons signed the Kirtland Camp Constitution. On July 6, 1838, those Mormons choosing to leave Kirtland in search of Smith set out on their journey for Missouri. Some members stayed in Kirtland.[73]

At first, the Missouri Mormons welcomed Smith and viewed the Kirtland debacle as their blessing. But Smith failed to find a more tolerant environment for his beliefs and practices. He ultimately fell victim to an angry mob that killed him in Carthage, Illinois, in 1844. Young then became the leader of the Mormons and in 1846 led them to Utah, which they called Deseret and considered to be their Zion. There, the Mormons re-created some of the unique practices they had begun in Kirtland, including communal ownership of property. They also embraced polygamy. In 1848, the Treaty of Guadalupe Hidalgo, which settled matters from the Mexican American War, brought the Mormons under the United States government. In the 1870s and 1880s, the United States Congress and the Supreme Court took action to force an end to the practice of polygamy.[74]

Eventually, the Kirtland temple reverted back to the Mormons. The effort to regain the property started in 1873, when the Mormons made attempts to begin again in Kirtland. In 1880, Joseph Smith III, son of the Prophet born in Kirtland, received a favorable ruling from Judge L. S.

Sherman of the Lake County Court of Common Pleas to take possession of the temple. The temple became part of the Reorganized Church of Jesus Christ of the Latter-Day Saints.[75] Kirtland thus served as home once again to the Mormons. The Western Reserve had provided Smith and the Mormons with the converts necessary to get the religious order off the ground.

Chapter 4

Secular Utopias in Ohio

WHILE THE MORMONS, ZOARITES, AND Shakers represented the powerful force of religious communitarianism in Ohio, they by no means constituted the entire utopian effort at work. Some utopianists established havens that emphasized new economic and social relationships rather than depending on religion as a guiding force. Although these utopias did not embrace religious doctrine, they did often coalesce around a particular philosophy. These utopias, which developed in the first half of the nineteenth century, attempted to address the ill effects of the Industrial Revolution, namely poor working and living conditions for laborers. Several utopianists in this period believed that it was possible to emphasize human cooperation rather than competition. These utopian socialists thought that havens could be created where private property did not exist, thus opening the way for new methods of social organization. The term "socialism" as used by these utopianists would later be equated with Marxism, albeit incorrectly, after the publication of *The Communist Manifesto* by Karl Marx and Friedrich Engels in 1848. During the antebellum period, many secular utopias emerged based on the socialist philosophies of two Europeans, Robert Owen of Great Britain and Charles Fourier of France. The ideals articulated by these men provided the foundation for the greatest number of utopias in the United States after 1825.[1]

Robert Owen had much to do with the emergence of secular utopias in the antebellum era. Born in 1771 in Wales, Owen managed a cotton mill in New Lanark, Scotland, where he earned a fortune and formulated his communitarian ideas. Because Owen had a share in the company that owned the mill, he found himself in a position to improve the living conditions and educational attainment of the residents. He also wanted to set limits on the use of child labor. His success, along with the reputation that he had acquired, buoyed him to continue his experiments.[2]

Owen attempted to further his concern by introducing to the British Parliament ideas concerning unemployment, relief for the poor, and working conditions. When these suggestions were ignored, Owen realized that the government would not function as an agent of social reform. Consequently, he took his proposals directly to the public. He published his philosophy in 1813 in *A New View of Society.* He also wrote to London newspapers, printed his ideas, and made speeches. He welcomed people to visit his factory to see his ideas at work.[3]

In his proposals, Owen called for the establishment of villages with populations of five hundred to two thousand people, where members would share the labor and the fruits of it. He suggested the layout of the communities as a parallelogram, with people enjoying a healthy living environment. Each community would have a school. Adults would have the opportunity to work in a wide array of jobs. Owen believed his vision provided a new society in which people would work for the prosperity of the whole. He thought his proposal provided a resolution to the problems of industrialization, as people could enjoy the wealth brought by manufacturing and yet help each other. Such ideas marked the origins of his communitarianism. Although he did not always think through his philosophies, Owen excited people with his suggestions for creating a perfect world. He attracted much attention in England because labor there had begun to unite. Owen's philosophy also offered key components to the socialist movement, including a critique of capitalism and emphasis on cooperation, education, and improvement of the environment.[4]

A controversial doctrine that Owen espoused included his assertion about environmentalism: a person's surroundings explained his or her character. Many disagreed with this assumption because it meant that people could blame their environment if they committed sins. Owen later altered this concept and stated that people held certain characteristics at birth that affected their character. Nonetheless, Owen's emphasis forced people to consider the effects of the environment on the individual.[5]

The utopian community proposed by Owen did not include religion, thus distinguishing it from the Shaker villages, Zoar, and the Mormons. Owen's haven centered on the laws of nature and science rather than the Bible. He offered members of his havens equality, promising that rank would not exist. Instead of the competition prevalent in capitalism, Owen wanted a society where members worked together. He hoped his havens would offer an alternative to capitalism without a revolution. Owen also believed that the community of families working and living together should replace the individual family. The social system implemented in his communities would result in the arrival of the millennium. The harmony of the societies would bring about a virtuous state.[6]

Although Owen offered an alternative to capitalism, his plans called for a community to prosper economically for survival. He limited the population so that enough members could work the land and help establish industry. While many of Owen's ideas, such as equality of members and an emphasis on education, coincided with the values of nineteenth-century American life, some of his other philosophies conflicted with them. His communalism, for example, went against the value Americans placed on private property.[7]

Owen brought his model for the perfect community to the United States in 1824; some American utopianists had already learned of his philosophy through various publications. Owen used his wealth to purchase the land owned by the Harmony Society, a community based on the principles of the German separatist George Rapp, in Indiana, which had decided to relocate back to Pennsylvania. Owen purchased the twenty thousand acres of land because it offered a community with two hundred buildings already in place, at a price he could not get in Great Britain. Owen enjoyed a warm reception in the United States and met intellectuals, business leaders, and Shakers. He also spoke before Congress twice, with outgoing president James Monroe and president-elect John Quincy Adams in attendance.[8]

The New Harmony Society faced difficulties from its inception. Because of the nationwide interest that Owen had generated, more than eight hundred people joined initially, when the community could house only seven hundred. Furthermore, many of the people lacked the discipline and ability to resolve conflicts necessary to succeed in the communal setting. Owen's indecisive leadership also caused problems. He did not adequately explain the circumstances regarding property ownership for members. Furthermore, he had not made decisions regarding the daily functions of the community. With such important questions left unanswered, he took the unwise action of traveling throughout the United States in 1825 rather than assisting the fledgling community.[9]

In 1826 Owen attempted to make up for his initial lack of leadership by offering some organization for New Harmony. He divided the settlement into groups dedicated to three specific functions: education, agriculture, and manufacturing. Instead of providing smooth direction for the society, the groups began to compete with each other for funds, threatening the life of the society. An investor in New Harmony, William MacClure, who was a teacher and geologist, sued Owen for failing to pay back loan money. The society thus disbanded quickly.[10]

But the philosophies of Owen did not subside, and more than twenty other communities emerged based on his ideals. Most of these were established in the United States, with others in Canada and Scotland. Of those in the United States, several took shape in Ohio: the Yellow Springs Community (1825–26); the Kendal Community (1826–29); Equity (1833–35); and Fruit Hills (1845–52).[11]

Several developments in the early nineteenth century helped to power the utopianist venture. Americans continued to move west, and they had to adapt to the forces of industrialization and the subsequent social changes. Initially, the economic growth brought wealth for many; however, falling agricultural prices and the decline in the value of land meant economic troubles for the country. The nation also experienced political change. The disputed election of 1824 led Andrew Jackson, who had fallen short of electoral votes in the election owing to what he called the "corrupt bargain," to solidify his support. By the next presidential election, the American two-party system had begun to reemerge with the Democrats and the National Republicans. In the midst of this change, between 1825 and 1826, the first Owenite communities were founded. The second wave of settlements began after the Panic of 1837.[12]

The Swedenborgians of Cincinnati contributed significantly to the establishment of the first Ohio Owenite community at Yellow Springs. Owen had visited Cincinnati on his way to New Harmony, Indiana, in December 1824, and had captured the imagination of a number of Swedenborgians.

The Swedenborgians adhered to the doctrines of Emanuel Swedenborg, an eighteenth-century Swedish noble, scientist, and writer who attempted to apply religion to everyday life. Swedenborg did not believe in predestination and salvation by faith alone, two of the central tenets of Protestantism. Owen found the Swedenborgians to be outstanding citizens of education and wealth. They formed the cornerstone of his community, with Daniel Roe acting as the leader.[13]

Owen had excited much activity in Cincinnati, and his books and pamphlets sold in quantity. The organizers of the Yellow Springs community purchased eight hundred acres on the Little Miami River. They anticipated a huge following, announcing that only two thousand people could join, but they attracted fewer than one hundred families. To begin their society, members constructed a line of buildings made of logs. Robert Owen offered both financial and moral support to Yellow Springs, making it the only Owenite community other than New Harmony to receive such aid. Members planned to focus their economic activity on manufacturing.[14]

Owen believed the Yellow Springs community would thrive because of the influence of the Swedenborgians, whom he considered intelligent, idealistic, and adept at business. But the community lasted only a year. Members realized that they held different ideas about the best way to run the community and they began to argue. The troubles they experienced mirrored the difficulties of Owen's New Harmony community. Members of Yellow Springs could not subordinate their individual needs for the good of the community. Secular utopias lacked the common faith and doctrine that provided strong incentives for cooperation in religious utopias.[15]

Also, the group did not have adequate funding to continue. They had accumulated a debt of four thousand dollars. When they disbanded, they owed half of the money that it cost to buy their property. Roe, along with the other members of the community, made an appeal in the *Xenia People's Press* in July 1826 asking for money to complete their land purchase. This did not work, and they never had complete ownership of the property. Owen tried to save the haven with a visit in December 1825, but he failed. Most of the members from Cincinnati had already returned home by Christmas. Some members had elected to go to other communal havens, including New Harmony and Shaker villages. But the end of the Owenite haven did not mean that Yellow Springs had forever lost its chance at becoming a utopia. In the 1850s, Thomas L. Nichols and Mary

S. Gove Nichols established a Fourierist community at Yellow Springs, which aroused much attention in the community.[16]

One of the most successful Ohio Owenite communities had its origins in 1825 when members of the New Harmony community visited Stark County, Ohio. Josiah Warren and Paul Brown sought to bring converts into the Owenite fold and establish a community in northeastern Ohio. These travels sparked the establishment of Kendal Community in 1826, near the present-day city of Massillon. The community began with more than two thousand acres of land purchased for twenty thousand dollars.[17]

On March 17, 1826, people from Portage and Stark Counties forged a constitution for the Friendly Association for Mutual Interests at Kendal. Organizers desired to create a community based on the principles of Robert Owen because "if the state of the human family should be changed for the better . . . we must abandon the present course and embrace a system of greater liberality and justice." They believed the whole society must be changed in order to accomplish this. Members of the community had to pledge themselves to pious, just, and benevolent living. They hoped their new organization would "increase happiness, arrest the progress of vice, and lead to all those virtues and graces which the Gospel enjoins." Such references to God and religion made the constitution of the society different from those of other Owenite communities. Owen himself criticized religion, but the Kendal group invoked God several times.[18]

Only male members signed the constitution, most likely indicating that only men contributed to its framework. The document outlined the specific goals and operations of the community. According to the constitution, male and female adult members of the community would hold meetings to determine the rules of the group as well as to carry out business. The community would also select members, including a treasurer and clerk, to conduct business. The community expected new recruits to contribute "their best services for the welfare of the company according to their age, experience and capacity, and if inexperienced in that which is requisite, they will apply diligently to acquire the knowledge of some useful occupation or employment." If the group did not have members with the skills required for their industries, they would hire outside laborers. Members could leave the group at will. Those who left by choice or by force would receive a share of the property value and all entered into the books at the time of departure.[19]

The framers of the community gave much attention to the issue of children. They stated their intention to construct buildings and find teachers "to instruct in the best physical and mental education all the children." In the preamble, they stated that in the event that parents died, the community would care for the children. Parents would not have to worry about their children becoming orphans because the community would "adopt them and amply provide for their comfort in the place of their natural parents." They would be "equally protected, educated and cherished with those living members." The education provided to the children would follow as closely as possible the guidelines of Owen. Men would receive an education in agriculture and a mechanical art while "the females are to be taught in a manner suitable for their sex." Monies to provide for the children would come out of the community funds.[20]

After the completion of the original document, members added by-laws to outline other significant functions and rules of the community. Adult members would receive an equal dividend each year from the community. Each family and person in Kendal would have necessities provided for by the community. Furthermore, the society would "furnish everything necessary for the laborers to pursue their several branches of industry for the general benefit of the whole." If one member had a grievance against another member, a committee would receive the complaint. Any person found guilty of committing a wrong would have to try to correct it or face expulsion from the society. As with the constitution, only men signed the by-laws.[21]

In the organization of the society, the establishment of the community of property received great attention since it meant a major shift in the conception of property ownership for members. When new members entered, the community would inventory any property brought by them, and that which was useful would be placed into the common stock. The society would keep records on such property. Individuals would get credit for the contributions and would "draw interest to be paid" on it. Regarding real estate, members agreed "to share equally in the loss or gain . . . in the sales of the property individually pledged or collectively given as security." Furthermore, members promised that "we will not sell, lease, rent or dispose of our individual shares of the real estate to any person or persons other than this Association."[22]

In contrast with religious utopias such as the Shakers and Zoar, the Owenites formulated laws on property that favored the individual who left the group. The Shakers generally would not allow departing members to leave with property, as new members promised not to make claims against the village. In Zoar, no communal property was divided among members until the community disbanded. The liberality of the departure laws at Kendal made it easier for the disaffected to withdraw.

While Robert Owen had supported more equal relations between the sexes, it seems that the Kendal community voiced their acceptance of this but backed it up with little action. Members accepted different roles for women and men, as indicated by their desire to educate females in areas "suitable for their sex." Although the Kendal community stipulated that women and men had the right to vote on affairs, men seemed to make the key decisions in the community. Men also made decisions concerning business. The records indicate that men held the important appointments, such as treasurer and chair.[23]

The disparate positions of men and women showed up in the economic functions of the community. Men were appointed to manage the woolen factory, blacksmith shop, and wagonmakers shop. At a meeting in December 1827, male members agreed to convene each evening for the purpose of learning about the business of the previous day.[24]

Only men were guaranteed a fixed monthly salary. Married men received ten dollars a month from community funds, while unmarried men received eight dollars a month. Men were expected to labor ten hours a day when in good health. Women, on the other hand, received pay based on the tasks they completed. Women earned twenty-five cents for eight hours of washing. They got seventy-five cents for a week's worth of housework. Their pay fell below that of men, indicating that their economic contributions to the society were not as highly valued. Women did, however, share equally in the loss or gain of property belonging to the common stock.[25]

In 1828, the society addressed some issues regarding the status of women. It voted to include in the community women who were married to members, if they signed the constitution. Furthermore, the society called for women to meet once a week to discuss the needs of the families. Women then had to report their findings to the commissioners.[26]

At the beginning of 1828, Kendal had approximately two hundred members, who came from different religious and ethnic backgrounds. According to the Kendal Constitution, members had to be "moral, sober, and industrious." The lack of unity in their religious convictions may have contributed to the decline of Kendal.[27]

In 1827, Kendal membership received a boost from the Forestville

Commonwealth, a New York experiment that had failed. Twenty-seven members of that community came to Kendal and entered the society in December 1827. From this group, Dr. Samuel Underhill rose to prominence at Kendal and served as a community commissioner. He also gave several public speeches to spread the philosophy of Owen. Because of Underhill's negative stance on religion, many people objected to his speeches and voiced their displeasure in local papers. One letter writer requested that Alexander Campbell, who would later lead the criticism of Mormonism, debate Underhill. Campbell refused because he viewed him as an insignificant figure. Instead, he wanted to debate Owen. The publicity generated by Underhill did not increase the membership but instead had the effect of adding to the negative feelings the local community had regarding Kendal.[28]

The community began experiencing difficulty in its first year. Members began to withdraw as early as January 1827. In February, the community attempted to settle a problem with the acting commissioner, James Freeman, which the community minutes do not explain. The following month, the community voted unanimously to negotiate a settlement for Freeman's removal from Kendal.[29]

The community's problems continued into 1828. Debt was a major concern. In February, the value of the community property was listed at more than twenty-six thousand dollars, while the community's debt was more than twenty-two thousand dollars. Furthermore, Kendal owed more than five thousand dollars to its members. Underhill indicated that the society needed to increase its capital by fifteen thousand dollars to develop its business and attract more members. He portrayed a different picture of the community to Robert Owen. Underhill communicated to Owen that Kendal enjoyed much prosperity and would begin the publication of a paper. Owen visited the community in 1828 and expected that the community would thrive.[30]

Another problem concerned community property and labor. Some members had been taking food from the garden without permission. The society voted to require the consent of the gardener to take such provisions. Also, some people had left Kendal to work elsewhere. To remedy this, the society stipulated that any person doing this "without the consent of the Commissioners shall be charged any amount that the Commissioners shall deem the damage to be to the interest of the Community." Several members withdrew from Kendal, taking with them both personal and work effects. Others followed suit in the winter.[31]

Because of the rapid decline in membership, the society contemplated leasing some or all of its property. As the numbers continued to dwindle throughout the winter, the society decided to disband. In January 1829, the society unanimously voted to end its business transactions and to sell personal property except for the machinery used in the woolen factory and clothing shop.[32]

The demise of the Kendal community occurred because of some of the same difficulties that other utopian experiments had encountered. The issue of debt played a large role in its short life. Beyond this, members of Kendal did not enjoy a unity of feeling, which led to disagreements and the withdrawal of members. Members had trouble placing the good of the community over their own self-interests.[33] Unlike religious communities where members united around faith, secular utopias had the difficulty of finding common bonds necessary to the unanimity of feeling for community property.[33]

The last Owenite community established in Ohio was founded in 1845 on the banks of the Miami River, twenty-six miles north of Cincinnati in Warren County. Orson S. Murray, the guiding hand behind the establishment of Fruit Hills, followed not only Owen's principles but also the anarchist philosophies of William Lloyd Garrison. The community lasted until 1852. During its existence, it enjoyed a close relationship with two utopian societies in Indiana, the Grand Prairie Community and the Kristeen Community.[34]

The havens based on Owen's ideals did not last long for a number of reasons. His philosophy contradicted some basic American convictions. Whereas Owen advocated that the environment determined the character of people, American individualism said otherwise; people shaped the environment. Whereas Owen downplayed religion, Americans embraced it. Owen called for people to share the wealth, and Americans viewed the attainment of individual wealth as the mark of success.[35]

Owen attempted to defend his ideals and his attitude toward religion in a debate with Alexander Campbell, a Baptist who later founded the Disciples of Christ. At the debate, held in 1829 in Cincinnati, each man asserted his own version of utopia. Owen's utopia lay in the secular world; Campbell saw utopia as connected with religion. Campbell received a warmer reception at the debate. Later that year, Owen went back to England. By that time, all of the original Owenite communities had closed. After the Panic of 1837, a new wave of Owenite associations began. At the same time, utopian experiments including the Oneida

Community of New York and the Fourierist groups emerged throughout the nation.[36]

Despite the short life of the Owenite communities, the effort to establish utopia held much importance. Owen's philosophy brought secular socialism to the nation in the 1820s. In the 1840s, Owenism was equated with socialism, a rejection of capitalism, and the acceptance of cooperative living as different communal theories emerged.

Another European whose philosophy inspired Americans to establish the perfect world was Charles Fourier. Born in France in 1772, Fourier (pronounced four-yay) was the son of a wealthy cloth merchant. He came of age as the French Revolution ravaged the nation. The swift changes brought by revolution probably influenced him to see the possibilities to alter society. During the siege of Lyon (1793), his property was confiscated, and he became a traveling salesman. Receiving no formal education, Fourier formulated his conception of utopia in the provinces and published three works, in 1808, 1819, and 1827. His theories reflected his dreams and aspirations, which stemmed from a desire to gain recognition from contemporaries and overcome his lack of education.[38]

Fourier based several of his societal ideals on mathematics. He displayed an affinity for numerology, commenting, for example, that seven scourges plagued civilization. He believed that Isaac Newton's explanation of the physical universe had a parallel in the natural social order. Each order consisted of eight ascending levels, and man could exhibit true emotion in the highest period, Harmony. Fourier sought to get rid of civilization, his word for contemporary society, because it was overtaken by individualism. He found civilization abhorrent because of the exploitation of the wage system and the excesses and waste of capitalism. Fourier believed that this stage of civilization represented one of thirty-two through which the world would pass. The current stage of civilization was necessary to evolve to Harmony. Man could skip various stages of development and reach Harmony by establishing communities, based on his model and called phalanxes, that met the needs of unchanging human nature. Fourier postulated that twelve passions influenced individuals in different degrees. These passions affected the type of work people liked to do, and the phalanx offered people the chance to labor in their selected field. Fourierism thus gave people a chance to be what nature wanted them to be because civilization had taken from them their ultimate destiny. Many communitarians attempted to create utopian havens in the United States because they subscribed to this belief, disclosing much about Americans' apprehension with either themselves or the plethora of antebellum reform efforts. Fourier postulated that women were kept from their true destiny because society prevented them from enjoying true liberty.[39]

Fourier thought that competition in trade led to dishonest dealings. In turn, this meant increased suffering for the poor, who were forced to pay for industrial inefficiencies. To alleviate this problem, Fourier proposed honesty in commerce by utilizing algebraic means. He advanced a system that paid the highest wages to workers who completed the least desirable tasks. Furthermore, he believed the establishment of trade unions would eliminate the corruption.[40]

To help man ascend to Harmony, Fourier proposed the creation of phalanxes, communities based on agriculture and cooperation. He painstakingly outlined his specifications for the phalanxes, giving much attention to numbers in his plans. For example, he recommended that 1,620 people live in the phalanx, the number that was double the 810 personality types he described. Members would enjoy a minimum income, work in agriculture, and experience happiness in their sexual relations. To prevent class competition between rich and poor, members would change their roles in the phalanxes, resulting in a more equal division of the wealth. A phalanx consisted of six thousand acres, and the community revolved around the phalanstery, a large building that would house the members and offer them opportunities for sexual unions. Because of the openness regarding sex, both children and older people lived away from the "galleries of association" where such activity might take place. Members would eat together in dining halls and could enjoy the orchards and gardens of the community. Fourier even included in his plans the places where different members would sleep. His devotion to detail seemed odd to many.[41]

Members of the phalanxes did not hold all property in common. Instead, people invested money in the phalanx and gained interest from economic endeavors. Agriculture mixed with light industry constituted the primary economic activities of the phalanxes. Fourier broke work into three categories: necessity, usefulness, and attractiveness. The phalanxes differed from ordinary joint-stock companies in that phalanx members viewed labor as a type of capital. This meant that the potential work contributed by a phalanx member was considered an investment. Fourierists also believed that those who contributed smaller investments to the phalanx should gain larger dividends than those who invested more.[42]

The French utopianist attempted to put his ideas into action by publishing them in a journal, *Le Phalanstère.* He did gain some converts, who created a phalanx in France in 1832. It failed, and Fourier insisted that the architect of the building was crazy and incompetent, thus explaining its lack of success. Fourier died in October 1837, just after the panic that sparked the establishment of phalanxes in the United States commenced.[43]

Fourier's ideas captured the attention of Albert Brisbane from the Burned-Over District of New York, who learned about the philosopher during his travels in Europe in 1833–34. When he returned to the United States, he attempted to raise money to establish phalanxes, but the onset of the Panic of 1837 inhibited this effort. The panic led to massive unemployment and deflation, which extended into the 1840s. Prices fell by 42 percent between 1837 and 1843. Brisbane published his Fourierist views during the economic crisis.[44]

The economic crisis, along with its social effects, led many people to search for a perfect world and express millennial beliefs. Some searched for answers in Fourierism, while others followed Robert Owen. Still others turned to William Miller, who calculated that Christ would return to earth in 1844. Those attracted to Fourierism believed phalanxes served as millennial havens or New Jerusalems, where members lived cooperatively to create the divine. Those who joined phalanxes stated that fears of an "industrial feudalism" led them to the communities, which were located predominantly in the industrial northeastern portion of the nation.[45]

Brisbane articulated his Fourierist views during the economic crisis. They appeared in articles in the *New York Tribune* with the support of its editor, Horace Greeley. In 1840, Brisbane published *The Social Destiny of Man,* which outlined his understanding of Fourier, adapted to American values. He overlooked Fourier's views on marriage and sexual relations and emphasized the economic aspects of the communities. Claiming that capitalists enjoyed an unfair share of the wealth, Brisbane called for people to work collectively and obtain an equal share for their labor. Founders of the Clermont Phalanx in Ohio claimed that their society was "based upon the Dignity of Labor, and the establishment of just relations between the three producing powers of man, which are Skill, Capital, and Labor, and of which Labor is the Chief."[46]

These ideas attracted largely people from the Northeast who suffered from the Panic of 1837 and those intellectuals in search of an end to social problems. In 1842, Brisbane worked to create a model phalanx and solicited financial contributions in the *New York Tribune.* He wanted to raise approximately five hundred thousand dollars by selling shares in the phalanxes for one thousand dollars each. Several phalanxes took shape in regions close to urban centers. Brisbane started a journal, the *Phalanx,* in 1843.[47]

According to its first issue, the *Phalanx* sought to devote its pages to an exposition and analysis of Fourier's ideas. Additionally, the journal would critique "the present false system of Society, and will expose its evils, and the defects of its leading social Institutions." Among other topics, the journal wanted to devote discourse to "the unjust and unnatural relation" established between Capital and Labor. The various phalanxes developing throughout the nation would report their progress in the journal.[48]

The publication did help to convert people to Fourierism. John D. Wilkins of Louisiana wanted to help with the number of followers by ensuring that college students had access to the *Phalanx.* He donated money so that every college would receive copies of the journal for six months. The students of Western Reserve College in Hudson, Ohio, wrote an acknowledgment for their copies in the *Phalanx,* indicating the paper did heighten their interest. The students wrote: we "return our grateful thanks to the gentleman who has shown such kind regard for the instruction of the rising generation, and benevolence in his endeavors to spread knowledge on the subject of Social Science." The students expressed "a deep and overwhelming interest" in the subject of association. They believed that social evils and moral corruption could be removed. They also felt it their duty as youths of America "to study well the principles on which a system promising so much, is based."[49]

The Fourierist movement attracted some communities that had organized earlier in Massachusetts. They accepted Fourierism and transformed their havens. These included Brook Farm, the Hopedale Community, and the Northampton Association. Brook Farm was the most famous phalanx to emerge in America because several prominent intellectuals had joined. The twenty-eight or so Fourierist communities that opened from 1841 to 1858 in states including Ohio, Michigan, Wisconsin, and Iowa did not, however, follow Fourier's designs precisely, as their populations were much smaller. The North American Phalanx at Red Bank, New Jersey, which had the longest life of any Fourierist colony, consisted of just over one hundred members during the peak years. Furthermore, members found it difficult to adhere to Fourier's philosophies, especially the establishment of association and harmony. In spite of their secular basis, members still clashed over religion.[50]

More than thirty Fourierist phalanxes were established between 1841 and 1870, and Ohio served as home to eight communities that embraced some elements of Fourierism. Only the state of New York equaled this statistic. These Ohio communities were Marlborough Association (1841–45); Social Reform Unity (1842–43); Ohio Phalanx (1844–45); Clermont Phalanx (1844–46); Trumbull Phalanx (1844–48); Columbian Phalanx (1845); Utopia [Trialville] (1847–58); and the Memnonia Institute (1856–57). The Fourierist J. P. Stuart offered an explanation concerning the growth of Fourierism in Ohio. He believed that the "Western Reserve is destined . . . to receive and carry out the Doctrines of Association with more promptness and earnestness than any other part of the great West" owing to its organization in towns. Influenced by the Yankee tradition, the towns of the Western Reserve offered meeting houses, schoolhouses, and other social institutions. This allowed the people to "keep up a brisk social intercourse and come together to speak freely on all matters of public interest. The Reserve is thus admirably adapted by its present mechanism, to the investigation of important Social questions." The people of the Western Reserve possessed strong character as "honest," "frugal," "hardworking and religious" people. They were not fanatical, but their religious discourse, Stuart thought, would lead them to the acceptance of Fourierism.[51]

In 1841, utopianists organized the Marlborough Association because they wanted to formulate a community to combat the poor condition of labor. While Brian J. L. Berry calls the Marlborough Association a Fourierist community, John Humphrey Noyes says it "had nothing to do with Fourier's philosophy." He also discloses that Abram Brooke, one of the founders, did not classify himself as a Fourierist or Owenite but rather lived in the way he believed to be correct. The community sought to correct the inequities suffered by laborers by holding property in common. Members would not buy or sell products from each other, but would share goods as needed.[52]

The organizers had first begun to plan for the community several years before it opened in Stark County, Ohio. The association was founded approximately six miles northwest of Alliance, which was about forty-five miles southeast of Cleveland. The founders started with two farms located a mile apart and donated by brothers Edward and Abram Brooke.[53]

The association faced several difficult circumstances. Most of those who joined had little property to contribute and little understanding of the hard work involved in obtaining it, and thus entered the group without the necessary attributes to make it successful. The amount of effort they put forth did not equal the force necessary to begin a haven from scratch. The land owned by the association needed to be cleared. Each farm had a house and barn, along with tenant houses and some horses, cattle, and sheep; however, members needed other materials and lacked sufficient funds to purchase them.[54]

As membership increased, the association bought the land to connect the two farms. The owner of the land asked a high price, which the members agreed to, thus incurring a large debt. They built a mansion on the land to serve as the residence for the members. Each family had its own apartment. The land did produce enough food for consumption, as one farm contained a sizable orchard. They also grew plenty of vegetables.[55]

Abram Brooke, one of the original donors of land, withdrew from the association during the planning stages. He had wanted to extend the philosophy of shared goods to those outside the community as well. When his brother Edward said that people would join out of selfish motives if the community adopted this ideology, Abram left. He did not want to join a group where the whole world was not part of the utopian experiment, but he let the association keep his land. After leaving Marlborough in 1843, he tried to organize an experimental community in Clinton County, Ohio, based on communal ownership of property and his philosophy that he would provide services and materials to people as needed. In return, he expected them to do the same for him. With few members, the community lasted only two years.[56]

In general, the members got along well at Marlborough. They did not hold religious services on Sundays but gathered to discuss ways to improve the community. They considered themselves to be a community of freethinkers. Although members did not quarrel, neither did they have a united corps of beliefs to guide them. New members did not have the same ideals as the founders, and some entered out of selfish motives.[57]

The death of a leading member, Joseph Lukens, a year and a half after the community was established led members to reevaluate the association. They decided to write a constitution, which forced them to consider important ideas about the community's nature. Members found that they had divergent views on the government of the association as well as the nature of communal ownership of property. Some of those members who had contributed to the community reevaluated their circumstances and left because of disappointment with the endeavor. Consequently, the association disbanded in 1845.[58]

Elijah Grant led another effort to establish a phalanx in Ohio. A graduate of Yale University, Grant practiced law in Ohio and had read Fourier closely. He traveled to Pittsburgh in 1843 to attend the Western Fourier Convention and meet utopianists similar to himself, but he grew frustrated because people wanted to deviate from Fourier's plans. Grant attempted to establish a phalanx based on Fourier's specifications. Grant believed Fourierism offered a "decisive attack upon the present state of strife and discord" and would build a "social temple in which the human soul may develop its faculties to their utmost capacity." Grant showed much optimism about the Fourierist movement: "A new light is beaming upon the world, and a higher and nobler faith is entering the souls of men." H. H. Van Amringe, who had helped with the establishment of the Trumbull Phalanx, worked with Grant.[59]

Initially, the association was called the American Phalanx. Members began the planning of the community in 1843 and opened it in February 1844 on two thousand acres in Westfield, Belmont County, Ohio, along the Ohio River, approximately eight miles south of Wheeling. The phalanx bought the land for thirty dollars per acre. Grant believed that the community would succeed financially, since supporters had pledged forty thousand dollars by the end of the first year and one hundred thousand dollars by the end of the second year. More than six hundred acres of the land purchased had already been used for agriculture. Other acreage included hilly areas, along with some regions that were heavily wooded. The property also offered a vein of coal that would provide fuel for steam engines and other endeavors. The land contained natural resources for construction, such as sandstone and limestone. Several buildings were located on the property, including two dwelling houses and ten log houses, but they could serve only as temporary shelters.[60]

The residents held much optimism for the community, reporting, "The domain is singularly beautiful, as well as fertile. . . . It is situated on one of the greatest thoroughfares in the world, the charming Ohio." This location gave the phalanx access to several markets. It also lay seven miles from the National Road. Associationists believed the phalanx would thrive because most members came from the Western Reserve and displayed such desirable qualities as intelligence, industry, frugality, and enterprise. Furthermore, they "understand well the difficulties to be encountered in the commencement of this important enterprise, and are prepared to meet and surmount them without murmuring." Organizers had designs for a temporary dwelling to house six to twelve families and plans to construct a hospital, a nursery, and a school, lecture, and church room. Still, they expected problems during the first year as members made mistakes because of their lack of experience in forging a "new order of society."[61]

After cementing the plans for organization, the Ohio Phalanx solicited membership applications in the *Phalanx*. It invited applicants to inform the community of their age, occupation, family members, and the amount of money or land they intended to invest in the community. Single men had to pay at least one hundred dollars and those with families two hundred dollars, which would go into the phalanx stock. Additionally, adult males would pay an admission fee of five dollars while women paid three dollars and children one dollar. The phalanx would use these funds for the organizational costs of the community and for books and other reading material for members. The Ohio group wanted to admit only "zealous friends of the cause" willing to make sacrifices for its success. In the announcement in the *Phalanx* they stipulated, "Applicants are expected to have their minds made up, and to be ready to co-operate at once in the experiment of a Social Reorganization." The Ohio Phalanx attracted committed Fourierists such as Mr. James Thornburgh, a lawyer known as the "Pioneer of Fourierism" because he "has ardently advocated it ever since he undertook its noble aims." The *Phalanx* considered him a "fine, good-hearted, and benevolent man, of good mind and energy" who held a strong commitment to Fourierism.[62]

In their quest for members, the Ohio Phalanx had to compete with both the Trumbull and the Columbian Phalanxes for people from eastern Ohio and Pittsburgh. This did not cause discord amongst the Fourierist groups, as they believed friendly rivalries would not impede their success. The establishment of so many communities did, however, speed along the demise of Fourierism.[63] If supporters had combined their efforts, energies, and financial resources, their communities might have enjoyed longer lives.

At the Fourth of July festivities in 1844, Grant disclosed the position of the society on several issues in a series of toasts he made. Phalanx members believed that the natural rights of man to life, liberty, and property could "be held and secured to all, only by individual association." He credited Fourier with being the "greatest discoverer who has ever existed" for introducing "the laws of social and industrial order, unity and harmony." He also called industrial phalanxes "armies for production . . . marked by peace, plenty, and joy; not by carnage, devastation, and tears." Grant called for a better status for women: "Every joy of man is increased by her participation; each grace and refinement are heightened by her aid; may the day be hastened, when her condition shall really be that which the beneficent Creator intended."[64]

Members of Grant's Ohio Phalanx argued over many of the same issues plaguing other associations, including religion and the social activities of some. Moreover, financial issues forced the members to disband. At its inception, the phalanx put down no money on the sixty-nine-thousand-dollar purchase price of the land. As with other phalanxes, when the community had to make payments on the debt, it did not have the financial resources to do so. In 1845, the phalanx owed more than four thousand dollars in interest. Many of the pledges that it had depended upon never materialized. When members could not make payments to James Shriver, who had allowed them to use his property without the down payment, he evicted them. The phalanx reorganized several times but dissolved after three new constitutions failed to rescue the community.[65]

Grant resigned as president, having lost one thousand dollars of his personal investment along with his hopes. He also had suffered the devastating loss of his infant son, Charles Fourier Grant, only days before he resigned. Grant believed several factors caused the failure of the Ohio Phalanx, including lack of funds, disagreements among the members, lack of leadership and skill, and lack of commitment to Fourierism. He despised that others did not understand the philosophy of Fourier, so he decided to give up the communal endeavor and work in civilization. He returned to Canton, Ohio, in 1846, working in business and banking. In 1868, he tried his hand at another communal endeavor in Kansas known as Silkville or the Prairie Home Colony, a project he left within a year. Grant died in 1874, before this community disbanded.[66]

Although Grant believed that the failure of the Ohio Phalanx meant Fourierist communities could not succeed, others thought they might. Former associationists at Ohio decided to join other utopian ventures, including the Clermont Phalanx and the Trumbull Phalanx. Grant, however, argued that even Brook Farm would suffer failure. Other Fourierist leaders like Brisbane insisted they would thrive. Grant had contributed to the closing of the Ohio Phalanx by adhering too closely to Fourier's specific plans, insisting that members act in a certain manner and think in a particular way. While attempting to conform to Fourier's precise model, he failed to see that the Ohio Phalanx had accumulated profits that could have led to a longer life for the community.[67]

The Clermont Phalanx began as a result of the following Fourierism acquired in Cincinnati. In 1843, Fourierists founded a local association called the Cincinnati Phalanx to spread Fourier's theories, and many members pushed for the establishment of phalanxes. With the encouragement and financial support of Horace Greeley, wealthy editor of the *New York Tribune,* and the encouragement of Brisbane, the local chapter moved to create phalanxes. In May 1844, a group of one hundred families and some single people left Cincinnati and traveled about thirty-five miles up the Ohio River to begin the Clermont Phalanx in Clermont County, Ohio. They settled on one thousand acres of land located on the Ohio River. Except for 150 acres, the land was filled with trees, including hickory, black walnut, and sugar maple. They anticipated that they could sell the timber and pay off the price of the property.[68]

The group began their haven with much fanfare and promise. They danced as the steamboat *Yucatan* took them to their new home. While they planned to adopt the labor ideals of Fourierism, they also planned to follow the great social law to "love thy neighbor as thyself." Most members did not have a vast knowledge of Fourier's ideals because they had only read Brisbane's writings on the French philosopher. After reaching the site, the group held ceremonies that included music, readings from Scripture, and an address by the president of the phalanx, Judge Wade Loofbourrow. Loofbourrow's speech contained many references to the millennialist tenets of Fourierism. He called the phalanx the "promised land" and "declared it to be the fulfillment of the Gospel of Jesus Christ, in the establishment of the kingdom of Heaven upon Earth, the reign of Universal Peace, and the restoration of Universal Unity."[69]

After the celebrations for the opening of the phalanx, the members began to construct an eighty-four-foot-long building that would include a dining hall and seven rooms on each side in which the families would live. The phalanstery was to be made of brick. During its construction, members lived in a barracks similar to a steamboat with the small rooms occupied by married couples or single persons. The members had left behind superior residences to these, but they initially accepted their dwellings without complaint.[70]

Members of the Clermont Phalanx experienced financial troubles during their first year. The *Phalanx* carried the following about those troubles: "We had received no account of it [Clermont Phalanx] lately, and as the last that we had was not very flattering in respect to its pecuniary condition, we should not have been surprised to hear of its dissolution." But the community managed to overcome these initial difficulties. It began its agricultural life by acquiring a stock of cattle, hogs, and sheep. Members also established shoe, tin, and tailor shops and constructed a sawmill and a gristmill. They planned to plant a large orchard, as A. H. Ernst had donated more than one thousand fruit trees. Those who had joined the community were knowledgeable in farming and mechanics.[71]

Another problem emerged during the first months of the phalanx. Members had begun to argue with each other. The community survived initially despite these troubles, and the Clermont Phalanx invited people of the "right character" to join. Prospective members were invited to visit the community. Any new members needed to have some funds "and if their families are large, the amount must be in proportion, and the members must be such as can make themselves useful." Clermont did accept new members, several of them from the Ohio Phalanx, which went out of existence in 1845.[72]

At the height of its association, Clermont had eighty people, not including the children. Members came from different religious backgrounds and contributed in different ways to the economic life of the community. They ate and worked together and took pride in the practicality of living together and sharing responsibilities.[73]

But the aspirations of the Clermont Phalanx did not prove substantial enough to maintain the community. In the fall of 1846, the phalanx went out of existence. A flood had damaged the community, and the phalanx had amassed a debt of more than fifteen thousand dollars. The debt problem also plagued other phalanxes, as most of these communities purchased too much land for the members they had to support. Many of the phalanxes made extravagant land purchases because supporters had pledged large sums of money. Subscribers had promised seventeen thousand dollars to Clermont, but the community received only six thousand. Another factor in Clermont's closing was jealousies among the members. Members began to sue each other. The phalanx also encountered problems with its president, Loofbourrow, who held the property deed for the community.[74]

After its dissolution, some members returned to Cincinnati, while others remained near the phalanx. Those remaining had the opportunity to try two other utopianist endeavors created on the ruins of Clermont. In 1846, John O. Wattles came to Clermont in search of a new venture. Wattles had established the short-lived Prairie Home Community in Logan County, Ohio, which began and ended in 1844. Wattles and Valentine Nicholson created the group after participating in a New York socialist convention in 1843. Prairie Home had attracted 130 members, many Hicksite Quakers. They lived by the rule to "do as you would be done by." They had no formal government.[75]

With J. D. Cornell, Wattles founded the Brotherhood, or Spiritualist Community, as an agricultural cooperative. Approximately one hundred people joined the group, including Swedenborgians. In addition to construction on the former Clermont site, they also built a store in Cincinnati where they sold their crops. Their buildings were destroyed in a flood in December 1847, and they were unable to recover from the natural disaster.[76]

After the failure of this second attempt at communitarianism at Clermont, Josiah Warren made a third effort. Warren had joined the Owenite community at New Harmony, Indiana, in 1825. He believed that New Harmony's failure rested in the establishment of a community of goods, which he thought went against personal responsibility. He had also founded another community, named Equity, in the Tuscarawas River Valley of Ohio in 1835. This group formulated a time-labor system. Epidemics led to the closing of the experiment in 1837. Warren came to the conclusion that a utopian community should have no government, and people should act as they chose, with members living with the consequences of their actions. He introduced individualism into a communal setting by emphasizing personal responsibility. This acceptance of individual responsibility in personal affairs would be combined with different economic relationships. People in his communities would engage in equitable commerce, meaning individuals would engage in trade with labor notes instead of the market value of the goods they produced. After the failure of Equity, Warren sought to implement his ideas at the former site of the Clermont Phalanx, hoping to attract those Fourierists disillusioned with Clermont's failure. This new community, called Utopia, opened in July 1847. Each of the twenty-four families that lived in Utopia owned its own house and followed Warren's ideas of "equitable commerce" when they seemed beneficial. Utopia lasted until 1858, collapsing since members had gradually given up on cooperative agriculture.[77]

The attraction of utopianists to Clermont and the set of people from different utopian experiments indicates the overlap of the nineteenth-century ventures. The progression of some Fourierists into anarchism indicates that utopianists had accepted a new set of beliefs both radical and conservative. Seemingly rejecting government, anarchists offered freedom of action to the individual and family. In acting against a community of property, however, they accepted an economic situation similar to laissez-faire concepts accepted in America at the time. As sectionalism heightened during the 1850s over slavery, anarchists exalted "free labor" as did other northerners. Utopianists in the decade came to glory in the freedoms of the nation rather than attempting to create a complete alternative.[78]

A Fourierist community founded on the Western Reserve developed into one of the most successful phalanxes in the country. The Trumbull Phalanx began with a meeting held on November 6, 1843, in Warren, Ohio, where organizers drew up the Fourierist principles by which they would live. Fourierists from Pittsburgh, Pennsylvania, took a leading role in creating the community. The association intended to offer shares for twenty-five dollars each to raise two hundred thousand dollars to start the phalanx. A board of directors would control the economic aspects of the community. The phalanx opened on April 1, 1844, led by Benjamin Robbins of Windham, Portage County, who served as president.[79]

The phalanx began with the purchase of land in Braceville, a town eight miles west of Warren and five miles north of Newton Falls. This location provided access to the Ohio and Pennsylvania Canal and a turnpike road. The community attracted a number of people from the Disciples of Christ, or Campbellites, who believed that Christians would establish a universal church to begin the millennium. Originally, thirty-five families founded the settlement by purchasing 280 acres of land from Eli Barnum. The land had rich soil, and, at the time of purchase, over half was under cultivation. Additionally, several working mills were located on the property, including a gristmill, an oil mill, and a sawmill, as well as a double-cording machine and cloth-dressing works. The phalanx could also benefit from the buildings already constructed on the land while it planned its phalanstery. During the first summer, the two-hundred-plus members lived in temporary dwellings in which "they are much crowded, residing in loose sheds, nevertheless, on no consideration would they exchange present relations for former ones." Eventually, the community would construct buildings for church and school, as well as a lecture hall and library.[80]

The phalanx members united in groups to complete part of the work of the community. According to the constitution of the Trumbull Phalanx, different work groups would have different pay. In practice, the community divided everything earned by the phalanx between members according to how much work each person completed. Boys in the phalanx worked together to establish a garden. Nathan C. Meeker of the phalanx praised this cooperation and claimed: "Those not accustomed to view the progress of combined labors will be astonished to see aggregates." Meeker completely believed in the potential of the phalanx to address the ills of capitalism. He exclaimed, "My eyes see men making haste to free the slave of all names, nations and tongues, and my ears hear them driving, thick and fast, nails into the coffin of Despotism." Meeker viewed the Trumbull Phalanx "as a step of as much importance as any which secured our Political independence." Despite his enthusiasm about the haven, it remained in question whether or not the families could live together in peace.[81]

During the fall and winter of 1844, the phalanx suffered from fever and ague. This led to problems with agricultural output, as members could not properly care for the crops. Consequently, the haven could not complete different plans for organization. Members still felt "harmony within and sympathy without." They believed themselves secure in mone-tary affairs because they paid off some of their debt. Both the president of the phalanx, Benjamin Robbins, and the secretary, H. N. Jones, thought that after a few years they would forge a blessed home where "the idler and the non-producer are unfelt and unknown."[82]

By 1845, the phalanx seemed quite successful. It had paid off more than eight thousand dollars of the eighteen-thousand-dollar debt accumulated by the purchase of the property. The community had made many other economic advances and offered the most diverse economic program among Fourierist communities. It had in operation a flouring mill, a sawmill, a shingle-machine, weaving machines, a blacksmith shop, and a hatter's shop. Members also planned to construct a wagon shop. In agriculture, the community had cultivated oats, corn, potatoes, and wheat in addition to its peach and apple orchards.[83]

Despite such successes, eight to ten families had left the phalanx by late summer 1845. Some of these people left because they said they "had been in the habit of living on better food"—members ate a coarse diet, at times having no meat. Others left because they no longer agreed with the Articles of Association. Consequently, the phalanx encouraged to join only those new members who studied Fourier and understood his principles. The phalanx had never prevented people from joining because of political or religious affiliation. Those who were fainthearted and could not make some sacrifices should not join. One prominent member of the phalanx, Nathan Meeker, advertised in the *Harbinger* that "we are prepared to receive members, who are desirous of uniting their interests with us, and of becoming truly devoted to the cause of Industrial Association." The Trumbull Phalanx did add many from Pittsburgh to its membership, and these people contributed substantially to the economic survival of the phalanx. However, they competed for support from Pittsburgh Associationists with the Ohio and Columbian Phalanxes.[84]

By 1847, the phalanx consisted of 250 members and had experienced some success. With help from supporters in Pittsburgh, the association paid off its debt. The community had succeeded in producing enough food and clothing to maintain its members, and each family lived in a convenient residence. In addition to these positive experiences, members had to endure some difficulties as ague and fever plagued them, especially during the rainy season.[85]

The phalanx gave much effort to establishing schools for the children—one a public school and the other a phalanx school. The teacher for both schools belonged to the phalanx. Nathan Meeker, known as the poet-laureate of the phalanx, and his wife, Arvilla Delight Smith Meeker, took the leadership roles in starting the school. The schools taught boys an industrial trade in addition to traditional subjects. Mrs. Meeker established in her family residence a nursery school considered to be the first in the Western Reserve.[86]

Because the phalanx had persevered through many trials, members expected it would ultimately lead them from the earthly domain to higher levels of liberty and love. These hopes were dashed, however, when the community announced its closing in 1847. Along with the North American and Wisconsin Phalanxes, Trumbull Phalanx represented one of the most successful Fourierist communities in the United States. Members made every effort to overcome their difficulties, and associationists from Pittsburgh offered their support. It closed for good in 1848. The phalanx had accepted members who were sick and in need. Such people could not contribute to the efficient running of the community. Also, the phalanx had accepted capital that brought nothing into the community except interest payments. Disgruntled members pointed to other reasons for the failure. One former phalanx member said that the community was located on swampy land difficult to cultivate, thus causing the ague and fever. Furthermore, some people entered the community with the idea that they would not have to work even though the constitution of the phalanx declared work a duty of the members. Members' arguments over religion worked against the prosperity of the community.[87]

Nathan Meeker, once a strong supporter of the phalanx he had joined in 1844 with his bride, wrote about the negative aspects of life in the phalanx in the *New York Tribune* in 1866. Meeker disclosed that the Fourierist philosophy did not prepare members for the problems of communal life, including the indolence and annoying habits of others. Meeker particularly found it unbearable that members could eavesdrop on conversations and then gossip about them. Also, because of the close quarters, members were subjected to disturbances from those who kept late hours.[88]

The group of Pittsburgh Associationists who helped to found the Trumbull and Ohio Phalanxes also gave their assistance in founding the Columbian Phalanx in 1845. This phalanx was located on the Muskingum River, seven miles north of Zanesville. It had attracted some members from the Integral Phalanx, a community initially located twenty-three miles north of Cincinnati. When the community moved to Illinois, some decided to stay in Ohio and join the Columbian group. This competition for support and members contributed to the end of the community in less than a year. Early reports suggested that the community ended because of lack of food. However, a visitor to the phalanx reported in August 1845 that such reports were false. The community had begun to take shape with thirty-two families. The report also stated that the phalanx had abundant crops of wheat, rye, corn, and oats. Furthermore, the community had no debt. Because of this success and plenty, the Columbian Phalanx invited people to join its haven.[89]

In spite of these glowing reports, the phalanx confronted serious problems, including the philosophical bent of members. Not all members of the Columbian group had studied and accepted Fourierism. The leading Fourierist attempted to act on the Frenchman's beliefs by laboring on Sunday, critiquing marriage, and advancing racial equality. The majority grew angry and exiled him, leading the other Fourierists to abandon the community. This sealed the fate of the endeavor.[90]

In the 1850s, the ideals of Fourier took root in a town that had once accepted the philosophy of Robert Owen. Yellow Springs served as a haven for a utopian venture led by Dr. Thomas L. Nichols and his wife, Mary S. Gove Nichols. In 1856, they founded the Memnonia Institute, whose name referred to the goddess of water, reflecting their support of hydropathy. Hydropathy was a health reform begun in Europe that consisted of purifying the body and curing it through bathing in and exposure to water. In 1851, the couple had established the American Hydropathic Institute, which tried to give legitimacy to hydropathy by establishing a curriculum that included science, medicine, and physiology. The two were career utopianists and reformers, having previously been involved in vegetarianism, phrenology, and Swedenborgianism. In fact, Mary Nichols served as a link between dietary reformers who followed the teachings of Sylvester Graham and hydropathy. In addition to Graham's recommendations for a bland diet of fruit, vegetables, and grain, he advocated bathing and exercise. In their search for a community with hydropathy at the core, the Nicholses had attempted to establish a colony in New York in 1851 but were forced to leave because of their advocacy of free love. The couple moved to Cincinnati and acted on the opportunity to lease the Yellow Springs Water Cure, where they created their institute in Greene County, Ohio. They hoped to establish a "School for Life" that included communitarianism.[91]

The Nicholses faced opposition in the establishment of the community from Horace Mann, the president of Antioch College, also located in Yellow Springs. Mann had earned a reputation as an educational reformer before coming to the new Antioch College in 1853. Antioch opened on new principles: it did not discriminate based on sex or race, and it was not affiliated with a religion. The Nicholses believed that the school's acceptance of different groups would lead them to accept Memnonia. However, Mann did not welcome them with enthusiasm when he learned from a circular that the institute was set to open. Mann feared the colony would promote free love and negatively influence his students. Students had already begun to read the Nicholses' writings, and one left the school because he encountered opposition for selling their works. Local newspapers also raised questions about the couple's plans.[92]

Mann attempted to excite enough opposition to prevent the colony from opening. He organized protests meant to convince the owner of the water cure, Dr. Ehrmann, not to lease it to the Nicholses, but failed in this effort. The Nicholses took possession of the property in July 1856. Almost immediately, the couple began to criticize the college for various reasons. They suggested that Antioch needed to relax the rules pertaining to relations between the sexes. Since Antioch would not work with the institute, the Nicholses wanted to establish their colony as a stronger center of learning.[93]

Just as the Nicholses had advocated a number of reforms throughout their lives, their colony at Yellow Springs embraced many principles advanced by nineteenth-century activists, including spiritualism, free love, socialism, and hydropathy. The couple spoke continuously of establishing Harmony at Memnonia and used Fourierism as the guideline to achieve it. At the heart of all of these doctrines was an optimistic belief in perfectionism, the idea that people could find a perfect state of life. Memnonia would not actually be the perfect state but would prepare people for utopia. In their statement of purpose, they outlined conditions people could expect at Memnonia: universal health, intelligence, wisdom, freedom, individuality, equality in relations, purity, life, and happiness.[94]

Although the idea of free love gained Memnonia much negative attention, the Nicholses did not intend for the colony to become a haven for unregulated sensual pleasure. The couple disclosed some of their ideas in their periodical, the *Nichols' Monthly,* especially in a novel, *Esperanza,* which appeared in the journal in serial form. The novel elaborated on the ideas of the perfect world they wanted to create at Memnonia. Dr. Nichols wrote the novel with help from his wife. The perfect world of Esperanza unfolds through the voice of Frank Wilson, who is led there by a beautiful woman whom he meets while traveling west. Esperanza is located on a tributary of the Mississippi River on rich land. The novel describes the layout of the community, including halls for festivities and science, a library, and a theater. The novel also focuses on the ideas of its leader, Vincent, who represents Thomas Nichols.[95]

Wilson learns about the key to harmony at Esperanza through his love for Melodia, the "beautiful preceptress," and Vincent. This love consists of elements of Christian charity including spirituality, universality, and selflessness. It is not based on sensual passions, but it does include the freedom to have more than one sexual partner without legal or moral restrictions. People do not have to accept only one partner, a practice meant to eliminate the possessiveness of love. Furthermore, women's control over sex prevents any coercion in such relations. Women enter into unions only for the purpose of conceiving a child and aiding the human race. Women adhere to the Law of Progression, which stipulates that sexual relations take place only to fulfill the highest order of humanity: to conceive a child. Women would not waste their time on sex only as a means for physical pleasure. According to the Law of Progression, men and women had to adhere to a ninety-day period of complete continence before engaging in limited sexual contact. In applying these ideas to the institute, the Nicholses practiced not free love based on lust but regulated sexual unions, just as John Humphrey Noyes and his Oneida Community had specific rules about sexual unions as they instituted the practice of complex marriage. The Nicholses' ideas earned the scorn of outsiders, who did not understand their practice of free love, and the ridicule of some members who considered the rules despotic.[96]

The Nicholses attracted people to their colony who had experienced problems in their personal lives, such as unfulfilled love or divorce. Many came from the eastern United States. Those who wanted to live by the principles of Memnonia had to pass first a trial period and then a probationary term. During the probationary period, members had to promise chastity and the quest for perfection. They had to work on overcoming their faults, and other members helped by pointing these out. They bathed on a daily basis, drank only water, and accepted vegetarianism but could consume dairy products and eggs. People could leave Memnonia as they pleased. Because the Nicholses needed money to keep the institute afloat, they also admitted hydropathic patients who wanted an education in the School of Life. The institute offered to members education in languages, math, art, music, science, and other fields. It also offered instruction in the ideas of socialists, including Fourier and Owen.[97]

Spiritualism played a prominent role at Memnonia, and members frequently participated in séances. Mrs. Nichols often received instruction from the spirit world concerning the everyday principles of living that guided the community. These communications from the spirit world ultimately became the undoing of the community.[98]

The beginning of the end of Memnonia occurred before the institute ever opened in September 1856. During a séance, Mrs. Nichols had received the instruction of a Jesuit who told her to learn about the history of the order. She did not follow this instruction. Six months later, another spirit dressed in Jesuit clothing reprimanded her for not listening. She then took action and educated herself about the Jesuits. During this education, she was visited by St. Ignatius of Loyola, the founder of the order, followed by St. Francis Xavier. Both spirits taught her about Catholic doctrine, including baptism, the incarnation and redemption given by Jesus Christ, and the sacrament of Holy Matrimony. After acquiring this information, the Nicholses verified that these were accurate representations of the Catholic faith. Learning that they had received accurate Catholic teachings convinced them to convert to the faith. In March 1857, the rector of St. Xavier College in Cincinnati presided over their conversion. Mrs. Nichols's daughter from a previous marriage, a former member of Memnonia, also entered into the Catholic faith with them. Subsequently, three other former followers joined. Memnonia closed on March 29, 1857, the day of the couple's baptism.[99]

The transformation of the Nicholses from various reforms to Catholicism was definitely remarkable. Yellow Springs was largely a Protestant community, and the Catholic religion did not enjoy widespread popularity during the 1850s. Several religious periodicals, including Catholic and Spiritualist ones, took notice of this fantastic conversion. The Nicholses had traded their communitarian experiment for the centuries-old Catholic Church. They gave up free love for monogamy. Dr. Nichols even began to accept that flirtations could lead to sin. The incredible lives of the Nicholses demonstrated the connections between intellectual currents, reforms, and socialism in the nineteenth century. Their transformation also indicated that anything was possible with the philosophies affecting the nation at the time. Interestingly, the Nicholses remained Catholic until their deaths.[100]

The Fourierist movement had dwindled by the mid-1850s because most phalanxes had failed. A major problem for the movement was that communities did not have a leader to unite them during times of crisis. In addition, the phalanxes in Ohio and other Western states lacked communication with the Eastern supporters. The absence of support partially stemmed from rivalries between the Eastern and Western associations. Elijah Grant of the Ohio Phalanx aspired to leadership of the Western communities by contributing frequently to the *Phalanx*. At the Fourth of July celebration in 1844, Grant offered a toast indicating the importance of a united movement: "We witness with joy the efforts of Associationists, to unite all the Phalanxes in a brotherly union; may a favoring Providence smile upon the design." But the quick dissolution of the Ohio Phalanx ended his efforts. Most of the Fourierist conventions were held in the East, and Western supporters wanted a closer connection with their counterparts. This never developed, and the lack of a national movement helped speed the end of Fourierism.[101]

As communities organized and closed with frequency, Fourierists found themselves moving from one community to another. H. H. Van Amringe, a Pittsburgh lawyer who had helped to introduce millennial thought to the Fourierist movement, joined the Ohio Phalanx. After it closed, he moved to the Trumbull Phalanx, then he went on to the Wisconsin Phalanx and lectured on Fourierism in the West.[102]

The closing of communities prompted Fourierist supporters to defend their philosophy. After the closing of the Ohio Phalanx, the *Phalanx* carried an article stating the failure of any phalanx "would be no argument against the principles of Association, to which they are devoted." The *Phalanx* rationalized this concept: "A thousand failures in the attempt to ignite damp gunpowder would by no means prove the absence of an explosive quality in the compound. Nor should we be surprised, if a social reform, demanding ample capital, scientific organization, and a rare combination of mental and moral powers in its leaders, should meet with temporary obstacles." Leaders of phalanxes, such as Grant, thought differently, however; the ends of their communities signified that Fourierism could not succeed.[103]

Whereas Fourierist and Owenite communities accounted for the largest number of utopias in Ohio, their philosophies did not enjoy a monopoly among the secular communities. Several other havens were established grounded on different principles. The association among utopianists influenced the founding of Rising Star Association in 1853. John S. Patterson founded the community in Stelvideo, Darke County, Ohio, on a large farm he had acquired as his inheritance. Patterson had consulted other utopianists, including Albert Brisbane and Thomas Nichols, in developing the haven. Females in the community adopted the new style of dress introduced by Amelia Bloomer, and the colony earned the name "Bloomertown." Several members relocated to Berlin Heights to join the free-love community after Patterson advocated the practice in his paper, the *Social Revolutionist*. Rising Star disbanded in 1857.[104]

The Free Lovers at Davis House joined together in community between 1854 and 1858 in Berlin Heights, Erie County, Ohio. The estimated thirty members looked different with their long hair and sleekness. They did not support the institution of marriage and declared war against it. Members practiced Spiritualism and free love. They lived on small fruit farms located on one side of the village. When residents of Berlin Heights expressed opposition to the group, members relocated to an area one mile from the village and lived together. The community's short life span probably had much to do with its deviation from the norm and the hostility of non-members to its presence. A year after the breakup of the Free Lovers at Davis House, a group of ten males and ten females reorganized to establish the Industrial Fraternity in 1860. The colony lasted until 1861.[105]

Subsequently, between 1861 and 1866, the Berlin Community, or Christian Republic, comprising twelve adults and six children, existed. Located in Berlin Heights, Erie County, the group supposedly had a connection to the other two havens based on free love at the location, but little information exists about the group.[106]

Just as the antebellum secular utopias must be viewed in the context of the era, the utopian efforts of the late nineteenth century reflect their period. Because of the powerful forces of industrialization and urbanization, reformers attempted to address the economic and social changes in a variety of ways. The Social Gospel Movement led by the Reverend Washington Gladden of Columbus, Ohio, served as the religious response to the transformations. Henry George, in *Progress and Poverty,* published in 1879, offered his solutions to the inequities of the industrial age. In response to the monopoly on valuable land held by big business, he proposed a single tax as a way to redistribute wealth and provide a proper standard of living for all Americans. Edward Bellamy, in *Looking Backward,* published in 1888, provided the United States with its most popular statements on utopian life. Bellamy envisioned a world ruled by nationalism, where community and cooperation defined the social and economic relations among people. People would work according to their abilities and live in social groups. Beyond these ideas, the nation listened to proponents of anarchism, syndicalism, and even anti-Catholicism to understand and offer solutions to the new questions.[107] Jacob Beilhart, a native-born Ohioan, offered his brand of religious philosophy and communitarianism, which received a lot of attention.

In 1899, a utopian haven based upon the religious and communal philosophy of Jacob Beilhart opened. The importance of Beilhart's leadership of the Spirit Fruit Society places the community in the charismatic perfectionist category, according to historian Robert S. Fogarty. Fogarty divides the post–Civil War utopian experiments into three groups based on an assessment of their leaders and members. The charismatic perfectionist communities lasted the longest. The basis of these groups rested on the sanctity of the group or its leader. The "perfectionist" element in the classification refers to the belief that members could achieve perfection in the community. Many of these groups emphasized religious elements and millennial philosophies. Fogarty's other groups are the cooperative colonizers and the political pragmatists. The cooperative colonizers believed they could improve their economic and moral condition by living communally. The political pragmatists hoped to establish an alternative to American democracy, which they believed could not come through the electoral process or through labor unions.[108]

The Spirit Fruit Society began in Ohio, where its leader grew up. Beilhart was born in 1867 in Columbiana County after most of the secular communities in Ohio had disbanded. Ohio still served as home to the religious communities of the Shakers and to Zoar. Beilhart came from a family of ten children. His parents had different religious backgrounds: his mother was a Mennonite, his father was a Lutheran. Born in the duchy of Wurtemberg, the region whence the Zoarites had come, Jacob's father emigrated after the German Revolutions of 1848. The children followed the faith of their father.[109]

Religion served as a guiding force in Beilhart's life. He had received little formal education and devoted his attention to farming. In his teens, he moved to Kansas with a relative. Here, religion came to dominate his life's work. Beilhart converted to Seventh-day Adventism through the influence of the Kansas family for whom he worked. He then served as a preacher and sought converts in California, Ohio, and Kansas. His new faith offered him the chance to obtain a higher education—he attended the Seventh-day Adventist college in Heildsburg, California.[110]

His adherence to Adventism afforded him the opportunity to pursue his aspiration of serving the sick. Beilhart entered into nursing studies at the Seventh-day Adventist Sanitarium in Battle Creek, Michigan. Upon completion of his education, he worked at the sanitarium as a staff nurse. Along with his medical knowledge, Beilhart came to believe that healing had as much to do with prayer as with diet. He prayed for a young girl sick with typhoid who recovered after he had anointed her. This increased his faith in the healing power of prayer and led him to reject the vegetarian diet of the Adventists. He continued in his studies of the Bible and withdrew from his Adventist beliefs. Subsequently, the officials of the sanitarium asked Beilhart to resign.[111]

Before he left, Beilhart underwent a further transformation. He had tended to the needs of C. W. Post, who later became a successful food manufacturer. At the time, Post ran LaVita Inn in Battle Creek, advocating healing through mental suggestion. According to Beilhart, Post led him to a belief in the healing powers of Christian Science. Beilhart's religious development continued as he left Christian Science to study Divine Science, Spiritualism, and Theosophy.[112]

In the 1890s, Beilhart built on his experience and knowledge in different religions to found his own faith, which he called the "Universal Life." Based on several aspects of Christian Science, he admonished jealousy and doubt as significant contributors to poor health; however, he rejected the materialism of Christian Science and claimed that people had to give up their possessions in order to achieve the "Fruit of the Universal Spirit."[113]

Based on his religious philosophy, Beilhart founded a utopia in 1899. While other communities at the time addressed political and economic concerns of the day, Beilhart did not. He sought to create a perfect society among a small group of people and advocated unconventional views such as his lack of acceptance of legal marriage. He encouraged people to achieve their highest natures. This might involve going against mainstream society, because Beilhart believed that convention inhibited the sexes. He wanted men to be men and to free women. His philosophy attracted people because it was liberal and erotic.[114]

Beilhart viewed himself as androgynous, having both male and female qualities. He traced this back to the death of his father when he was six years old. At this time, he grew closer to his mother. His mother influenced him greatly, giving him a feminine sensitivity that he claimed caused much trouble for him. Beilhart stated that his masculine side developed later than his feminine side. In his writings, he seemed to accept homosexuality by paraphrasing quotations from Walt Whitman and making references to the English socialist and homosexual advocate Edward Carpenter. Beilhart described himself as possessing the masculine nature living in the feminine state so that she might be free. Beilhart thought a woman could find her "spirit voice" through her lover and spiritual guide. Such beliefs led Beilhart's utopia to be called a "free love" community.[115]

Beilhart established his community in Lisbon, Ohio, with emphasis on a communal lifestyle and his religious faith. Beilhart had selected a site near his childhood home that offered a good population of Spiritualists from which to draw converts. Also, he purchased land that had access to railroad transportation at an affordable price. To promote the haven, Beilhart published *Spirit Fruit* and later *Spirit's Voice,* which came out each month. Beilhart began the community with his wife of six years, Loruma, their two children, and his sister Mary.[116]

The community grew slowly. In 1901, the state officially recognized the society as a corporation dedicated to showing man how to act on the truths taught by Christ. Subsequently, membership grew, but slowly. Between 1901 and 1904, when the society left Lisbon for Chicago, Illinois, twelve more people joined. The new members came from different places, including Lisbon, South Carolina, and Boston. Four people joined Spirit Fruit from Chicago. Although the new members were diverse—a farmer, a plumber, a teacher, and a physician—they held one characteristic in common. All seemed to have experienced some dramatic personal loss or to lack a sense of belonging in life. Kate Waters, who graduated in 1897 from the University of Chicago and was a trained physician, suffered the sudden loss of her fiancé, a physician, who succumbed to an epidemic disease. She turned first to alcohol and drugs and grew dependent. After ridding herself of the addiction, she joined the faculty of Campbell University in Holton, Kansas. One of her friends had read Beilhart's work and told Waters about it. Fascinated with his beliefs, Waters visited Spirit Fruit and then joined. The community also excited a number of visitors, including future U.S. president Warren G. Harding.[117]

Spirit Fruit did not initially attract a lot of attention. The small group provided for itself and sold agricultural products. Friends contributed gifts to the community as well. Discord did not take over the society as it had in other secular groups, probably because Beilhart served as the leader and made all decisions of consequence.[118]

But the serene existence did not last. Rumors began to circulate that Beilhart's community sanctioned "free love." The sexual practices at Spirit Fruit deviated from the norm, though members did not advocate sexual relations with a variety of partners. Nor did they claim that the importance of sexual pleasure superseded its role in procreation. Beilhart did emphasize tolerance in sexual attitudes. In general, members paired off and formed exclusive relationships, usually for long periods of time. Since the society did not demand legal marriage, members could exit an exclusive relationship and enter another. Beilhart appears to be the only person who had more than one sexual partner at a given time. Throughout several years, Beilhart lived with both his wife and his lover, Virginia Moore, a Lisbon resident. His wife apparently tolerated the affair for a time but ultimately left Beilhart, though they never divorced.[119]

The accusations of free love began when Beilhart's sister Mary had two children by two different fathers, neither of whom she married. In August 1900, she gave birth to Evelyn Gladys, daughter of Ralph Galbreath, and in May 1904, she had a boy, Robert, fathered by Ed Knowdell.[120]

During the controversy over Mary Beilhart's children, another event brought the group under scrutiny. A Mrs. Bailey was reported missing by her husband, Dr. Bailey, a well-known physician from Chicago. Apparently, Mrs. Bailey had traveled east to visit relatives. When she did not return to Chicago, Dr. Bailey hired investigators, who found her at Spirit Fruit. When her family could not convince her to go back home, Dr. Bailey attempted to gain a writ of habeas corpus but failed. He then tried to have the courts declare her mentally unbalanced. After her hearing in Lisbon, she realized her husband was serious about having her declared mentally unstable, so she agreed to go back. On the day she left, Beilhart went to the train station to say goodbye. Dr. Bailey slapped Beilhart in the face several times. Beilhart turned the other cheek for him. Dr. Bailey did no more harm to Beilhart and left with his wife.[121]

The newspapers covered the story of the Baileys, and several large urban newspapers, including the *Cleveland Press* and the *Chicago American,* carried negative articles about Beilhart and Spirit Fruit. They alleged that Beilhart sanctioned free love and communal ownership of everything, including humans, against all American values. Beilhart answered the questions of reporters and seemed to sanction such unaccepted practices as divorce. The Reverend J. P. Anderson of Lisbon's First Presbyterian Society had long tried to force Beilhart out of town and applauded the press coverage. In actuality, the press had exaggerated its accounts in order to sell newspapers. Later, several newspapers apologized for their inaccurate stories. The public had a voracious appetite for learning about the society that had gone against the values of Victorian America.[122]

The press began to portray Spirit Fruit as a society preying on young women. In 1904, Katherine Herbeson, an eighteen-year-old woman who was well educated, talented, and attractive, joined Spirit Fruit. She had heard Beilhart speak in Ohio and wanted to leave the tension at home as her divorced parents competed for control of her. Her father and brother-in-law went to Lisbon to get her to return home. Beilhart did not interfere, but the press blamed the community for abducting or brainwashing young women. The Lisbon newspaper, the *Buckeye State,* carried such articles and began a campaign to force the commune to leave. Feelings ran so high that members feared a mob attack. Residents of Lisbon printed a warning to Spirit Fruit that a mob intended to attack the community and use tar and feathers to scare Beilhart out of town.[123]

Beilhart took the warning seriously and left his Ohio haven for Chicago. He decided to move Spirit Fruit there permanently. As he settled his affairs in Ohio, the press criticized him further as his wife sued for divorce. The press argued that the Spirit Fruit cult could not be right because of the domestic problems it caused.[124]

After leaving its Ohio home, the utopia relocated to Ingleside, Illinois, about forty-five miles northwest of Chicago. The location made sense, as the society hoped to add members from the second largest city in the country. Spirit Fruit had enough funds to purchase ninety acres of land, with access to railroad transportation, from the sale of the Lisbon community and from the donations of Irwin E. Rockwell, the prosperous leader of Idaho Consolidated Mines.[125]

By 1906, the community consisted of eight men and five women. They enjoyed a harmonious relationship in their new home and worked hard constructing the buildings. They also grew crops and raised a dairy herd. The society faltered, however, after the death of its leader. Beilhart died in November 1908, days after emergency surgery to treat appendicitis. Spirit Fruit continued on without its leader for more than twenty-one years, but no one satisfactorily replaced Beilhart. In 1915, the community left Illinois for Santa Cruz County, California. Its new home consisted of eighty acres known as Hilltop Ranch. The economic difficulties helped to weaken the society, and the remaining eleven members disbanded in the 1920s.[126]

The collapse of Spirit Fruit followed the same pattern as those of other groups that relied upon a single leader who sought to attain a perfectionist haven. The society probably enjoyed a long harmonious life because the group was small, with fewer people to please. Also, many of the members shared family and marital bonds.[127]

The number of secular utopias in Ohio in the nineteenth century indicates the influence of new philosophies like those advocated by Robert Owen and Charles Fourier. The new ideas did move people to action, especially during times of economic change and trouble. Without a firm religious base, many of the communities quickly dismantled because of problems arising over financial issues, differences of opinion, and lack of leadership. The antebellum secular utopias missed the strong presence of leaders. In contrast, the Spirit Fruit society of the late nineteenth century had such a leader. Its controversial practices, however, made it unwelcome in Lisbon, and it had to relocate. After the death of its leader, the society failed to thrive. While Ohio provided a home for these ventures, none of them lasted long enough or attained enough influence to effect meaningful change in society.

Conclusion

The Perfect World in Ohio

THROUGHOUT THE NINETEENTH CENTURY, OHIO PROVIDED A home for many communities attempting to establish perfect societies. Ohio attracted so many utopianists because of the availability of cheap land and the cultural diversity of the state, which provided a more tolerant atmosphere. Still, the utopianists did not escape the threat or the wrath of the mob when they deviated too far from the established norms.

Migration patterns affected the prominence of utopias in Ohio as descendents of activist Yankees found their way into Ohio. If western New York was "burned over," the Western Reserve of Ohio found itself "brushed over" as the wildfires of New York spread into her borders with less intensity. The area along the Ohio River near Cincinnati was also greatly affected by communal experiments, indicating that access to transportation routes, along with the social and economic changes affecting the region, contributed to the establishment of utopias. The religious excitement of this region heated up with the Kentucky Revivals of the early nineteenth century. The region also underwent industrial changes in the early part of the century as cotton and woolen mills were opened. These factors made Cincinnati the largest city in the state in the first half of the century, earning it the label "Queen of the West." It was the hub of commercial activity and home to the largest number of immigrants in the state. Its location on the Ohio River made it a thoroughfare for people in search of the perfect world.[1]

The utopianists who came to Ohio had various goals. Some, such as the Shakers, Zoarites, and Mormons, attempted to establish utopias based on religious doctrines. Others, such as the Owenites and Fourierists, looked to secular socialism as the underpinning of their communities. The religious utopianists held a greater commitment to their endeavors because the group was bound by faith. Furthermore, the Shakers, Zoarites, and Mormons had suffered, to various degrees, the disdain of outside society, which made their determination stronger. The persecution the Zoarites had known in Germany gave them resolve to stay together in their Ohio lands. The secular utopianists often disagreed on principles or their interpretations of Owen and Fourier. Since their conversion did not penetrate to the soul, they could walk away from the endeavor without much personal affliction.

Leaders, and the groups' attitudes toward them, were crucial to the success of the utopias. The Shakers had a hierarchical leadership that sustained the various villages even when prominent leaders died. Joseph Bimeler was the guiding hand behind the establishment of Zoar and all of its successes. After his passing, the community went into a steady decline. Joseph Smith, the Mormon Prophet, worked with others who came to Kirtland and joined his flock to weave together a viable religious order. Ohioan Sidney Rigdon and Brigham Young of Vermont proved invaluable to the Mormon success. Smith had enough intelligence to determine when Kirtland and Ohio could help his fledgling religion, and he possessed the acumen to know that the time had come to depart in 1838. After Smith's death at the hands of a mob in Illinois in 1844, Young stepped forward to lead the order. The Owenite and Fourierist communities did not have strong leadership, a factor that contributed to their short life spans. Furthermore, the communities throughout the nation did not establish strong ties with each other. This was markedly different from the close associations among the many Shaker villages throughout the nation. Elders and eldresses frequently visited each other, and the villages cooperated. The secular settlement of Spirit Fruit enjoyed a strong leader in the person of Jacob Beilhart. He was the author of the communal religion of Spirit Fruit. After his death, the community continued to exist but did not evolve and grow.

The attitude toward community property also affected these utopias. The Shakers and the Zoarites succeeded in outlining the functioning of communal ownership of property and shared labor. They also represented the success of utopias in keeping up with invention and industry in the first half of the nineteenth century. Part of the reason for the decline of the Shaker villages and of Zoar in the last half of the nineteenth century was their inattention to changing technology. The secular utopias never seemed to get communal ownership of property right. They put it down on paper in their constitutions, and it sounded plausible. But they were unable to get the members to put communal ownership into practice. Self-interested individuals often could not let go of their inclinations. Without this unique economic factor, little motivation existed for the community to remain in existence.

The utopian communities also experimented with new gender roles. Women in both Shaker villages and at Zoar enjoyed unique positions of participation. In Shaker villages, women held leadership roles over the female sides of the families; however, the average female Shaker did not enjoy decision-making power. Furthermore, women did not have control over the economic wealth of the communities. At Zoar, all women could vote on community affairs, making the average female's participation in government greater than it was in Shaker villages. Again, however, women did not serve as leaders or have control over community property. In theory, women of Owenite communities and Fourierist phalanxes enjoyed greater roles than they did in outside society. They could give their opinions and vote on matters, but men held roles as leaders and controllers of the community wealth. In the Mormon order, women lacked decision-making and economic power. The unique sexual practices of the Mormons also subjected women more to the designs of men.

Along with the different roles for women, the utopianists introduced different concepts of sexual relations. The Shaker villages institutionalized celibacy, and the sexes remained separate to maintain this doctrine. Zoar went through a period where it accepted celibacy, but altered this belief when it went against the personal wishes of Bimeler. The Mormons began to develop the concept of polygamy or plural marriage in Kirtland, and this evolved further after they moved to Utah. Secular utopias often embraced different variations on the idea of free love, although this often meant some regulation regarding sexual activity but without the framework of marriage. The unique relations between the sexes often attracted much attention from the outside world and led to the undoing of some havens, as with the Mormons and the free-love communities.

The combination of religious excitement, reform activity, and economic change in the first half of the nineteenth century shook the nation and moved many to attempt to shape their environment. The northern part of the United States, and Ohio in particular, afforded individuals the opportunity to attempt to create a perfect world on earth. American individualism, economic realities, and lack of leadership were forces too difficult to overcome, and the utopias ceased to exist.

In the late nineteenth century, rapid industrialization swept across the nation, causing vast social changes, and reformers attempted to influence some of them. In Ohio, few looked to utopias as the solution. Some reformers believed they could find answers in the government—by altering it either completely or in part. The combination and intensity of religious, reform, and utopian activity was unique to the nineteenth century. The millennial spirit had not died, but it would never again reach the fervor, intensity, and religious base it had in this century.[2]

Notes

INTRODUCTION

1. Alice Felt Tyler, *Freedom's Ferment: Phases of American Social History from the Colonial Period to the Outbreak of the Civil War* (1944; New York: Harper and Row, 1962), 1; Lawrence Foster, *Religion and Sexuality: Three American Communal Experiments of the Nineteenth Century* (New York: Oxford University Press, 1981), 10–12.

2. Foster, *Religion and Sexuality,* 6; George M. Marsden, *Religion and American Culture* (Fort Worth: Harcourt Brace College Publishers, 1990), 8.

3. Arthur Bestor, *Backwoods Utopias: The Sectarian Origins and the Owenite Phase of Communitarian Socialism in America, 1663–1829* (1953; Philadelphia: University of Pennsylvania Press, 1970), 4; Ronald G. Walters, *American Reformers, 1815–1860* (1978; New York: Hill and Wang, 1987), 39; Foster, *Religion and Sexuality, 6–7.*

4. Bestor, *Backwoods Utopias,* 5; Michael Barkun, *Crucible of the Millennium: The Burned-Over District of New York in the 1840s* (Syracuse: Syracuse University Press, 1986), 63; Walters, *American Reformers,* 40–41; Robert S. Fogarty, *All Things New: American Communes and Utopian Movements, 1860–1914* (Chicago: University of Chicago Press, 1990), 5; Foster, *Religion and Sexuality,* 6.

5. Barkun, *Crucible of Millennium,* 63; Walters, *American Reformers,* 40–41; Fogarty, *All Things New,* 5.

6. Barkun, *Crucible of Millennium,* 70; Grace I. LeMaster, "A Study of the North Union, Ohio, Society of Believers" (M.A. thesis, University of Akron, 1950), 10.

7. Barkun, *Crucible of Millennium,* 64; Walters, *American Reformers,* 73.

8. Barkun, *Crucible of Millennium,* 63; Walters, *American Reformers,* 40.

9. Barkun, *Crucible of Millennium,* 84; Fogarty, *All Things New,* 22–23; Foster, *Religion and Sexuality,* 17.

10. Barkun, *Crucible of Millennium,* 82–83; Bestor, *Backwoods Utopias,* 235; Brian J. L. Berry, *America's Utopian Experiments: Communal Havens from Long-Wave Crises* (Hanover: University Press of New England, 1992), xvi; Fogarty, *All Things New,* 1–2. For a listing of the communities see Robert S. Fogarty, *Dictionary of American Communitarian and Utopian History,* appendix A.

11. Barkun, *Crucible of Millennium,* 63.

12. Barkun, *Crucible of Millennium*, 2–3, 83; Whitney R. Cross, *The Burned-Over District: The Social and Intellectual History of Enthusiastic Religion in Western New York, 1800–1850* (New York: Harper & Row, 1950), ix, 3.

13. Barkun, *Crucible of Millennium*, 85–86; George W. Knepper, *Ohio and Its People* (1989; Kent, Ohio: Kent State University Press, 1997), 50, 58, 178.

14. Knepper, *Ohio*, 112; R. Douglas Hurt, *The Ohio Frontier: Crucible of the Old Northwest, 1720–1830* (Bloomington: Indiana University Press, 1996), xiii.

15. Tyler, *Freedom's Ferment*, 140–41.

16. Knepper, *Ohio*, 179; Tyler, *Freedom's Ferment*, 128–30; Hurt, *Ohio Frontier*, 302, 305.

17. Knepper, *Ohio*, 177; Tyler, *Freedom's Ferment*, 94–95, 98, 106.

18. Berry, *America's Utopian Experiments*, 57; Tyler, *Freedom's Ferment*, 196–98, 200.

19. Berry, *America's Utopian Experiments*, 86; Tyler, *Freedom's Ferment*, 217–18.

20. Berry, *America's Utopian Experiments*, 143.

CHAPTER I

1. Michael Barkun, *Crucible of the Millennium: The Burned-Over District of New York in the 1840s* (Syracuse: Syracuse University Press, 1986), 69–70; Robert S. Fogarty, *Dictionary of American Communal and Utopian History* (Westport, Conn.: Greenwood Press, 1980), xxii; Alice Felt Tyler, *Freedom's Ferment: Phases of American Social History from the Colonial Period to the Outbreak of the Civil War* (1944; New York: Harper and Row, 1962), 141–42.

2. Fogarty, *Dictionary of Utopian History*, 67; Tyler, *Freedom's Ferment*, 142; Lawrence Foster, *Women, Family, and Utopia* (Syracuse: Syracuse University Press, 1991), 63; Lawrence Foster, *Religion and Sexuality: Three American Communal Experiments of the Nineteenth Century* (New York: Oxford University Press, 1981), 24; Ronald G. Walters, *American Reformers, 1815–1860* (1978; New York: Hill and Wang, 1987), 45.

3. Walters, American Reformers, 45; Tyler, *Freedom's Ferment*, 142–43; Fogarty, *Dictionary of Utopian History*, 67; Foster, *Women, Family, and Utopia*, 6; Foster, *Religion and Sexuality*, 25.

4. Tyler, *Freedom's Ferment*, 142–43; Fogarty, *Dictionary of Utopian History*, 67; Walters, *American Reformers*, 45; Barkun, *Crucible of Millennium*, 64.

5. Tyler, *Freedom's Ferment*, 142–43; Walters, *American Reformers*, 45; Barkun, *Crucible of Millennium*, 45; Foster, *Religion and Sexuality*, 27.

6. Tyler, *Freedom's Ferment*, 143–44; Walters, *American Reformers*, 45; Fogarty, *Dictionary of Utopian History*, 67; Foster, *Religion and Sexuality*, 27; Marjorie Procter-Smith, *Women in Shaker Community and Worship: A Feminist Analysis of the Uses of Religious Symbolism* (Lewiston, Maine: Edwin Mellen Press, 1985), 18; for quote, see "Mother's Gospel," 1819 VII, B, v. 242, Shaker Manuscript Collection, MSS 3944, Western Reserve Historical Society, Cleveland, Ohio (hereafter cited as Shaker MSS, WRHS).

7. Tyler, *Freedom's Ferment*, 144; Priscilla J. Brewer, "The Shakers of Mother Ann Lee," in Donald E. Pitzer, ed., *America's Communal Utopias* (Chapel Hill: University of North Carolina Press, 1997), 42.

8. For quote, see "Mother's Gospel," 1819, VII, B, v. 242, Shaker MSS, WRHS; "Covenant of Church at Watervliet," 1814, I, B, v. 74, Shaker MSS, WRHS; Procter-Smith, *Women in Shaker Community,* 43, 47.

9. Tyler, *Freedom's Ferment,* 145; Walters, *American Reformers,* 46; Brewer, "Shakers of Mother Ann," 42–43; Foster, *Religion and Sexuality,* 36; Foster, *Women, Family, and Utopia,* 20.

10. Foster, *Religion and Sexuality,* 28–29, 36; Foster, *Women, Family, and Utopia,* 27; "Covenant of Church at Watervliet," I, B, v. 74 in Shaker MSS, WRHS; Notes by Richard W. Pelham on third edition of *The Testimony of Christ's Second Appearing* (1823), VII, B, v. 243, Shaker MSS, WRHS, 68.

11. Essay on Nature and Character of Jesus Christ by Harvey L. Eads, 1856, 21, 22, 84, VII, B, v. 245, Shaker MSS, WRHS; Barkun, *Crucible of Millennium,* 64; Tyler, *Freedom's Ferment,* 146.

12. Foster, *Religion and Sexuality,* 37.

13. Foster, *Religion and Sexuality,* 38; Tyler, *Freedom's Ferment,* 148.

14. Foster, *Religion and Sexuality,* 26, 29; Brewer, "Shakers of Mother Ann," 44.

15. John P. MacLean, *Shakers of Ohio: Fugitive Papers Concerning the Shakers of Ohio, with Unpublished Manuscripts* (1907; Philadelphia: Porcupine Press, 1975), 19; Procter-Smith, *Women in Shaker Community,* 51–52; Brewer, "Shakers of Mother Ann," 44; Priscilla J. Brewer, *Shaker Communities, Shaker Lives* (Hanover: University Press of New England, 1986), 33–35; Records of Church Family at Union Village, V, B, v. 230, Shaker MSS, WRHS.

16. MacLean, *Shakers of Ohio,* 61, 63–64, 92; for quote, Covenant of the Church of Union Village, 1812, I, B, v. 67, Shaker MSS, WRHS.

17. MacLean, *Shakers of Ohio,* 190, 199.

18. Grace I. LeMaster, "A Study of the North Union, Ohio, Society of Believers" (M.A. thesis, University of Akron, 1950), 13–14, 17; Caroline B. Piercy, *The Valley of God's Pleasure: A Saga of the North Union Shaker Community* (New York: Stratford House, 1951), 9, 16–17; for quote, see "The History of North Union" by James S. Prescott, second edition, VII, B, v. 221, Shaker MSS, WRHS (hereafter Prescott, "History of North Union").

19. LeMaster, "Study of North Union," 14–15; "North Union: A Brief Record of Its Rise and Progress, 1822–1855," V, B, Folder 176, Shaker MSS, WRHS.

20. LeMaster, "Study of North Union," 16–18, 25.

21. MacLean, *Shakers of Ohio,* 230–31.

22. Prescott, "History of North Union," 27; Brian J. Berry, *America's Utopian Experiments: Communal Havens from Long-Wave Crises* (Hanover: University Press of New England, 1992), 37–38; Procter-Smith, *Women in Shaker Community,* 68; Foster, *Women, Family, and Utopia,* 24; Tyler, *Freedom's Ferment,* 149; LeMaster, "Study of North Union," 26–27; Priscilla J. Brewer, "'Tho' of the Weaker Sex': A Reassessment of Gender Equality among the Shakers," in Wendy E. Chmielewski, Louis J. Kern, and Marlyn Klee-Hartzell, eds., *Women in Spiritual and Communitarian Societies in the United States* (Syracuse: Syracuse University Press, 1993), 135.

23. Tyler, *Freedom's Ferment,* 149; LeMaster, "Study of North Union," 10–11, 27.

24. Brewer, "Shakers of Mother Ann," 49; for quote, see Covenant of the Church at Union Village, I, B, v. 67, Shaker MSS, WRHS.

25. Fogarty, *Dictionary of Utopian History,* 93; Barkun, *Crucible of Millennium,* 86–87; "A Sketch of the Life and Religious Experience of Richard W. Pelham, written by himself," VI, B, v. 46, Shaker MSS, WRHS.

26. Testimony of Luther Gould, VI, A, Folder 7, Shaker MSS, WRHS.

27. Barkun, *Crucible of Millennium,* 86–87; James Prescott, General Epistle to all Saints at Watervliet, December 25, 1860, IV. A, Folder 51, Shaker MSS, WRHS; Fogarty, *Dictionary of Utopian History,* 94–95.

28. For quote, see "Account of the Rise and Progress of the Church at North Union, 1822–1886," V, B, Folder 177 (hereafter "Rise of North Union"), Shaker MSS, WRHS; Tyler, *Freedom's Ferment,* 150; Covenant of Church at Union Village, 1812, I, B, v. 67, Shaker MSS, WRHS.

29. LeMaster, "Study of North Union," 24; Prescott, "History of North Union"; Brewer, "Shakers of Mother Ann," 49; Records of Church Family, Union Village, March 31, 1879, V, B, v. 232, Shaker MSS, WRHS.

30. LeMaster, "Study of North Union," 14–15, 31; Tyler, *Freedom's Ferment,* 150; Barkun, *Crucible of Millennium,* 86.

31. For quote, see "Covenant of the Church at Union Village," I, B, v. 67, Shaker MSS, WRHS; Fogarty, *Dictionary of Utopian History,* 93; for quote, see Sketch of Richard Pelham, Shaker MSS, WRHS.

32. Covenant of the Church with signatures, I, B, v. 73; Covenant, 1829, I, B, v. 70, both in Shaker MSS, WRHS; Tyler, *Freedom's Ferment,* 150; Brewer, "Shakers of Mother Ann," 44.

33. Brewer, "Shakers of Mother Ann," 45–46, 48; "A Declaration of the Law and Order of God in the heirship of Children and Youth," I, A, Folder 19, Shaker MSS, WRHS; LeMaster, "Study of North Union," 32–33.

34. MacLean, *Shakers of Ohio,* 379–80.

35. Ibid., 382–84.

36. Procter-Smith, *Women in Shaker Community,* 21.

37. Covenant of Church at Watervliet, 1814, I, B, v. 74; for quotes see, "Covenant of the Church at Union Village," I, B, v. 67, both in Shaker MSS, WRHS; Tyler, *Freedom's Ferment,* 150.

38. Prescott, "History of North Union."

39. Ibid.

40. Copy of an act for the relief and support of women who may be abandoned by their husbands, 1807, I, A, Folder 19, Shaker MSS, WRHS.

41. Ibid.

42. MacLean, *Shakers of Ohio,* 367–68; R. Douglas Hurt, *The Ohio Frontier: Crucible of the Old Northwest* (Bloomington: Indiana University Press, 1996), 295–96.

43. MacLean, *Shakers of Ohio,* 369–70.

44. Ibid., 370–77.

45. Ibid., 377–79.

46. State of Ohio, Warren County, October 8, 1812; Richard Whemar, Affidavit for a Habeas Corpus; Return of the Habeas Corpus, October 14, 1812, all in I, A, Folder 19, Shaker MSS, WRHS.

47. Richard Whemar, Notes from Trial, I, A, Folder 19, Shaker MSS, WRHS.

48. Ibid.

49. Barkun, *Crucible of Millennium,* 86–87.

50. David (North Union) to Ministry, June 12, 1838, IV, A, Folder 51, Shaker MSS, WRHS.

51. Tyler, *Freedom's Ferment,* 147, 150; Covenant of Church at Watervliet, 1814, I, B, v. 74, Shaker MSS, WRHS.

52. Procter-Smith, *Women in Shaker Community,* 40; Prescott, "History of North Union"; Covenant of Church with signatures, I, B, v. 73, Shaker MSS, WRHS.

53. Brewer, *Shaker Communities,* 91; Covenant between William and Robert Wilson and Malcolm Worley, 1806, I, A, Folder 19; Thomas Cohoon Statement, November 2, 1843, I, A, Folder 12; Covenant of the Church at Union Village, 1812, I, B, v. 67; quote see Henry Rickerd statement, November 9, 1846, I, A, Folder 12; see also Susannah Rickert statement in same folder, July 3, 1848, all in Shaker MSS, WRHS.

54. "Law Case Tried at Cleveland, Ohio," I, A, Folder 12, Shaker MSS, WRHS.

55. Ibid.

56. LeMaster, "Study of North Union," 17–21; "Rise of North Union," Shaker MSS, WRHS.

57. Prescott, "History of North Union"; LeMaster, "Study of North Union," 29–30, 43; MacLean, *Shakers of Ohio,* 135.

58. Prescott, "History of North Union"; LeMaster, "Study of North Union," 40–41; Book of Records, 1778–1884, Union Village, I, B, v. 72; Dates of Buildings, Watervliet, I, A, Folder 21, both in Shaker MSS, WRHS.

59. LeMaster, "Study of North Union," 41–42.

60. Ibid., 49–50.

61. Testimony of Chester Risley, December 23, 1843, VI, A, Folder 7; Prescott, "History of North Union," both in Shaker MSS, WRHS.

62. "Rise of North Union"; for quote, see Prescott, "History of North Union," both in Shaker MSS, WRHS; Procter-Smith, *Women in Shaker Community,* 22; Walters, *American Reformers,* 47.

63. Sketch of Richard Pelham; Covenant of the Church at Union Village, 1812, I, B, v. 67, both in Shaker MSS, WRHS; Walters, *American Reformers,* 47; Foster, *Women, Family, and Utopia,* 18.

64. Procter-Smith, *Women in Shaker Community,* 22; Foster, *Women, Family, and Utopia,* 18, 27–28; Karen E. Nickless and Pamela J. Nickless, "Sexual Equality and Economic Authority: The Shaker Experience, 1784–1900," in Wendy E. Chmielewski, Louis J. Kern, and Marlyn Klee-Hartzell, eds., *Women in Spiritual and Communitarian Societies in the United States* (Syracuse: Syracuse University Press, 1993), 123.

65. Nickless and Nickless, "Sexual Equality," 123; LeMaster, "Study of North Union," 25; Procter-Smith, *Women in Shaker Community,* 56–58, 68; Prescott, "History of North Union," Shaker MSS, WRHS.

66. Brewer, *Shaker Community,* 65–68; Foster, *Religion and Sexuality,* 58–59.

67. Foster, *Religion and Sexuality,* 59–60.

68. Foster, *Religion and Sexuality,* 60–61; Archibald Mencham to Rufus Bishop, March 15, 1838, IV, A, Folder 86, Shaker MSS, WRHS.

69. Archibald Mencham to Rufus Bishop, March 15, 1838, IV, A, Folder 86; "North

Union, Brief Record of its Rise and Progress, 1822–1855," V, B, Folder 176, both in Shaker MSS, WRHS; Foster, *Religion and Sexuality,* 61; LeMaster, "Study of North Union," 11–12.

70. LeMaster, "Study of North Union," 55–56, 59; for quote, see Archibald Mencham to Rufus Bishop, March 15, 1838, IV, A, Folder 86, Shaker MSS, WRHS.

71. LeMaster, "Study of North Union," 59; Common place book of Philander C. Cramer, VIII, B, v. 218, Shaker MSS, WRHS.

72. LeMaster, "Study of North Union," 59; "North Union, Brief History of its Rise," V, B, Folder 176, Shaker MSS, WRHS.

73. "Rise of North Union," for quote, see "A Declaration of the Law and Order of God in the Heirship of Children and Youth," 1816, I, A, Folder 19, both in Shaker MSS, WRHS; for quote, see "Children's Order Book," North Union, December 2, 1846, in Shaker Papers, MSS 119, Ohio Historical Society, Columbus, Ohio; Brewer, *Shaker Communities,* 74–76.

74. Brewer, *Shaker Communities,* 74–75; Procter-Smith, *Women in Shaker Community,* 60; "Rise of North Union."

75. Foster, *Religion and Sexuality,* 61; Prescott, "History of North Union"; LeMaster, "Study of North Union," 32; MacLean, *Shakers of Ohio,* 69, 237.

76. LeMaster, "Study of North Union," 32; "Rise of North Union"; Prescott, "History of North Union."

77. Brewer, *Shaker Communities,* 74–76; Foster, *Religion and Sexuality,* 61–62.

78. MacLean, *Shakers of Ohio,* 67, 100, 150; Edward Deming Andrews, *The People Called Shakers: A Search for the Perfect Society* (New York: Oxford University Press, 1953), 266; Military Service, Signed, 1813, I, A, Folder 19, Shaker MSS, WRHS; LeMaster, "Study of North Union," 9–10.

79. Records of Church Family at Union Village, November 17, 1862, V, B, v. 231, Shaker MSS, WRHS.

80. MacLean, *Shakers of Ohio,* 100; Records of Church Family at Union Village, November 12, 1861 and September 3, 1862, V, B, v. 231, Shaker MSS, WRHS.

81. Nickless and Nickless, "Sexual Equality," 120; Foster, *Women, Family, and Utopia,* 26; Procter-Smith, *Women in Shaker Community,* 60–61.

82. Foster, *Religion and Sexuality,* 59; LeMaster, "Study of North Union," 48.

83. LeMaster, "Study of North Union," 48–49; Records of Church Family at Union Village, V, B, v. 232, Shaker MSS, WRHS.

84. Prescott, "History of North Union"; LeMaster, "Study of North Union," 35–37, 39–40.

85. MacLean, *Shakers of Ohio,* 66, 237; Records of Church Family at Union Village, June 5, 1876, October 31, 1876, V, B, v. 232, Shaker MSS, WRHS.

86. MacLean, *Shakers of Ohio,* 97; Prescott, "History of North Union"; LeMaster, "Study of North Union," 35, 43–44.

87. LeMaster, "Study of North Union," 37, 39–40.

88. Records of Church Family at Union Village, December 27, 1876, V, B, v. 232; General Annual Report of Business Conditions, Center Family, North Union, 1881, II, A, Folder 10, both in Shaker MSS, WRHS.

89. Nickless and Nickless, "Sexual Equality," 127; LeMaster, "Study of North Union," 47–48.

90. Nickless and Nickless, "Sexual Equality," 127; LeMaster, "Study of North Union," 45–46; Charles O. Lee, "The Shakers as Pioneers in the American Herb and Drug Industry," unpublished paper, 1959, MSS qL477RMV, Cincinnati Historical Society, Cincinnati, Ohio.

91. Journal of Accounts pertaining to Mill Family, 1845–1868, North Union, II, B, v. 46; Shaker MSS, WRHS; LeMaster, "Study of North Union," 46–47; MacLean, *Shakers of Ohio,* 101.

92. Journal of Accounts Pertaining to Mill Family, North Union, II, B, v. 46; Records of Church Family at Union Village, June 15, 1876, July 12, 1876, V, B, v. 232, both in Shaker MSS, WRHS.

93. Procter-Smith, *Women in Shaker Community,* 66–68; East Family Sisters Cash Account, North Union, II, A, Folder 10; Center Family Sisters Account, North Union, II, A, Folder 10, both in Shaker MSS, WRHS; Nickless and Nickless, "Sexual Equality," 119, 128.

94. Nickless and Nickless, "Sexual Equality," 124–26; Frederick William Evans, *Autobiography of a Shaker and Revelation of the Apocalypse* (1888; New York: AMS Press, 1973), 14–17.

95. Ibid., 129–30; Andrews, *People Called Shakers,* 230.

96. Brewer, *Shaker Communities,* 74.

97. Inspired Writings, North Union, 1841, VIII, B, v. 205, Shaker Papers, WRHS; Prescott, "History of North Union."

98. James S. Prescott, "Report on Convention of Shakers and Spiritualists in Cleveland, Ohio, 1871," VII, A, Folder 16, Shaker MSS, WRHS.

99. Clarke Garrett, *Spirit Possession and Popular Religion: From the Camisards to the Shakers* (Baltimore: Johns Hopkins University Press, 1987), 154–55, 195–96.

100. Nickless and Nickless, "Sexual Equality," 124; Unnamed to Brother Rufus Bishop, February 25, 1835, IV, A, Folder 51, Shaker MSS, WRHS.

101. Brewer, *Shaker Communities,* 115.

102. Ibid., 116.

103. Jean M. Humez, ed., *Mother's First-Born Daughters: Early Shaker Writings on Women and Religion* (Bloomington: Indiana University Press, 1993), 210–11; Brewer, *Shaker Communities,* 115–16.

104. MacLean, *Shakers of Ohio,* 93–94

105. Ibid., 93; "North Union, Brief Record of Its Rise and Progress, 1822–1855," V, B, Folder 176; "Rise of North Union," both in Shaker MSS, WRHS.

106. John P. Root, December 20, 1843, VII, A, Folder 16, Shaker MSS, WRHS.

107. Records of Church Family at Union Village, V, B, v. 230, Shaker MSS, WRHS.

108. Inspired Writings, VIII, B, v. 205, Shaker MSS, WRHS.

109. Brewer, *Shaker Communities,* 122; Inspired Writings, VIII, B, v. 205, 207, Shaker MSS, WRHS.

110. Inspired Writings, VIII, B, v. 205, 207, 209 Shaker MSS, WRHS; Brewer, *Shaker Communities,* 122–23.

111. Inspired Writings, VIII, B, v. 283, Shaker MSS, WRHS.

112. Inspired Messages, 1845, VIII, A, Folder 48, Shaker MSS, WRHS.

113. Brewer, *Shaker Communities,* 124–25, 131–33; MacLean, *Shakers of Ohio,* 93; Walters, *American Reformers,* 148.

114. George W. Knepper, *Ohio and Its People* (1989; Kent, Ohio: Kent State University Press, 1997), 177; MacLean, *Shakers of Ohio*, 97.

115. Brewer, *Shaker Communities*, 153–54; Walters, *American Reformers*, 163–65; "Rise of North Union"; Records of Church Family at Union Village, February 4, 1850, V, B, v. 230, both in Shaker MSS, WRHS.

116. Brewer, "Shakers of Mother Ann," 48; for quote, see O. C. Hampton for Eldress Lydia Cramer to Eldress Lydia Dole, June 18, 1882, IV, A, Folder 51, Shaker MSS, WRHS.

117. Brewer, "Shakers of Mother Ann," 48.

118. Prescott, "Report of Convention of Shakers and Spiritualists in Cleveland, Ohio, 1871," VII, A, Folder 16, Shaker MSS, WRHS.

119. Ibid.

120. Brewer, *Shaker Communities*, 204–5.

121. LeMaster, "Study of North Union," 50–52.

122. Methodist Home for the Aged, July 30, 1909, I, A, Folder 19, Shaker MSS, WRHS.

123. Brewer, "Shakers of Mother Ann," 49.

CHAPTER 2

1. Edgar B. Nixon, "The Society of Separatists of Zoar" (Ph.D. diss., Ohio State University, 1933), 2–3, 5; Emilius O. Randall, *History of the Zoar Society from Its Commencement to Its Conclusion; a Sociological Study in Communism* (1904; New York: AMS Press, 1971), 2–3; Hilda Dischinger Morhart, *The Zoar Story* (1968; Dover, Ohio: Seibert Printing, 1969), 11.

2. Randall, *History of Zoar*, 2–3; Nixon, "Society of Separatists," 5–6; Morhart, *Zoar Story*, 11.

3. Nixon, "Society of Separatists," 4–5; Ohio Historical Society, *Zoar: An Ohio Experiment in Communalism* (Columbus: Ohio Historical Society, 1970), 13.

4. Randall, *History of Zoar*, 4.

5. Morhart, *Zoar Story*, 12; Nixon, "Society of Separatists," 9–12.

6. Nixon, "Society of Separatists," 7–9; Morhart, *Zoar Story*, 12.

7. Ibid., 13–14.

8. Ibid., 15–17; Petition of Separatists to the Royal Minister of the Interior of Wurtemberg, May 20, 1816, in Zoar Papers, MSS 110, Ohio Historical Society, Columbus, Ohio (hereafter Zoar Papers, OHS).

9. Nixon, "Society of Separatists," 6–7, 17–18; Randall, *History of Zoar*, 5; Ohio Historical Society, *Zoar*, 14.

10. Morhart, *Zoar Story*, 14; Randall, *History of Zoar*, 5, Catherine R. Dobbs, *Freedom's Will: The Society of the Separatists of Zoar: An Historical Adventure of Religious Communism in Early Ohio* (New York: William Frederick Press, 1947), 16; Nixon, "Society of Separatists," 18; Robert S. Fogarty, *Dictionary of American Communal and Utopian History* (Westport, Conn.: Greenwood Press, 1980), 14. Bimeler is the English version of the name Baumler, by which he was originally known.

11. Randall, *History of Zoar,* 5; Thomas P. Cope to Thomas Rotch and George Brantingham, February 6, 1818, typescript; John James to J. Michael Baumler, November 30, 1818, both in Zoar Papers, OHS.

12. Morhart, *Zoar Story,* 14; Randall, *History of Zoar,* 14; Nixon, "Society of Separatists," 20–21; Thomas P. Cope to Thomas Rotch and George Brantingham, typescript, February 6, 1818; Thomas P. Cope to Thomas Rotch, copy, both in Zoar Papers, OHS.

13. Nixon, "Society of Separatists," 21–22.

14. Thomas P. Cope to Thomas Rotch and George Brantingham, February 6, 1818, typescript, Zoar MSS, OHS.

15. Nixon, "Society of Separatists," 22; Randall, *History of Zoar,* 6; Ohio Historical Society, *Zoar,* 17.

16. Nixon, "Society of Separatists," 24; Randall, *History of Zoar,* 6.

17. Hanna Fisher to Thomas Rotch, March 16, 1818, Zoar MSS, OHS; Randall, *History of Zoar,* 6; Nixon, "Society of Separatists," 24; Philip E. Webber, "Jakob Sylvan's preface to the Zoarite Anthology *Die Wahre Separation, oder die Widergeburt* as an introduction to un(der)studied separatist principles," *Communal Societies* 19 (1999), 107–8.

18. Thomas P. Cope to Thomas Rotch, June 4, 1818, typescript; Thomas Rotch to the German Separatists, undated, typescript; J. M. Bimeler to the Community of Friends, July 14, 1818, typescript translation, all in Zoar MSS, OHS; Nixon, "Society of Separatists," 24–26.

19. Nixon, "Society of Separatists," 26–28; *The Nugitna,* January 27, 1896, in Randall, *History of Zoar,* 59–60; Ohio Historical Society, *Zoar,* 18.

20. Nixon, "Society of Separatists," 28–29; Randall, *History of Zoar,* 7–11; Dobbs, *Freedom's Will,* 43. A translated copy of the original Constitution, written in German, can be found in Randall, *History of Zoar,* 8–10, and Nixon, "Society of Separatists," 238–43. The original Articles of Association, April 19, 1819, are in German in Zoar MSS, OHS.

21. Nixon, "Society of Separatists," 29–30; Articles of Association, 1819, in Randall, *History of Zoar,* 8–10.

22. Articles of Association, 1819, in Randall, *History of Zoar,* 8–11.

23. Articles of Association, 1819, in Randall, *History of Zoar,* 8–11; Nixon, "Society of Separatists," 238–43.

24. Articles of Association, 1819, in Randall, *History of Zoar,* 9–10, 84–85; Nixon, "Society of Separatists," 243. The original Articles of Agreement, October 14, 1833, are in German in Zoar MSS, OHS. Translations appear in Randall, *History of Zoar,* 88–96, and Nixon, "Society of Separatists," 243–51.

25. Randall, *History of Zoar,* 10–11; Articles of Agreement, 1833, in Nixon, "Society of Separatists," 248.

26. Randall, *History of Zoar,* 11–13; Articles of Agreement, 1833, in Nixon, "Society of Separatists," 244, 246, 247, 249.

27. Randall, *History of Zoar,* 95–96; Nixon, "Society of Separatists," 56–58, 247, 250.

28. Articles of Agreement, 1833, in Nixon, "Society of Separatists," 249.

29. Ibid., 250.

30. Nixon, "Society of Separatists," 30–31.

31. Randall, *History of Zoar,* 13–14.

32. Ibid., 16, 18.

33. Randall, *History of Zoar,* 14, 16–18; Nixon, "Society of Separatists," 101–2.

34. Randall, *History of Zoar,* 17–19.

35. Ibid., 17–18, 21–22.

36. Ibid., 20; Nixon, "Society of Separatists," 33–34.

37. Randall, *History of Zoar,* 20.

38. Ibid.; Nixon, "Society of Separatists," 35, 83–84.

39. Membership Applications, Nixon Family Papers, MSS 680, Ohio Historical Society, Columbus, Ohio (hereafter Nixon Papers, OHS).

40. Edgar B. Nixon, "The Zoar Society: Applicants for Membership," *Ohio State Archaeological and Historical Quarterly* 45 (January 1936), 342; Nixon, "Society of Separatists," 168; Randall, *History of Zoar,* 11.

41. Randall, *History of Zoar,* 11; Nixon, "Zoar Society," 343, 345.

42. Nixon, "Zoar Society," 344–45, 348, 350; Nixon, "Society of Separatists," 179; Carl Archut, April 25, 1876; Karl Gustav Andler, April 22, 1875, translation, both in Nixon Papers, OHS.

43. A. J. Randall to Ackerman, November 30, 1872, in Nixon Papers, OHS: Nixon, "Zoar Society," 350.

44. Nixon, "Zoar Society," 343, 346.

45. Nixon, "Society of Separatists," 51–53.

46. Ibid., 31–32; Ohio Historical Society, *Zoar,* 29; Accounting Information for blacksmith shop, sawmill, in Zoar MSS, OHS.

47. George W. Knepper, *Ohio and Its People* (1989; Kent, Ohio: Kent State University Press, 1997), 149–51, 153; Nixon, "Society of Separatists," 36; James Robertson to Joseph Bimeler, June 11, 1834, Society of Separatists of Zoar Records, MSS 1663, Western Reserve Historical Society, Cleveland, Ohio (hereafter Zoar Papers, WRHS); Ohio Historical Society, *Zoar,* 30–31; Morhart, *Zoar Story,* 25; Proceedings of Meeting regarding Canal, December 11, 1833, Nixon Papers, OHS.

48. Nixon, "Society of Separatists," 36; Ohio Historical Society, *Zoar,* 29, 31; Morhart, *Zoar Story,* 26; Ledger for Zoar Canal Mill, Zoar MSS, OHS.

49. Morhart, *Zoar Story,* 26; Nixon, "Society of Separatists," 38–39.

50. Ohio Historical Society, *Zoar,* 27; Nixon, "Society of Separatists," 85–86, 119–20, 129; Randall, *History of Zoar,* 32–33; J. M. Bimeler to Lewis F. Birk, May 3, 1845, Nixon Papers, OHS.

51. Ohio Historical Society, *Zoar,* 29; Nixon, "Society of Separatists," 71–72; Accounting Information for team and farm, Zoar Papers, WRHS; Morhart, *Zoar Story,* 61.

52. Nixon, "Society of Separatists," 136–39, 141; Furnace Account Book, Zoar Papers, WRHS; J. M. Bimeler to Lewis F. Birk, May 3, 1845, Nixon Papers, OHS.

53. Ohio Historical Society, *Zoar,* 29–30; Nixon, "Society of Separatists," 63, 145–46.

54. Ohio Historical Society, Zoar, 27; Brewers' Record of Fermented Liquors, 1870–1873, 1875–1877, 1882–1884, Zoar MSS, OHS; Morhart, *Zoar Story,* 116; Nixon, "Society of Separatists," 72, 130; Randall, *History of Zoar,* 40.

55. Unlabeled Journal of Accounts, January 1880–December 1894, Zoar MSS, OHS; William Brehm to C. Wiebel, undated, Nixon Papers, OHS; Ohio Historical Society, *Zoar,* 32; Randall, *History of Zoar,* 36.

56. Ohio Historical Society, *Zoar,* 32–33; J. M. Bimeler (by C. Weebel) to Peter Kaufmann, undated and June 8, 1844; J. M. Bimeler (by Lewis F. Birk) to Peter Kaufmann, February 14, 1845, both in Peter Kaufmann Papers, MSS 136, Ohio Historical Society, Columbus, Ohio (hereafter Kaufmann Papers, OHS); W. L. J. Kinderlen to Ludwig Birk, December 15, 1850, in Nixon Papers, OHS.

57. Ohio Historical Society, *Zoar,* 33; Miscellaneous Letters and Documents, Zoar Papers, WRHS.

58. Nixon, "Society of Separatists," 148–49, 226–27; Randall, *History of Zoar,* 70.

59. Nixon, "Society of Separatists," 65, 67, 69, 77; Randall, *History of Zoar,* 35.

60. Nixon, "Society of Separatists," 124–25.

61. Randall, *History of Zoar,* 35.

62. Ludwig F. Birk to Christian Bauer, July 21, 1848, in Nixon Papers, OHS.

63. Nixon, "Society of Separatists," 74–76.

64. Ibid.

65. Randall, *History of Zoar,* 20–21; Contract of Thomas White, 1836, in Nixon Papers, OHS; Webber, "Jakob Sylvan's preface," 103.

66. Nixon, "Society of Separatists," 77–78, 82–83, 87–89; Randall, *History of Zoar,* 37.

67. Randall, *History of Zoar,* 32–35.

68. Nixon, "Society of Separatists," 188–90.

69. Randall, *History of Zoar,* 23.

70. Nixon, "Society of Separatists," 191–93; Goesele v. Bimeler, typescript notes, in Nixon Papers, OHS.

71. Ibid., 193–95.

72. Ibid., 195.

73. Goesele et al. v. Bimeler et al. in Nixon Papers, OHS; Randall, *History of Zoar,* 23.

74. Randall, *History of Zoar,* 24–26; Goesele v. Bimeler, typescript, in Nixon Papers, OHS.

75. Randall, *History of Zoar,* 27–29.

76. Goesele et al. v. Bimeler et al. in Nixon Papers, OHS.

77. Goesele et al. v. Bimeler et al., Supreme Court of the United States, December 1852, in Zoar MSS, OHS.

78. Randall, *History of Zoar,* 30–31.

79. Randall, *History of Zoar,* 33–34; Nixon, "Society of Separatists," 93.

80. Nixon, "Society of Separatists," 200.

81. Ibid., 44, 114.

82. Nixon, "Society of Separatists," 117–18, 132; Memorandum of articles furnished soldiers now in Potomac Army, Zoar MSS, OHS.

83. Randall, *History of Zoar,* 35–36.

84. Nixon, "Society of Separatists," 201, 206–7.

85. Ibid., 206–8, 210; Alexander Gunn, *The Hermitage-Zoar notebook and journal of travel* (New York, 1902), 51.

86. Ohio Historical Society, *Zoar,* 68–70; Nixon, "Society of Separatists," 208–13.

87. Nixon, "Society of Separatists," 213–16.

88. Ibid., 218; Randall, *History of Zoar,* 51–52; Railroad Item, January 1, 1854, in Nixon Papers, OHS; Ohio Historical Society, *Zoar,* 63, 66.

89. Randall, *History of Zoar,* 53–54; *Nugitna,* December 30, 1895, in Randall, *History of Zoar,* 55–57; Ohio Historical Society, *Zoar,* 71.

90. *Nugitna,* January 27, 1896, February 24, 1896, March 23, 1896, in Randall, *History of Zoar,* 59–68.

91. Nixon, "Society of Separatists," 225.

92. An Agreement recorded in Tuscarawas County Deed Records, November 9, 1900, Zoar MSS, OHS.

93. Nixon, "Society of Separatists," 226–28; Randall, *History of Zoar,* 69–70, 100–105.

94. Nixon, "Society of Separatists," 228–30; Randall, *History of Zoar,* 71–72.

CHAPTER 3

1. Anne B. Prusha, *A History of Kirtland, Ohio* (Mentor, Ohio: Lakeland Community College Press, 1982), 38; Alice Felt Tyler, *Freedom's Ferment: Phases of American Social History from the Colonial Period to the Outbreak of the Civil War* (1944; New York: Harper and Row, 1962), 86.

2. Richard L. Bushman, *Joseph Smith and the Beginnings of Mormonism* (Urbana: University of Illinois Press, 1984), 18, 30, 36, 40; Tyler, *Freedom's Ferment,* 86.

3. Fawn M. Brodie, *No Man Knows My History: The Life of Joseph Smith, the Mormon Prophet* (1945; New York: Alfred A. Knopf, 1971), 10; Bushman, *Joseph Smith,* 43, 45, 47; Brian J. L. Berry, *America's Utopian Experiments: Communal Havens from Long-Wave Crises* (Hanover: University Press of New England, 1992), 64.

4. Bushman, *Joseph Smith,* 48–51, 54; Brodie, *No Man Knows,* 5, 16, 18, 34–35; Berry, *America's Utopian Experiments,* 64.

5. Brodie, *No Man Knows,* 21–23.

6. Berry, *America's Utopian Experiments,* 64; Bushman, *Joseph Smith,* 56–57, 61–62.

7. Berry, *America's Utopian Experiments,* 64; Bushman, *Joseph Smith,* 62–63.

8. Berry, *America's Utopian Experiments,* 64; Bushman, *Joseph Smith,* 63–64.

9. Berry, *America's Utopian Experiments,* 64–65; Brodie, *No Man Knows,* 43.

10. Bushman, *Joseph Smith,* 107–11, 119.

11. Berry, *America's Utopian Experiments,* 65.

12. Bushman, *Joseph Smith,* 143–44, 149, 151.

13. Ibid., 120–21, 170; Prusha, *Kirtland,* 40.

14. Bushman, *Joseph Smith,* 149–50.

15. Berry, *America's Utopian Experiments,* 48–49, 67; Prusha, *Kirtland,* 39–41; Brodie, *No Man Knows,* 94.

16. *Painesville Telegraph,* November 16, 1830; Brodie, *No Man Knows,* 95.

17. Prusha, *Kirtland,* 41–42.

18. Berry, *America's Utopian Experiments,* 67; F. Mark McKiernan, *The Voice of One Crying in the Wilderness: Sidney Rigdon, Religious Reformer, 1793–1876* (1971; Independence, Mo.: Herald House, 1979), 33–34; for quote, see "Mormonism" manuscript in A. C. Williams Papers, MSS 593, Western Reserve Historical Society, Cleveland, Ohio (hereafter Williams Papers, WRHS).

19. Bushman, *Joseph Smith,* 173–74.

20. Ibid., 179; B. Fowles, Copy of typescript letter to Postmaster at Kirtland, Ohio, with some reminiscences of Joseph Smith and Mormon Temple at Kirtland, 1946, MSS Vertical File F, Western Reserve Historical Society, Cleveland, Ohio (hereafter Fowles MSS, WRHS).

21. Brodie, *No Man Knows,* 99.

22. Brodie, *No Man Knows,* 97; "Mormonism" in Williams Papers, WRHS; Max H. Parkin, "Conflict at Kirtland: A Study of the Nature and Causes of External and Internal Conflict of the Mormons in Ohio between 1830 and 1838" (M.A. thesis, University of Utah, 1966), 97.

23. Parkin, "Conflict at Kirtland," 47, 99; McKiernan, *Voice of One,* 48–49; Prusha, *Kirtland,* 42–43.

24. Prusha, *Kirtland,* 41–42, 59; Wesley Perkins to Jacob Perkins, February 11, 1832, MSS Vertical File P, Western Reserve Historical Society, Cleveland, Ohio.

25. *Cleveland Herald,* November 25, 1830; *Painesville Telegraph,* November 16, 1830; March 22, 1831.

26. McKiernan, *Voice of One,* 27–28, 41.

27. Bushman, *Joseph Smith,* 181–82.

28. Ibid., 125–27, 1818; Prusha, *Kirtland,* 39, 41.

29. Bushman, *Joseph Smith,* 140–41, 151.

30. Lucia A. Goldsmith, Sidney Rigdon, the first Mormon Elder MSS, Vertical File G, Western Reserve Historical Society, Cleveland, Ohio (hereafter Goldsmith MSS, WRHS); "Mormonism" in Williams Papers, WRHS.

31. "Mormonism" in Williams Papers, WRHS.

32. Brodie, *No Man Knows,* 108, 110, 114–15.

33. Prusha, *Kirtland,* 43; Fowles MSS, WRHS.

34. Prusha, *Kirtland,* 43.

35. Prusha, *Kirtland,* 42–44; Brodie, *No Man Knows,* 119–20.

36. Brodie, *No Man Knows,* 120.

37. Ibid., 124–25.

38. Prusha, *Kirtland,* 44.

39. For quote, see C. C. Goodwin, "The Truth about Mormons," 1899, in Williams Papers, WRHS; "Kirtland Temple" in *Historic American Buildings,* no. 6, Alfred Mewett Papers, MSS 3124, Container 11, Western Reserve Historical Society, Cleveland, Ohio (hereafter Mewett Papers, WRHS), 178.

40. Fowles MSS, WRHS.

41. "Kirtland Temple," 178 in Mewett Papers, WRHS; Parkin, "Conflict at Kirtland," 201–2.

42. "Kirtland Temple," 178, in Mewett Papers, WRHS; Prusha, *Kirtland,* 45–46, 60.

43. Goldsmith MSS, WRHS.

44. "Kirtland Temple," 179, in Mewett Papers, WRHS.

45. Parkin, "Conflict at Kirtland," 84–85; Brodie, *No Man Knows,* 178–80.

46. "Kirtland Temple," 178, in Mewett Papers, WRHS; Prusha, *Kirtland,* 49.

47. Brodie, *No Man Knows,* 128.

48. Prusha, *Kirtland,* 58.

49. Ibid., 47; Brodie, *No Man Knows,* 131–38.

50. Brodie, *No Man Knows,* 135, 146–58; Milton V. Backman Jr., *A Profile of Latter-Day Saints of Kirtland, Ohio, and Members of Zion's Camp, Vital Statistics and Sources* (Provo, Utah: Brigham Young University, 1983), vii.

51. Brodie, *No Man Knows,* 140–41.

52. Prusha, *Kirtland,* 48, 59–60; *Painesville Telegraph,* January 31, 1834.

53. Parkin, "Conflict at Kirtland," 122–23; Bushman, *Joseph Smith,* 126–27.

54. Parkin, "Conflict at Kirtland," 125–26; Prusha, *Kirtland,* 41, 59–60; *Painesville Telegraph,* January 31, 1834.

55. Undated, Untitled History of Mormonism, in Williams Papers, WRHS.

56. "Mormonism," in Williams Papers, WRHS.

57. Berry, *America's Utopian Experiments,* 69; Prusha, *Kirtland,* 48; Bushman, *Joseph Smith,* 183; Goldsmith MSS, WRHS.

58. Brodie, *No Man Knows,* 182–86, 458–59; Parkin, "Conflict at Kirtland," 166–67; Lawrence Foster, *Religion and Sexuality: Three American Communal Experiments of the Nineteenth Century* (New York: Oxford University Press, 1981), 139, 145–46.

59. Brodie, *No Man Knows,* 182–86; Prusha, *Kirtland,* 55; Goldsmith MSS, WRHS.

60. Brodie, *No Man Knows,* 182–83; Prusha, *Kirtland,* 56.

61. Prusha, *Kirtland,* 56; Foster, *Religion and Sexuality,* 139, 145–46.

62. Brodie, *No Man Knows,* 203.

63. Parkin, "Conflict at Kirtland," 191–93.

64. Ibid., 196–97.

65. Brodie, *No Man Knows,* 169–73.

66. Ibid., 166–67.

67. Prusha, *Kirtland,* 61; Brodie, *No Man Knows,* 188–89.

68. Prusha, *Kirtland,* 58; "Mormonism" in Williams Papers, WRHS; Berry, *America's Utopian Experiments,* 49, 69; *Painesville Telegraph,* February 24, 1837.

69. Berry, *America's Utopian Experiments,* 49, 69; Promissory Notes, September 1, 1837, and January 30, 1838, of Joseph Smith, Sidney Rigdon, Oliver Cowdery, Brigham Young, Hyrum Smith, and other notables of the Church of Jesus Christ of the Latter Day Saints, Joseph Smith Papers, VFM, MSS 1431, Ohio Historical Society, Columbus, Ohio.

70. Prusha, *Kirtland,* 64; "Kirtland Temple," 178 in Mewett Papers, WRHS.

71. *Painesville Telegraph,* June 30, 1837; Brodie, *No Man Knows,* 203.

72. Berry, *America's Utopian Experiments,* 49, 69; Prusha, *Kirtland,* 65–66.

73. Backman, *A Profile of Latter-Day Saints,* vii; Prusha, Kirtland, 67; Brodie, *No Man Knows,* 205–7.

74. Parkin, "Conflict at Kirtland, 329; Tyler, *Freedom's Ferment,* 106–7.

75. "Kirtland Temple," 178 in Mewett Papers, WRHS.

CHAPTER 4

1. Alice Felt Tyler, *Freedom's Ferment: Phases of American Social History from the Colonial Period to the Outbreak of the Civil War* (1944; New York: Harper and Row, 1962),

196–97; Ronald G. Walters, *American Reformers, 1815–1860* (New York: Hill and Wang, 1978), 64.

2. Walters, *American Reformers,* 61–62; Brian J. L. Berry, *America's Utopian Experiments: Communal Havens from Long-Wave Crises* (Hanover: University Press of New England, 1992), 56–57.

3. Walters, *American Reformers,* 62; Berry, *America's Utopian Experiments,* 57.

4. Walters, *American Reformers,* 62–63; Berry, *America's Utopian Experiments,* 57.

5. Walters, *American Reformers,* 63.

6. Berry, *America's Utopian Experiments,* 58; Richard J. Cherok, "No Harmony in Kendal: The Rise and Fall of an Owenite Community, 1825–1829," in *Ohio History* 108 (winter–spring 1999), 26.

7. Walters, *American Reformers,* 64.

8. Tyler, *Freedom's Ferment,* 198–99.

9. Ibid., 200; Berry, *America's Utopian Experiments,* 60.

10. Walters, *American Reformers,* 66–67.

11. Berry, *America's Utopian Experiments,* 57.

12. Ibid., 56, 63.

13. Ophia D. Smith, "The Beginnings of the New Jerusalem Church in Ohio," in *Ohio Archaeological and Historical Quarterly* 61 (1952), 236, 238, 239, 250–51; Don Hutslar, "Yellow Springs once home of 'unharmounious' commune," in *Echoes* 37 (August 1998), 5.

14. Smith, "Beginnings," 251–53; Hutslar, "Yellow Springs," 5.

15. Hutslar, "Yellow Springs," 5–6; Smith, "Beginnings," 252–53; Robert S. Fogarty, *Dictionary of American Communal and Utopian History* (Westport, Conn.: Greenwood Press, 1980), 179.

16. Smith, "Beginnings," 252–54; Hutslar, "Yellow Springs," 6; Fogarty, *Dictionary of Utopian History,* 151–52.

17. Fogarty, *Dictionary of Utopian History,* 180; Wendall P. Fox, "The Kendal Community," in *Ohio Archaeological and Historical Publications* 20 (April–July 1911), 177. The Fox article includes the reprinted manuscript of the Kendal Constitution and also records of the Society's meetings.

18. Constitution of the Friendly Association for Mutual Interests at Kendal, Ohio, in Fox, "Kendal," 179; Cherok, "No Harmony," 28–29.

19. Constitution for Kendal in Fox, "Kendal," 181–82.

20. Consitution for Kendal and Reports of Meetings, August 19, 1826, May 5, 19, 1827, in Fox, "Kendal," 179, 181–82, 187, 196.

21. Reports of Meetings, August 19, 1826, in Fox, "Kendal," 186–88.

22. Constitution for Kendal and Reports of Meetings, August 19, 1826, in Fox, "Kendal," 181, 188–89.

23. Reports of Meetings, May 18, 1826, August 7, 19, 1826, January 2, 1827, April 19, 1827, in Fox, "Kendal," 184–85, 189, 191, 194.

24. Reports of Meetings, April 19, 1827, December 22, 1827, in Fox, "Kendal," 194, 202–3.

25. Reports of Meetings, April 19, 1827, May 19, 1827, in Fox, "Kendal," 194–95, 197.

26. Reports of Meetings, April 27, 1828, in Fox, "Kendal," 209–10.

27. Preface, Constitution for Kendal, and Reports of Meetings, August 19, 1826, in Fox, "Kendal," 177, 180, 186; Cherok, "No Harmony," 34.

28. Cherok, "No Harmony," 32–34.

29. Cherok, "No Harmony," 31; Reports of Meetings, February 10, 1827, March 31, 1827, in Fox, "Kendal," 192–93.

30. Inventory of Property, Improvements in Property, Schedule of Debts, Value of Household Goods, in Fox, "Kendal," 216–19; Cherok, "No Harmony," 34–35.

31. Reports of Meetings, May 24, 1828, July 26, 1828, September 10, 11, 1828, October 5, 6, 1828, in Fox, "Kendal," 211–13.

32. Reports of Meetings, October 11, 12, 1828, January 1, 3, 6, 1829, in Fox, "Kendal," 214–16.

33. Cherok, "No Harmony," 28, 37–38.

34. Fogarty, *Dictionary of Utopian History,* 192.

35. Berry, *America's Utopian Experiments,* 62–63.

36. Ibid., 63.

37. Ibid.

38. Ibid., 84–85, 87; Carl J. Guarneri, *The Utopian Alternative: Fourierism in Nineteenth-Century America* (Ithaca, New York: Cornell University Press, 1991), 17.

39. Walters, *American Reformers,* 69–70; Berry, *America's Utopian Experiments,* 85–87; Guarneri, *Utopian Alternative,* 17.

40. Berry, *America's Utopian Experiments,* 85–86; Walters, *American Reformers,* 68.

41. Berry, *America's Utopian Experiments,* 87; Walters, *American Reformers,* 68; Guarneri, *Utopian Alternative,* 19.

42. Walters, *American Reformers,* 68–69.

43. Berry, *America's Utopian Experiments,* 88.

44. Ibid.; Tyler, *Freedom's Ferment,* 217.

45. Berry, *America's Utopian Experiments,* 84–85, 88; Guarneri, *Utopian Alternative,* 4.

46. *Phalanx,* June 1, 1844; Berry, *America's Utopian Experiments,* 83.

47. Berry, *America's Utopian Experiments,* 83, 88–89.

48. *Phalanx,* October 5, 1843.

49. Ibid., March 1, 1844.

50. Berry, *America's Utopian Experiments,* 89; Walters, *American Reformers,* 69–70.

51. Berry, *America's Utopian Experiments,* 83, 86; *Phalanx,* November 4, 1843.

52. John Humphrey Noyes, *History of American Socialisms* (1870; New York: Dover Pubications, 1966), 309–10, 312, 314–15.

53. Fogarty, *Dictionary of Utopian History,* 183; Noyes, *History of Socialisms,* 309–10.

54. Noyes, *History of Socialisms,* 310, 313.

55. Ibid., 311; Fogarty, *Dictionary of Utopian History,* 183.

56. Noyes, *History of Socialisms,* 312–13, 315; Fogarty, *Dictionary of Utopian History,* 187.

57. Noyes, *History of Socialisms,* 311, 313.

58. Ibid., 311–14; Fogarty, *Dictionary of Utopian History,* 183.

59. Carlton Smith, "Elijah Grant and the Ohio Phalanx: A Study in American Utopianism" (M.A. thesis, University of Chicago, 1950), 5; Guarneri, *Utopian Alternative,* 156; Noyes, *History of Socialisms,* 354; both quotes from the *Phalanx,* October 5, 1843.

60. *Phalanx,* December 5, 1843.

61. Ibid.

62. Ibid., March 1, 1844; May 18, 1844.

63. Guarneri, *Utopian Alternative,* 156–57.

64. *Phalanx,* July 27, 1844.

65. Smith, "Elijah Grant," 139, 141–43; Guarneri, *Utopian Alternative,* 156, 159–60.

66. Guarneri, *Utopian Alternative,* 156; Smith, "Elijah Grant," 141–42; 144–45, 150; Fogarty, *Dictionary of Utopian History,* 43.

67. Smith, "New Beginnings," 154; Fogarty, *Dictionary of Utopian History,* 188, 189.

68. Guarneri, *Utopian Alternative,* 36, 155; *Phalanx,* April 1, 1844, May 18, 1844, June 1, 1844.

69. Guarneri, *Utopian Alternative,* 179; *Phalanx,* June 1, 1844.

70. *Phalanx,* June 1, 1844; Noyes, *History of Socialisms,* 369.

71. *Phalanx,* June 1, 1844, May 3, 1845; *Harbinger,* June 14, 1845; Noyes, *History of Socialisms,* 369.

72. *Phalanx,* May 3, 1845; *Harbinger,* June 14, 1845; Noyes, *History of Socialisms,* 372.

73. Noyes, *History of Socialisms,* 372–73.

74. Guarneri, *Utopian Alternative,* 158, 163; Noyes, *History of Socialisms,* 373; *Harbinger,* October 2, 1847.

75. *Harbinger,* October 2, 1847; Fogarty, *Dictionary of Utopian History,* 187, 193.

76. Noyes, *History of Socialisms,* 374–76; Guarneri, *Utopian Alternative,* 352; Fogarty, *Dictionary of Utopian History,* 193.

77. Guarneri, *Utopian Alternative,* 364; Fogarty, *Dictionary of Utopian History,* 181, 194.

78. Noyes, *History of Socialisms,* 375–76; Guarneri, *America's Utopian Alternative,* 366–67.

79. Trumbull Phalanx Manuscript, c. 1938, VFM 3141, Ohio Historical Society, Columbus, Ohio (hereafter Trumbull Phalanx MSS, OHS).

80. Guarneri, *Utopian Alternative,* 72; Fogarty, *Dictionary of Utopian History,* 189; *Phalanx,* June 29, 1844, August 10, 1844; Trumbull Phalanx MSS, OHS.

81. *Phalanx,* August 10, 1844; Guarneri, *Utopian Alernative,* 189.

82. Trumbull Phalanx MSS, OHS; *Phalanx,* December 9, 1844.

83. Noyes, *History of Socialisms,* 335–36; Guarneri, *Utopian Alternative,* 183; *Harbinger,* August 23, 1845.

84. Noyes, *History of Socialisms,* 339; Trumbull Phalanx MSS, OHS; *Harbinger,* October 4, 1845.

85. Noyes, *History of Socialisms,* 339–42, 345; Guarneri, *Utopian Alternative,* 156–57; *Harbinger,* October 4, 1845.

86. Trumbull Phalanx MSS, OHS; *Harbinger,* January 2, 1847; Guarneri, *Utopian Alternative,* 213.

87. Fogarty, *Dictionary of Utopian History,* 189; Guarneri, *Utopian Alternative,* 201, 390

88. Guarneri, *Utopian Alternative,* 201, 390.

89. Fogarty, *Dictionary of Utopian History,* 191–92; *Harbinger,* August 15, 1845; Guarneri, *Utopian Alternative,* 157.

90. Guarneri, *Utopian Alternative,* 162.

91. Fogarty, *Dictionary of Utopian History,* 151–52, 199; Philip Gleason, "From Free-Love to Catholicism: Dr. and Mrs. Thomas L. Nichols at Yellow Springs," *Ohio*

Historical Quarterly 70 (October 1961), 283–84; Walters, *American Reformers,* 147–48, 153–55.

92. Gleason, "From Free-Love," 285–86.

93. Ibid., 287, 289–90.

94. Ibid., 290–92.

95. Ibid., 292–96.

96. Ibid., 294–96.

97. Ibid., 296–97.

98. Ibid., 297–98.

99. Ibid., 298–300; Fogarty, *Dictionary of Utopian History,* 151–52.

100. Gleason, "From Free-Love," 301–7.

101. Walters, *American Reformers,* 71; Guarneri, *Utopian Alternative,* 231; *Phalanx,* July 27, 1844.

102. Guarneri, *Utopian Alternative,* 71, 231.

103. *Phalanx,* May 3, 1845.

104. Fogarty, *Dictionary of Utopian History,* 197–98.

105. Ibid., 199, 201.

106. Ibid., 202.

107. H. Roger Grant, "Jacob's Ohio Utopia," *Timeline* 2 (December 1985–January 1986), 23; Robert H. Wiebe, *The Search for Order, 1877–1920* (New York: Hill and Wang, 1967), 45, 65, 69, 70, 137.

108. Robert S. Fogarty, *All Things New: American Communes and Utopian Movements, 1860–1914* (Chicago: University of Chicago Press, 1990), 16–18; Robert S. Fogarty and H. Roger Grant, "Free Love in Ohio: Jacob Beilhart and the Spirit Fruit Colony," *Ohio History* 89 (Winter 1980), 206.

109. Fogarty and Grant, "Free Love in Ohio," 208; H. Roger Grant, *Spirit Fruit: A Gentle Utopia* (DeKalb: Northern Illinois University Press, 1988), 10.

110. Fogarty and Grant, "Free Love in Ohio," 208; H. Roger Grant, "The Spirit Fruit Society: A Perfectionist Utopia in the Old Northwest, 1899–1915," *The Old Northwest* 9 (Spring 1983), 24.

111. Fogarty and Grant, "Free Love in Ohio," 209; Grant, "Spirit Fruit Society," 25.

112. Fogarty and Grant, "Free Love in Ohio," 209–10; Grant, "Spirit Fruit Society," 25.

113. Fogarty and Grant, "Free Love in Ohio," 210.

114. Grant, "Jacob's Ohio Utopia," 20; Fogarty and Grant, "Free Love in Ohio," 217–20; Grant, "Spirit Fruit Society," 32.

115. Fogarty and Grant, "Free Love in Ohio," 217–19.

116. Ibid., 211.

117. Grant, "Spirit Fruit Society," 26, 28; Fogarty and Grant, "Free Love in Ohio," 211; Grant, "Jacob's Ohio Utopia," 19; Grant, *Spirit Fruit,* 64.

118. Fogarty and Grant, "Free Love in Ohio," 211; Grant, "Spirit Fruit Society," 28.

119. Grant, *Spirit Fruit,* 50–51, 71.

120. Grant, "Spirit Fruit Society," 29.

121. Fogarty and Grant, "Free Love in Ohio," 212–13.

122. Grant, "Spirit Fruit Society," 29; Fogarty and Grant, "Free Love in Ohio," 211–12; Grant, "Jacob's Ohio Utopia," 24, 27; James L. Murphy, *The Reluctant Radicals:*

Jacob L. Beilhart and the Spirit Fruit Society (New York: University Press of America, 1989), 76–77.

123. Grant, "Spirit Fruit Society," 29; Fogarty and Grant, "Free Love in Ohio," 213–14.

124. Fogarty and Grant, "Free Love in Ohio," 214.

125. Fogarty and Grant, "Free Love in Ohio," 214–15; Grant, "Spirit Fruit Society," 29.

126. Fogarty and Grant, "Free Love in Ohio," 215–16; Grant, "Spirit Fruit Society," 30–31, 33–34.

127. Murphy, *Reluctant Radicals*, 57, 79.

CONCLUSION

1. Francis P. Weisenburger, *The Passing of the Frontier: 1825–1850*, vol. 3, in Carl Wittke, ed., *The History of the State of Ohio* (Columbus: Ohio State Archaeological and Historical Society, 1941), 26–27, 30.

2. Michael Barkun, *Crucible of the Millennium: The Burned-Over District of New York in the 1840s* (Syracuse: Syracuse University Press, 1986), 150–51.

Bibliography

MANUSCRIPT COLLECTIONS

Cincinnati Historical Society

Charles O. Lee, "The Shakers as Pioneers in the American Herb and Drug Industry," unpublished paper

John Patterson MacLean Papers

Ohio Historical Society, Columbus, Ohio

Peter Kaufmann Papers

Nixon Family Papers

Shaker Papers

Joseph Smith Papers

Trumbull County Phalanx Manuscript

Zoar Manuscript Papers

Western Reserve Historical Society, Cleveland, Ohio

B. Fowles Letter

Lucia A. Goldsmith, Sidney Rigdon, the first Mormon Elder

Alfred Mewett Papers

Wesley Perkins letter, 1832

Shaker Manuscript Collection

Society of Separatists of Zoar Records

A. C. Williams Papers

NEWSPAPERS

Cleveland Herald
Harbinger
Painesville Telegraph
Phalanx

BOOKS

Andrews, Edward Deming. *The People Called Shakers: A Search for the Perfect Society.* New York: Oxford University Press, 1953.

Backman, Milton V. Jr. *A Profile of Latter-Day Saints of Kirtland, Ohio and Members of Zion's Camp, Vital Statistics and Sources.* Provo, Utah: Brigham Young University, 1983.

Barkun, Michael. *Crucible of the Millennium: The Burned-Over District of New York in the 1840s.* Syracuse: Syracuse University Press, 1986.

Berry, Brian J. L. *America's Utopian Experiments: Communal Havens from Long-Wave Crises.* Hanover: University Press of New England, 1992.

Bestor, Arthur. *Backwoods Utopias: The Sectarian Origins and the Owenite Phase of Communitarian Socialism in America: 1663–1829.* 1950; Philadelphia: University of Pennsylvania Press, 1970.

Brewer, Priscilla J. *Shaker Communities, Shaker Lives.* Hanover: University Press of New England, 1986.

Brodie, Fawn M. *No Man Knows My History: The Life of Joseph Smith, the Mormon Prophet.* 1945; New York: Alfred A. Knopf, 1971.

Bushman, Richard L. *Joseph Smith and the Beginnings of Mormonism.* Urbana and Chicago: University of Illinois Press, 1984.

Chmielewski, Wendy E., Louis J. Kern, and Marlyn Klee-Hartzell, eds. *Women in Spiritual and Communitarian Societies in the United States.* Syracuse: Syracuse University Press, 1993.

Dobbs, Catherine R. *Freedom's Will: The Society of the Separatists of Zoar: An Historical Adventure of Religious Communism in Early Ohio.* New York: William Frederick Press, 1947.

Evans, Frederick W. *Autobiography of a Shaker, and Revelation of the Apocalypse.* 1888; New York, AMS Press, 1973.

Fogarty, Robert S. *All Things New: American Communes and Utopian Movements, 1860–1914.* Chicago: University of Chicago Press, 1990.

———. *Dictionary of American Communal and Utopian History.* Westport, Conn.: Greenwood Press, 1980.

Foster, Lawrence. *Religion and Sexuality: Three American Communal Experiments of the Nineteenth Century.* New York and Oxford: Oxford University Press, 1981.

———. *Women, Family, and Utopia: Communal Experiments of the Shakers, the Oneida Community, and the Mormons.* Syracuse: Syracuse University Press, 1991.

Garrett, Clarke. *Spirit Possession and Popular Religion: From the Camisards to the Shakers.* Baltimore: Johns Hopkins University Press, 1987.

Grant, H. Roger. *Spirit Fruit: A Gentle Utopia.* DeKalb: Northern Illinois Press, 1988.

Guarneri, Carl J. *The Utopian Alternative: Fourierism in Nineteenth-Century America.* Ithaca: Cornell University Press, 1991.

Gunn, Alexander. *The Hermitage-Zoar Notebook and Journal of Travel.* New York, 1902.

Humez, Jean M., ed. *Mother's First-Born Daughters: Early Shaker Writings on Women and Religion.* Bloomington: Indiana University Press, 1993.

Hurt, R. Douglas. *The Ohio Frontier: Crucible of the Old Northwest, 1720–1830.* Bloomington: Indiana University Press, 1996.

Knepper, George W. *Ohio and Its People.* 1989; Kent, Ohio: Kent State University Press, 1997.

MacLean, J. P. *Shakers of Ohio: Fugitive Papers Concerning the Shakers of Ohio, with Unpublished Manuscripts.* 1907; Philadelphia: Porcupine Press, 1975.

Marsden, George M. *Religion and American Culture.* Fort Worth: Harcourt Brace Jovanovich, 1990.

McKiernan, F. Mark. *The Voice of One Crying in the Wilderness: Sidney Rigdon, Religious Reformer, 1793–1876.* 1971; Independence, Mo.: Herald House, 1979.

Morhart, Hilda Dischinger. *The Zoar Story.* 1968; Dover, Ohio: Seibert Printing, 1969.

Murphy, James L. *The Reluctant Radicals: Jacob L. Beilhart and the Spirit Fruit Society.* New York: University Press of America, 1989.

Noyes, John Humphrey. *History of American Socialiasms.* 1870; New York: Dover Publications, 1966.

Ohio Historical Society. *Zoar: An Experiment in Communalism.* Columbus: Ohio Historical Society, 1970.

Piercy, Caroline B. *The Valley of God's Pleasure: A Sage of the North Union Shaker Community.* New York: Stratford House, 1951.

Pitzer, Donald, ed. *America's Communal Utopias.* Chapel Hill: University of North Carolina Press, 1997.

Procter-Smith, Marjorie. *Women in Shaker Community and Worship: A Feminist Analysis of the Uses of Religious Symbolism.* Lewiston, N.Y.: Edwin Mellen Press, 1985.

Prusha, Anne B. *A History of Kirtland, Ohio.* Mentor, Ohio: Lakeland Community College Press, 1982.

Randall, Emilius Oviatt. *History of the Zoar Society: From Its Commencement to Its Conclusion: A Sociological Study in Communism.* 1904; New York: AMS Press, 1971.

Tyler, Alice Felt. *Freedom's Ferment: Phases of American Social History from the Colonial Period to the Outbreak of the Civil War.* 1944; New York: Harper, 1962.

Walters, Robert G. *American Reformers, 1815–1860.* New York: Hill and Wang, 1978.

Weisenberger, Francis P. *The Passing of the Frontier: 1825–1850,* vol. 3 in Carl Wittke, ed., *The History of the State of Ohio.* Columbus: Ohio State Archaeological and Historical Quarterly, 1941.

Wiebe, Robert H. *The Search for Order, 1877–1920.* New York: Hill and Wang, 1967.

ARTICLES

Cherok, Richard J. "No Harmony in Kendal: The Rise and Fall of an Owenite Community." *Ohio History* 108 (1999): 26–38.

Fogarty, Robert S., and H. Roger Grant. "Free Love in Ohio: Jacob Beilhart and the Spirit Fruit Colony." *Ohio History* 108 (Winter–Spring 1980): 206–21,

Fox, Wendall P. "The Kendal Community." *Ohio Archaeological and Historical Society* 20 (April-July 1911): 176–219.

Gleason, Philip. "From Free-Love to Catholicism: Dr. and Mrs. Thomas L. Nichols at Yellow Springs." *Ohio Historical Quarterly* 70, no. 4 (October 1961): 283–307.

Grant, H. Roger. "'Jacob's' Ohio Utopia." *Timeline* 2 (1985–86): 18–27.

———. "The Spirit Fruit Society: A Perfectionist Utopia in the Old Northwest, 1899–1915." *Old Northwest* 9 (1983): 23–36.

Hutslar, Don. "Yellow Springs once home of "unharmonious" commune." *Echoes* 37, no. 8 (August 1998): 5–6.

Nixon, Edgar B. "The Zoar Society: Applicants for Membership." *Ohio State Archaeological and Historical Quarterly* 45 (January 1936): 341–50.

Smith, Ophia D. "Adam Hurdus and the Swedenborgians in Early Cincinnati." *Ohio Archaeological and Historical Quarterly* 53 (1944): 106–34.

———. "The Beginnings of the New Jerusalem Church in Ohio." *Ohio Archaeological and Historical Quarterly* 61 (1952): 235–61.

Webber, Philip E. "Jakob Sylvan's preface to the Zoarite Anthology *Die Wahre Separation, oder die Widergeburt* as an introduction to un(der)studied separatist principles." *Communal Societies* 19 (1999): 101–28.

UNPUBLISHED THESES AND DISSERTATIONS

LeMaster, Grace I. "A Study of the North Union, Ohio, Society of Believers." M.A. thesis, University of Akron, 1950.

Nixon, Edgar B. "The Society of Separatists of Zoar." Ph.D. diss., Ohio State University, 1933.

Parkin, Max H. "The Nature and Cause of Internal and External Conflict of the Mormons in Ohio between 1830 and 1828." M.A. thesis, Brigham Young University, 1966.

Smith, Carlton. "Elijah Grant and the Ohio Phalanx: A Study in American Utopianism." M.A. thesis, University of Chicago, 1950.

Index